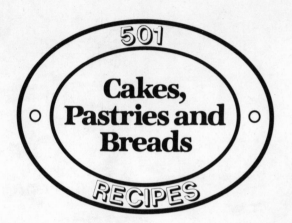

501
Cakes,
Pastries and
Breads
RECIPES

501
Cakes, Pastries and Breads
RECIPES

Edited by
Norma MacMillan

Notes

All measurements in this book are given in Metric,
Imperial and American. Follow one set only because
they are not interchangeable.

Standard spoon measurements are used in all recipes
1 tablespoon = one 15 ml spoon
1 teaspoon = one 5 ml spoon
All spoon measurements are level.

Ovens should be preheated to the specified temperature or heat setting.

This edition first published 1981 by
Octopus Books Limited
59 Grosvenor Street
London W1

HARDBACK ISBN   –   0 7064 1514 0
PAPERBACK ISBN   –   0 7064 1855 7

Printed in Czechoslovakia
50 474

Contents

Cakes

Rich Madeira Cake

Metric/Imperial
225 g/8 oz plain flour
½ teaspoon baking powder
¼ teaspoon salt
225 g/8 oz butter, softened
225 g/8 oz caster sugar
grated rind of 1 small lemon
1 teaspoon vanilla essence
4 eggs
1 strip crystallized citron peel
  (optional)

American
2 cups all-purpose flour
½ teaspoon baking powder
¼ teaspoon salt
16 tablespoons (2 sticks) butter,
  softened
1 cup sugar
grated rind of 1 small lemon
1 teaspoon vanilla extract
4 eggs
1 strip candied citron peel (optional)

Sift together the flour, baking powder and salt. Cream the butter with the sugar, lemon rind and vanilla until light and fluffy. Beat in the eggs, one at a time, adding a tablespoon of flour with each egg. Fold in the remaining flour.

Pour into a greased and lined 18 cm/7 inch round deep cake pan or a 1 kg/2 lb (9 × 5 × 3 inch) loaf pan. Place the citron peel on top, if using. Bake in a preheated moderate oven (160°C/325°F, Gas Mark 3) for 1¾ to 2 hours or until a skewer inserted into the centre comes out clean.

Cool in the pan for 10 minutes, then turn out onto a wire rack to cool completely.

Whisked Sponge Cake

Metric/Imperial
3 eggs
75 g/3 oz caster sugar
75 g/3 oz plain flour, sifted

American
3 eggs
6 tablespoons sugar
¾ cup all-purpose flour, sifted

Beat the eggs and sugar together until the mixture is pale and very thick and will make a ribbon trail on itself when the beater is lifted. Fold in the flour. Pour the mixture into a greased and floured 23 cm/9 inch or 20 cm/8 inch cake pan and bake in a preheated moderately hot oven (190°C/375°F, Gas Mark 5) for 15 to 20 minutes (25 to 35 minutes for the smaller pan) until risen and firm to the touch. Cool on a wire rack.

Variations:

Orange Whisked Sponge Cake: Add the grated rind of 1 to 2 oranges to the egg and sugar mixture, and fold in 1 tablespoon hot orange juice after the flour. Bake as above and cool. Sandwich together with marmalade and whipped cream. Decorate the top with more whipped cream, sweetened and flavoured with orange liqueur.

Lemon Whisked Sponge Cake: Make as for orange whisked sponge cake, using lemon rind and juice. Sandwich together with lemon curd and whipped cream, and flavour the cream for the decoration with apricot brandy.

Spiced Honey Cake

Metric/Imperial
500 g/1 lb honey
250 ml/8 fl oz oil
2 teaspoons instant coffee powder
150 ml/¼ pint boiling water
225 g/8 oz dark brown sugar
4 eggs, beaten
500 g/1 lb self-raising flour
1 heaped teaspoon ground
   cinnamon
1 heaped teaspoon ground mixed
   spice
1 teaspoon ground ginger
1 teaspoon bicarbonate of soda

American
1⅓ cups honey
1 cup oil
2 teaspoons instant coffee powder
⅔ cup boiling water
1 cup dark brown sugar
4 eggs, beaten
4 cups self-rising flour
1 heaped teaspoon ground
   cinnamon
1 heaped teaspoon ground allspice
1 teaspoon ground ginger
1 teaspoon baking soda

Mix the honey with the oil. Dissolve the coffee in the water and add to the honey mixture with the sugar and eggs. Mix well.

Sift the flour with the spices and soda and stir into the honey mixture. Pour into a greased 30 × 25 cm/12 × 10 inch cake pan.

Bake in a moderate oven (160°C/325°F, Gas Mark 3) for 1 to 1¼ hours.

Genoese Sponge Cake

Metric/Imperial
3 eggs
75 g/3 oz caster sugar
50 g/2 oz butter, melted
75 g/3 oz plain flour, sifted 3 times

American
3 eggs
6 tablespoons sugar
4 tablespoons butter, melted
¾ cup all-purpose flour, sifted 3 times

Beat the eggs and sugar together until the mixture is pale and very thick and will make a ribbon trail on itself when the beater is lifted. Pour the melted butter around the edge of the egg mixture and fold it in gently. Fold in the flour in two batches.

Divide the batter between two greased and floured or lined 18 cm/7 inch sandwich tins (layer cake pans). Bake in a preheated moderately hot oven (190°C/375°F, Gas Mark 5) for 20 to 25 minutes or until well risen, golden and firm. Turn out onto a towel-covered wire rack and leave to cool.

Sandwich the cake layers together with jam, whipped cream, buttercream (see page 41) or an icing or frosting of your choice.

Variation:
Oil Sponge Cake: Substitute 3 tablespoons corn oil for the melted butter.

Vanilla Chiffon Cake

Metric/Imperial
100 g/4 oz self-raising flour
150 g/5 oz caster sugar
½ teaspoon salt
4 tablespoons corn oil
3 eggs, separated
5 tablespoons water
1 teaspoon vanilla essence
½ teaspoon cream of tartar

American
1 cup self-rising flour
⅔ cup sugar
½ teaspoon salt
¼ cup corn oil
3 eggs, separated
5 tablespoons water
1 teaspoon vanilla extract
½ teaspoon cream of tartar

Sift the flour, sugar and salt into a bowl. Make a well in the centre and add the oil, egg yolks, water and vanilla. Stir briskly until the batter is smooth.

Beat the egg whites with the cream of tartar until stiff. Fold the egg whites into the batter very gently. Spoon into a deep, 18 to 20 cm/7 to 8 inch, ring tin (tube pan) with sloping sides. Bake in a preheated moderate oven (160°C/325°F, Gas Mark 3) for 1¼ hours.

Invert the tin (pan) over a large funnel or bottle and leave to cool completely. To remove the cake from the tin (pan), loosen the edges with a knife, then tap the base of the tin (pan) sharply.

Variation:
Lemon Chiffon Cake: Use only ½ teaspoon vanilla essence (extract) and add the finely grated rind of ½ lemon with the vanilla.

Chestnut and Rum Swiss Gâteau

Metric/Imperial
3 eggs
75 g/3 oz caster sugar
50 g/2 oz butter, melted
75 g/3 oz plain flour, sifted 3 times

Filling:
1 small can unsweetened chestnut
  purée
1 egg yolk
100 g/4 oz icing sugar, sifted
1–2 tablespoons rum
Icing:
1 egg white
275 g/10 oz icing sugar, sifted
chocolate leaves to decorate

American
3 eggs
½ cup sugar
4 tablespoons butter, melted
¾ cup all-purpose flour, sifted 3
  times

Filling:
1 small can unsweetened chestnut
  purée
1 egg yolk
1 cup confectioners' sugar, sifted
1–2 tablespoons rum
Frosting:
1 egg white
2½ cups confectioners' sugar, sifted
chocolate leaves to decorate

Beat the eggs and sugar together until the mixture is pale and very thick and will make a ribbon trail on itself when the beater is lifted. Pour the melted butter around the edge of the egg mixture and fold it in gently. Fold in the flour in two batches.

Bake in a greased and lined Swiss (jelly) roll pan, in a preheated moderately hot oven (190°C/375°F, Gas Mark 5) for 12 to 15 minutes. Turn out onto a sugared sheet of greaseproof (wax) paper and roll up the cake with the paper inside. Cool.

For the filling, mix together the chestnut purée, egg yolk, icing (confectioners') sugar and the rum. Unroll the cake, discard the paper and spread with the chestnut mixture. Roll up the cake again.

Beat the egg white until frothy and gradually beat in the icing (confectioners') sugar to make a soft, flowing icing. Swirl over the cake and leave to set. Decorate with chocolate leaves.

Almond Meringue Cake

Metric/Imperial	American
100 g/4 oz self-raising flour	1 cup self-rising flour
pinch of salt	pinch of salt
100 g/4 oz butter	8 tablespoons (1 stick) butter
275 g/10 oz caster sugar	1¼ cups sugar
1 teaspoon vanilla essence	1 teaspoon vanilla extract
4 eggs, separated	4 eggs, separated
4–5 tablespoons milk	4–5 tablespoons milk
2 tablespoons caster sugar	2 tablespoons sugar
½ teaspoon ground cinnamon	½ teaspoon ground cinnamon
25 g/1 oz flaked almonds	¼ cup slivered almonds

Sift the flour and salt together. Cream the butter with 100 g/4 oz (½ cup) of the sugar and vanilla until light and fluffy. Beat in the egg yolks, one at a time, adding a tablespoon of flour with each yolk. Mix in the milk and fold in the remaining flour.

Pour into a 20 cm/8 inch round deep cake pan. Beat the egg whites until stiff, then gradually beat in 175 g/6 oz (¾ cup) of the sugar. Spread the meringue over the cake batter. Mix the remaining 2 tablespoons of sugar with the cinnamon and sprinkle over the meringue, followed by the almonds. Bake in a preheated moderate oven (180°C/350°F, Gas Mark 4) for 60 to 65 minutes. Test with a skewer.

Orange, Carrot and Nut Cake

Metric/Imperial	American
100 g/4 oz butter	8 tablespoons (1 stick) butter
175 g/6 oz caster sugar	¾ cup sugar
1 teaspoon ground cinnamon	1 teaspoon ground cinnamon
1 teaspoon grated orange rind	1 teaspoon grated orange rind
2 eggs, beaten	2 eggs, beaten
75 g/3 oz carrot, grated	¾ cup grated carrot
50 g/2 oz walnuts, finely chopped	½ cup finely chopped walnuts
1 tablespoon orange juice	1 tablespoon orange juice
225 g/8 oz self-raising flour	2 cups self-rising flour
pinch of salt	pinch of salt

Cream the butter with the sugar, cinnamon and orange rind until light and fluffy. Beat in the eggs, then stir in the carrot, walnuts and orange juice. Sift over the flour and salt and fold into the creamed mixture.

Pour into a greased 20 cm/8 inch round deep cake pan. Bake in a preheated moderate oven (160°C/325°F, Gas Mark 3) for 45 to 55 minutes or until the cake springs back when lightly pressed. Cool on a wire rack.

Swiss (Jelly) Roll

Metric/Imperial
1 quantity whisked sponge cake
    batter (see page 7)
4 tablespoons jam or lemon curd

American
1 quantity whisked sponge cake
    batter (see page 7)
¼ cup jam or lemon cheese

Pour the batter into a greased and lined 30 × 20 cm/12 × 8 inch Swiss (jelly) roll pan. Bake in a preheated moderately hot oven (200°C/400°F, Gas Mark 6) for 10 to 12 minutes or until well risen and golden.

Turn out the cake onto a sheet of greaseproof (wax) paper that has been liberally sprinkled with sugar and placed on a damp towel. Peel away the lining paper and trim the crusty edges from the cake.

Spread the cake quickly with the jam or lemon curd (cheese), then roll it up tightly, lifting it with the paper and towel. Hold it in place for 1 to 2 minutes so it doesn't unroll, then leave to cool.

Variations:

Cream-Filled Swiss (Jelly) Roll: After trimming off the crusty edges, roll up the cake with paper inside to prevent the cake sticking to itself. Cover with a damp cloth and leave to cool. Unroll the cake, remove the paper and spread with whipped cream, slightly sweetened with icing (confectioners') sugar. Roll up again and hold in position for 1 to 2 minutes.

Chocolate Swiss (Jelly) Roll: Make up the whisked sponge cake batter substituting 1 tablespoon cocoa powder (unsweetened cocoa) for 1 tablespoon of the flour. Continue as above, filling the cake with whipped cream.

Yule Log: Make a chocolate Swiss (jelly) roll as above, then cover with chocolate frosting (see page 44), all over including the ends. Mark with a fork to resemble bark. When set, sprinkle with icing (confectioners') sugar to resemble snow and decorate with Christmas decorations such as holly.

Honey Roll: Make up the whisked sponge cake batter using only 50 g/2 oz (¼ cup) sugar and adding 2 tablespoons clear honey (beat it with the eggs and sugar). Stir in ½ teaspoon bicarbonate of soda (baking soda) dissolved in 1 tablespoon hot water, followed by the flour increased to 100 g/4 oz (1 cup). Add 1 teaspoon ground cinnamon. Pour into a 35 × 25 cm/14 × 10 inch Swiss (jelly) roll pan and bake in a preheated moderately hot oven (190°C/375°F, Gas Mark 5) for 12 to 15 minutes. Fill with whipped cream.

Genoa Cake

Metric/Imperial	American
100 g/4 oz currants	⅔ cup seedless white raisins
100 g/4 oz raisins	⅔ cup raisins
75 g/3 oz mixed candied peel, chopped	½ cup chopped mixed candied peel
2 tablespoons glacé cherries, chopped	2 tablespoons chopped candied cherries
25 g/1 oz blanched almonds, finely chopped	¼ cup finely chopped blanched almonds
1 quantity basic or rich Madeira cake batter (see pages 6 and 13)	1 quantity basic or rich Madeira cake batter (see pages 6 and 13)

Fold the mixed fruit and nuts into the cake mixture.

Bake in a preheated cool oven (150°C/300°F, Gas Mark 2) for 2 to 2½ hours. Cool in the pan for 15 minutes before turning out to cool completely on a wire rack.

Battenburg Cake

Metric/Imperial	American
double quantity Victoria sandwich cake batter (see page 16)	double quantity Victoria layer cake batter (see page 16)
red food colouring	red food coloring
apricot jam, melted	apricot jam, melted
225 g/8 oz almond paste	½ lb almond paste

Divide the batter in half. Add a few drops of red food colouring to one half to tint it a fairly deep pink.

Grease and line a 30 × 20 cm/12 × 8 inch Swiss (jelly) roll pan, making sure the paper extends about 2.5 cm/1 inch above the rim of the pan. Divide the tin (pan) in half lengthways by standing a wide band of cardboard covered in foil down the centre to form a wall. Put the pink batter in one half and the plain batter in the other.

Bake in a preheated moderate oven (180°C/350°F, Gas Mark 4) for 35 to 45 minutes or until well risen and firm. Cool in the pan for 5 minutes, then turn out onto a wire rack to cool completely.

Trim both pieces of cake to the same size, if necessary, then cut each piece lengthways in half. Spread the four pieces of cake all over with jam, and form them into a block, alternating the colours.

Roll out the almond paste to an oblong about 20 × 25 cm/8 × 10 inches. Brush the cake all over with jam again, then place it on the almond paste. Wrap the paste around the cake, pressing the join well together to seal. Crimp the edges and make criss-cross cuts on top to decorate.

Madeira Cake

Metric/Imperial
225 g/8 oz plain flour
2 teaspoons baking powder
¼ teaspoon salt
175 g/6 oz butter, softened
175 g/6 oz caster sugar
grated rind of 1 small lemon
1 teaspoon vanilla essence
3 eggs
2 tablespoons milk
1 strip crystallized citron peel
 (optional)

American
2 cups all-purpose flour
2 teaspoons baking powder
¼ teaspoon salt
12 tablespoons (1½ sticks) butter,
 softened
¾ cup sugar
grated rind of 1 small lemon
1 teaspoon vanilla extract
3 eggs
2 tablespoons milk
1 strip candied citron peel (optional)

Sift together the flour, baking powder and salt. Cream the butter with the sugar, lemon rind and vanilla until light and fluffy. Beat in the eggs, one at a time, adding a tablespoon of the flour with each egg. Fold in the remaining flour alternately with the milk.

Pour the batter into a greased and floured or lined 18 cm/7 inch round deep cake pan or a 1 kg/2 lb (9 × 5 × 3 inch) loaf pan. Place the citron peel on top, if using. Bake in a preheated moderate oven (160°C/325°F, Gas Mark 3) for 1½ to 1¾ hours or until a skewer inserted into the centre comes out clean.

Cool in the pan for 10 minutes, then turn out onto a wire rack to cool completely.

Variations:

Caraway Seed Cake: Omit the lemon rind and add 4 to 6 teaspoons caraway seeds. Do not use the citron peel.

Marble Cake: Follow the rich Madeira cake recipe, but after adding the eggs divide the batter in half. Fold half the flour into one half. Sift 1 tablespoon cocoa powder (unsweetened cocoa) with the remaining flour and fold into the second portion of batter, alternately with 1 tablespoon milk. Drop alternate spoons of both mixtures into the pan and bake as above.

Fruit and Nut Loaf: Add 225 g/8 oz (1⅓ cups) mixed dried fruit to the basic or rich Madeira cake batter. Pour into a greased and floured or lined loaf pan and cover with 2 tablespoons flaked (slivered) almonds. Bake as above.

Butterscotch Sponge Cake

Metric/Imperial
100 g/4 oz self-raising flour
pinch of salt
1 teaspoon baking powder
75 g/3 oz soft margarine
100 g/4 oz soft brown sugar
2 eggs
1 tablespoon water
little crushed butterscotch for
  decoration
Icing:
50 g/2 oz butter
1 tablespoon golden syrup
100 g/4 oz icing sugar, sifted

American
1 cup self-rising flour
pinch of salt
1 teaspoon baking powder
6 tablespoons soft margarine
⅔ cup light brown sugar
2 eggs
1 tablespoon water
little crushed butterscotch for
  decoration
Icing:
4 tablespoons butter
1 tablespoon light corn syrup
1 cup confectioners' sugar, sifted

Sift the flour, salt and baking powder into a bowl. Add the margarine, sugar, eggs and water and beat to make a smooth, pale batter. Pour into a greased and floured or lined 20 cm/8 inch square deep cake pan.

Bake in a preheated moderate oven (160°C/325°F, Gas Mark 3) for about 45 minutes or until well risen and firm to the touch. Turn out onto a wire rack to cool.

For the icing, cream the butter with the syrup until softened, then gradually beat in the sugar. If the icing is too stiff to spread, add a few drops of water.

Cover the top and sides of the cake with the icing and decorate with crushed butterscotch.

Coffee Walnut Layer Cake

Metric/Imperial
175 g/6 oz butter
150 g/5 oz caster sugar
25 g/1 oz soft brown sugar
3 large eggs
1 egg yolk
1 tablespoon strong black coffee
175 g/6 oz self-raising flour, sifted
75 g/3 oz walnuts, finely chopped
⅔ quantity simple buttercream (see page 41)
½ quantity boiled white frosting (see page 43)
few walnut halves to decorate

American
12 tablespoons (1½ sticks) butter
⅔ cup sugar
2½ tablespoons light brown sugar
3 eggs
1 egg yolk
1 tablespoon strong black coffee
1½ cups self-rising flour, sifted
¾ cup finely chopped walnuts
⅔ quantity simple buttercream (see page 41)
½ quantity boiled white frosting (see page 43)
few walnut halves to decorate

Cream the butter with the sugars until fluffy. Gradually beat in the eggs, egg yolk and coffee. Fold in the flour and walnuts. Divide the batter between two greased and floured 18 cm/7 inch sandwich tins (layer cake pans).

Bake in a preheated moderate oven (180°C/350°F, Gas Mark 4) for about 25 minutes or until firm to the touch. Cool on a wire rack.

Cut each cake into two layers and sandwich the four layers together with the buttercream. Spread the frosting over the top and sides of the cake and decorate the top with walnut halves.

Variation:
Omit the buttercream. Use the whole recipe quantity of boiled frosting and use half of it to sandwich together the cake layers.

Cherry Coconut Cake

Metric/Imperial
175 g/6 oz self-raising flour
100 g/4 oz butter
175 g/6 oz caster sugar
50 g/2 oz desiccated coconut
75 g/3 oz glacé cherries, halved
2 eggs, beaten

American
1½ cups self-rising flour
8 tablespoons (1 stick) butter
¾ cup sugar
⅔ cup shredded coconut
½ cup halved candied cherries
2 eggs, beaten

Sift the flour into a bowl and rub in the butter. Stir in the sugar, coconut and about two-thirds of the cherries, then bind with the eggs. Pour into a greased and floured 20 cm/8 inch round deep cake pan. Press the rest of the cherries into the top.

Bake in a preheated moderate oven (180°C/350°F, Gas Mark 4) for about 1 hour or until firm to the touch.

Victoria Sandwich (Layer) Cake

Metric/Imperial
100 g/4 oz self-raising flour
pinch of salt
100 g/4 oz butter
100 g/4 oz caster sugar
1 teaspoon vanilla essence
2 eggs

American
1 cup self-rising flour
pinch of salt
8 tablespoons (1 stick) butter
½ cup sugar
1 teaspoon vanilla extract
2 eggs

Sift the flour and salt together. Cream the butter with the sugar and vanilla until light and fluffy. Beat in the eggs, one at a time, adding a tablespoon of flour with each egg. Fold in the remaining flour.

Divide the batter between two greased and floured or lined 18 cm/7 inch sandwich tins (layer cake pans). Bake in a preheated moderate oven (180°C/350°F, Gas Mark 4) for 25 to 30 minutes or until well risen and golden. Cool in the tins (pans) for 5 minutes, then turn out and cool completely on a wire rack.

Sandwich together the cake layers with jam, whipped cream and jam, or buttercream (see page 41) and sprinkle the top with sugar.

Variations:

Orange or Lemon Sandwich (Layer) Cake: Omit the vanilla and replace with 2 teaspoons grated orange or lemon rind. Sandwich together the two layers with lemon curd (cheese) and dust the top with icing (confectioners') sugar.

Iced Fancies: Make a slab cake as above, cool and cut into fingers, squares, diamonds or other decorative shapes. Spread the tops with glacé icing (see page 42), buttercream (see page 41) or whipped cream and decorate with nuts, glacé (candied) cherries, angelica, chocolate drops (chips), vermicelli (chocolate sprinkles) or crystallized flower petals.

Coconut Squares: Make a slab cake as above, cool and cut into squares. Brush all over with melted plum or apricot jam and coat with desiccated (shredded) coconut.

Fairy Cakes: Add 3 to 4 tablespoons of currants to the basic cake batter after the eggs.

Divide between 20 to 24 fluted paper cake cases and place in bun tins (cup cake pans). Bake in a preheated moderately hot oven (190°C/375°F, Gas Mark 5) for 20 minutes or until well risen and golden.

Madeleines: Divide the basic cake batter between 12 well greased castle pudding or dariole moulds. Bake in a preheated moderate oven (180°C/350°F, Gas Mark 4) for 20 to 25 minutes or until well risen and golden. Cool, then cut a slice off the widest part of each madeleine so it stands upright. Brush the top and sides of each cake with melted apricot jam, then coat with desiccated (shredded) coconut. Top each with a halved glacé (candied) cherry and 2 angelica leaves.

Plum Cake

Metric/Imperial
150 g/5 oz butter
100 g/4 oz sugar
1 egg
200 g/7 oz self-raising flour
pinch of salt
500 g/1 lb plums, stoned and sliced
lemon juice
2 tablespoons apricot or plum jam,
    melted
sifted icing sugar to dredge

American
10 tablespoons butter
½ cup sugar
1 egg
1¾ cups self-rising flour
pinch of salt
1 lb plums, pitted and sliced
lemon juice
2 tablespoons apricot or plum jam,
    melted
sifted confectioners' sugar to dredge

Cream the butter with 75 g/3 oz (6 tablespoons) of the sugar until light and fluffy. Beat in the egg. Sift the flour with the salt and fold into the creamed mixture. Spread three-quarters of the dough over the bottom of a greased 18 cm/7 inch round deep cake pan.

Arrange the plum slices on the dough and sprinkle them with lemon juice and the remaining sugar. Brush with the jam.

Take small pieces of the remaining dough and roll into strips. Arrange in a lattice pattern over the fruit.

Bake in a preheated moderate oven (160°C/325°F, Gas Mark 3) for 1 hour. Dredge with icing (confectioners') sugar and cool.

Variations:

Other fruits, such as apples, cherries, apricots or gooseberries, may be used instead of plums.

Quick Mix Chocolate Cake

Metric/Imperial
100 g/4 oz soft margarine
100 g/4 oz sugar
2 drops of vanilla essence
150 g/5 oz self-raising flour, sifted
1 teaspoon baking powder
50 g/2 oz cocoa powder
2 eggs
3 tablespoons hot water

American
½ cup soft margarine
½ cup sugar
2 drops of vanilla extract
1¼ cups self-rising flour, sifted
1 teaspoon baking powder
½ cup unsweetened cocoa
2 eggs
3 tablespoons hot water

Put all the ingredients in a bowl and beat until creamy. Pour into a greased 18 cm/7 inch square cake pan.

Bake in a preheated moderate oven (180°C/350°F, Gas Mark 4) for 45 minutes.

ocolate Nut Cake

Imperial	American
50 g/2 oz self-raising flour	½ cup self-rising flour
pinch of salt	pinch of salt
100 g/4 oz butter	8 tablespoons (1 stick) butter
100 g/4 oz caster sugar	½ cup sugar
2 eggs	2 eggs
50 g/2 oz hazelnuts, ground and toasted	½ cup ground, toasted hazelnuts
25 g/1 oz plain chocolate, grated	2 tablespoons grated dark sweet chocolate
1 quantity coffee buttercream (see page 41)	1 quantity coffee buttercream (see page 41)
sifted icing sugar	sifted confectioners' sugar

Sift the flour and salt together. Cream the butter with the sugar until light and fluffy. Beat in the eggs, one at a time, adding a tablespoon of flour with each egg. Fold in the remaining flour, the hazelnuts and the chocolate.

Divide the batter between two greased 15 cm/6 inch sandwich tins (layer cake pans) that have been floured or lined. Bake in a preheated moderate oven (180°C/350°F, Gas Mark 4) for 25 to 30 minutes or until well risen and golden. Cool, then sandwich the cake layers with coffee buttercream (see page 41) and dust the top of the cake with sifted icing (confectioners') sugar.

Basic Butter Cake

Metric/Imperial	American
100 g/4 oz butter	8 tablespoons (1 stick) butter
175 g/6 oz caster sugar	¾ cup sugar
1 teaspoon vanilla essence	1 teaspoon vanilla extract
2 eggs	2 eggs
225 g/8 oz self-raising flour	2 cups self-rising flour
pinch of salt	pinch of salt
3–4 tablespoons milk	3–4 tablespoons milk

Cream the butter with the sugar and vanilla until light and fluffy. Beat in the eggs one at a time, adding a tablespoon of flour with each egg. Sift over the remaining flour and the salt and fold in with the milk. Pour into a greased and lined, deep, 18 to 20 cm/7 to 8 inch, round cake pan. Bake in a preheated moderate oven (180°C/350°F, Gas Mark 4) for 50 to 60 minutes.

Variation:
One-Egg Butter Cake: Reduce the butter to 75 g/3 oz (6 tablespoons) and increase the sugar to 225 g/8 oz (1 cup). Use plain (all-purpose) flour with 2½ teaspoons baking powder. Use only 1 egg and increase the milk to 4 to 5 tablespoons. Bake as above.

Walnut Raspberry Roll

Metric/Imperial
4 large eggs
75 g/3 oz caster sugar
40 g/1½ oz plain flour
large pinch of ground cinnamon
40 g/1½ oz ground walnuts
25 g/1 oz butter, melted
walnut halves for decoration
Filling:
75 g/3 oz seedless raspberry jam
50 g/2 oz butter
100 g/4 oz icing sugar, sifted
large pinch of ground cinnamon

American
4 eggs
6 tablespoons sugar
6 tablespoons all-purpose flour
large pinch of ground cinnamon
⅓ cup ground walnuts
2 tablespoons butter, melted
walnut halves for decoration
Filling:
¼ cup raspberry jelly
4 tablespoons butter
1 cup confectioners' sugar, sifted
large pinch of ground cinnamon

Beat the eggs and sugar together until the mixture is pale and thick and makes a ribbon trail on itself when the beater is lifted. Sift the flour and cinnamon together twice and fold into the egg mixture with the ground walnuts and melted butter. Pour into a greased and lined 30 × 25 cm/ 12 × 10 inch Swiss (jelly) roll pan.

Bake in a preheated moderately hot oven (190°C/375°F, Gas Mark 5) for 15 to 20 minutes or until just firm and springy.

Turn out the cake onto a sheet of greaseproof (wax) paper that has been sprinkled with icing (confectioners') sugar. Peel off the lining paper and trim the edges. Roll up with the paper inside and cool.

Unroll the cake and spread with the jam (jelly). Cream the butter with the sugar and cinnamon. Spread half this mixture over the cake and roll it up again. Dredge with more icing (confectioners') sugar, then pipe the remaining buttercream down the centre. Decorate with walnut halves.

Variation:
Fill and decorate the cake with whipped cream and fresh raspberries.

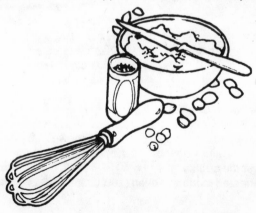

Chocolate Sandwich (Layer) Cake

Metric/Imperial	American
150 g/5 oz self-raising flour	1¼ cups self-rising flour
25 g/1 oz custard powder	¼ cup cornstarch
25 g/1 oz cocoa powder	¼ cup unsweetened cocoa
175 g/6 oz butter	12 tablespoons (1½ sticks) butter
175 g/6 oz caster sugar	¾ cup sugar
3 eggs	3 eggs
2 tablespoons milk	2 tablespoons milk
1 quantity chocolate buttercream (see page 40)	1 quantity chocolate buttercream (see page 40)

Sift the flour, custard powder (cornstarch) and cocoa powder (unsweetened cocoa) into a bowl. Cream the butter with the sugar until light and fluffy. Beat in the eggs one at a time, adding a tablespoon of the flour mixture with each one. Fold in the remaining flour mixture alternately with the milk.

Divide the batter between two greased and floured or lined 20 cm/8 inch sandwich tins (layer cake pans). Bake in a preheated moderate oven (180°C/350°F, Gas Mark 4) for 30 to 35 minutes or until well risen and firm. Cool in the tins (pans) for 5 minutes, then turn out onto a wire rack to cool completely. Sandwich together with the buttercream.

Apple Teacake

Metric/Imperial	American
50 g/2 oz butter	4 tablespoons butter
115 g/4½ oz caster sugar	½ cup plus 1 tablespoon sugar
1 egg	1 egg
175 g/6 oz self-raising flour	1½ cups self-rising flour
pinch of salt	pinch of salt
120 ml/4 fl oz milk	½ cup milk
2 apples, peeled, cored and thinly sliced	2 apples, peeled, cored and thinly sliced
2 teaspoons ground cinnamon	2 teaspoons ground cinnamon

Cream the butter with 100 g/4 oz (½ cup) of the sugar until light and fluffy. Beat in the egg. Sift over the flour and salt and fold in followed by the milk. Pour into a greased and floured 20 cm/8 inch sandwich tin (layer cake pan).

Arrange the apple slices on top. Mix the remaining sugar with the cinnamon and sprinkle over the apples.

Bake in a preheated moderate oven (180°C/350°F, Gas Mark 4) for about 45 minutes.

Orange Marmalade Cake

Metric/Imperial
225 g/8 oz self-raising flour
½ teaspoon baking powder
pinch of salt
100 g/4 oz butter
50 g/2 oz caster sugar
grated rind of ½ orange
2 eggs, beaten
2 tablespoons orange marmalade
about 2 tablespoons orange juice

American
2 cups self-rising flour
½ teaspoon baking powder
pinch of salt
8 tablespoons (1 stick) butter
¼ cup sugar
grated rind of ½ orange
2 eggs, beaten
2 tablespoons orange marmalade
about 2 tablespoons orange juice

Sift the flour, baking powder and salt into a bowl and rub in the butter. Stir in the sugar and orange rind, then mix in the eggs, marmalade and enough orange juice to make a soft dropping consistency. Pour into a greased and lined 15 cm/6 inch deep cake pan.

Bake in a preheated moderate oven (180°C/350°F, Gas Mark 4) for about 1 hour or until well risen and firm to the touch.

Chocolate Fudge Cake

Metric/Imperial
150 g/5 oz self-raising flour
25 g/1 oz cocoa powder
175 g/6 oz butter
175 g/6 oz soft brown sugar
3 eggs, beaten
50 g/2 oz plain chocolate, melted
1 teaspoon vanilla essence
orange chocolate frosting (see page 44)

American
1¼ cups self-rising flour
¼ cup unsweetened cocoa
12 tablespoons (1½ sticks) butter
1 cup light brown sugar
3 eggs, beaten
⅓ cup semi-sweet chocolate chips, melted
1 teaspoon vanilla extract
orange chocolate frosting (see page 44)

Sift together the flour and cocoa. Cream the butter with the sugar until light and fluffy. Beat in the eggs one at a time, adding a tablespoon of the flour mixture after each egg. Beat in the chocolate and vanilla, then fold in the remaining flour mixture.

Pour into a greased and floured 20 cm/8 inch round deep cake pan. Bake in a preheated moderate oven (180°C/350°F, Gas Mark 4) for 1 to 1¼ hours or until a skewer inserted into the centre of the cake comes out clean. Cool the cake in the pan for 10 minutes, then turn out onto a wire rack to cool completely.

Cut the cake into two layers, then sandwich together with some of the frosting and use the rest to cover the top and sides.

Devil's Food Cake

Metric/Imperial	American
175 g/6 oz plain flour	1 1/2 cups all-purpose flour
1/4 teaspoon baking powder	1/4 teaspoon baking powder
1/4 teaspoon bicarbonate of soda	1/4 teaspoon baking soda
50 g/2 oz cocoa powder	1/2 cup unsweetened cocoa
100 g/4 oz butter	8 tablespoons (1 stick) butter
275 g/10 oz caster sugar	1 1/4 cups sugar
2 eggs	2 eggs
6 tablespoons water	6 tablespoons water
whipped cream or buttercream (see page 41)	whipped cream or buttercream (see page 41)

Sift together the flour, baking powder, soda and cocoa. Cream the butter with the sugar until light and fluffy. Beat in the eggs one at a time, adding a tablespoon of the flour mixture with each one. Fold in the remaining flour mixture alternately with the water.

Divide the batter between two greased and floured or lined 20 cm/8 inch sandwich tins (layer cake pans). Bake in a preheated moderate oven (180°C/350°F, Gas Mark 4) for 50 to 60 minutes or until risen and firm.

Cool in the tins (pans) for 5 minutes, then turn out onto a wire rack to cool completely.

Sandwich together the layers with whipped cream or buttercream (see page 41) and cover the top and sides of the cake with an icing or frosting of your choice.

Slab Cake

Metric/Imperial	American
175 g/6 oz self-raising flour	1 1/2 cups self-rising flour
pinch of salt	pinch of salt
175 g/6 oz butter	12 tablespoons (1 1/2 sticks) butter
175 g/6 oz sugar	3/4 cup sugar
3 eggs	3 eggs

Sift the flour and salt together. Cream the butter with the sugar until light and fluffy. Beat in the eggs, one at a time, adding a tablespoon of flour with each egg. Fold in the remaining flour.

Spread out the batter in a greased and floured or lined Swiss (jelly) roll pan and bake in a preheated moderate oven (180°C/350°F, Gas Mark 4) for 20 to 25 minutes or until well risen and golden. Cool, then cut in half and sandwich together with a filling to make a square cake.

Chocolate Raisin Sponge Cake

Metric/Imperial
150 g/5 oz self-raising flour
25 g/1 oz cocoa powder
150 g/5 oz caster sugar
5 tablespoons corn oil
5 tablespoons water
2 large eggs, separated
50 g/2 oz raisins
Icing:
275 g/10 oz icing sugar, sifted
3 tablespoons corn oil
2–3 tablespoons top of the milk
rum essence
To decorate:
chocolate drops
raisins

American
1¼ cups self-rising flour
¼ cup unsweetened cocoa
⅔ cup sugar
5 tablespoons corn oil
5 tablespoons water
2 eggs, separated
⅓ cup raisins
Icing:
2½ cups confectioners' sugar, sifted
3 tablespoons corn oil
2–3 tablespoons half-and-half
rum flavoring
To decorate:
chocolate chips
raisins

Sift the flour and cocoa into a bowl and stir in the sugar. Add the oil, water and egg yolks and beat until smooth and glossy. Beat the egg whites until stiff and fold into the batter with the raisins. Divide the batter between two greased and floured 18 cm/7 inch sandwich tins (layer cake pans).

Bake in a preheated moderate oven (180°C/350°F, Gas Mark 4) for about 30 minutes or until firm to the touch. Turn out onto a wire rack to cool.

For the icing, mix the sugar with the oil and enough of the top of the milk (half-and-half) to make a spreading consistency. Flavour with rum. Use half the icing to sandwich the cake layers together, then cover the top of the cake with the remaining icing. Decorate with chocolate drops (chips) and raisins.

Honey Orange Cake

Metric/Imperial
175 g/6 oz butter
6 tablespoons clear honey
50 g/2 oz caster sugar
finely grated rind of 2 oranges
3 eggs
225 g/8 oz plain flour
1 teaspoon baking powder
pinch of salt
Topping:
1 orange, thinly sliced
150 ml/¼ pint water
100 g/4 oz sugar

American
12 tablespoons (1½ sticks) butter
6 tablespoons clear honey
¼ cup sugar
finely grated rind of 2 oranges
3 eggs
2 cups all-purpose flour
1 teaspoon baking powder
pinch of salt
Topping:
1 orange, thinly sliced
⅔ cup water
½ cup sugar

Cream the butter with the honey and sugar until light and fluffy. Beat in the orange rind. Beat in the eggs one at a time, adding a tablespoon of flour with each one. Sift the remaining flour with the baking powder and salt and fold into the creamed mixture. Pour into a greased and lined 18 cm/7 inch round deep cake pan.

Bake in a preheated moderate oven (160°C/325°F, Gas Mark 3) for about 1¼ hours or until well risen and firm to the touch. Turn out onto a wire rack and leave to cool.

For the topping, poach the orange slices in the water in a frying pan for about 10 minutes. Stir in the sugar until dissolved, then continue to simmer until the syrup is thick. Cool slightly, then arrange the orange slices around the top of the cake. Spoon or brush over the syrup and leave until cold.

Coffee Almond Torte

Metric/Imperial
1 quantity whisked sponge cake
   batter (see page 7)
300 ml/½ pint whipping cream
1 tablespoon strong black coffee
sifted icing sugar
flaked almonds

American
1 quantity whisked sponge cake
   batter (see page 7)
1¼ cups whipping cream
1 tablespoon strong black coffee
sifted confectioners' sugar
slivered almonds

Pour the batter into two 18 cm/7 inch sandwich tins (layer cake pans) and bake in a preheated moderate oven (180°C/350°F, Gas Mark 4) for 15 to 20 minutes. Cool. Whip the cream with the coffee and sugar to taste, until thick. Sandwich the layers together with some of the cream and use the rest to cover the top and sides. Press flaked (slivered) almonds against the sides.

Siena Cake

Metric/Imperial	American
75 g/3 oz toasted hazelnuts, chopped	¾ cup chopped toasted hazelnuts
75 g/3 oz blanched almonds, chopped	¾ cup chopped blanched almonds
175 g/6 oz chopped mixed peel	1 cup chopped mixed candied peel
25 g/1 oz cocoa powder	¼ cup unsweetened cocoa
50 g/2 oz plain flour, sifted	½ cup all-purpose flour, sifted
½ teaspoon ground cinnamon	½ teaspoon ground cinnamon
¼ teaspoon ground mixed spice	¼ teaspoon ground allspice
100 g/4 oz caster sugar	½ cup sugar
100 g/4 oz honey	⅓ cup honey
Topping:	**Topping:**
2 tablespoons icing sugar	2 tablespoons confectioners' sugar
1 teaspoon ground cinnamon	1 teaspoon ground cinnamon

Mix together the nuts, peel, cocoa, flour and spices. Put the sugar and honey in a saucepan and heat gently, stirring to dissolve the sugar. Boil until the mixture reaches 115°C/240°F on a sugar thermometer. Remove from the heat and stir in the nut mixture.

Pour into a greased and lined 20 cm/8 inch flan ring on a baking sheet or a tart pan. Spread out evenly.

Bake in a preheated cool oven (150°C/300°F, Gas Mark 2) for 30 to 35 minutes. Cool in the pan. Sprinkle with the icing (confectioners') sugar mixed with the cinnamon and cut into wedges to serve.

Lamingtons

Metric/Imperial	American
1 quantity basic butter cake batter (see page 18)	1 quantity basic butter cake batter (see page 18)
Icing:	**Frosting:**
500 g/1 lb icing sugar	4 cups confectioners' sugar
5 tablespoons cocoa powder	5 tablespoons unsweetened cocoa
1½ tablespoons melted butter	1½ tablespoons melted butter
6–8 tablespoons warmed milk	6–8 tablespoons warmed milk
desiccated coconut	shredded coconut

Bake the basic butter cake batter in a 28 × 18 cm/11 × 7 inch cake pan in a preheated moderate oven (180°C/350°F, Gas Mark 4) for 30 to 40 minutes. Cool, then cut into squares.

Sift the icing (confectioners') sugar and cocoa powder (unsweetened cocoa) into a bowl. Add the melted butter and warm milk to make a smooth coating consistency. Dip the cake squares in the icing (frosting), then coat with the coconut.

Iced Cherry Cake

Metric/Imperial	American
175 g/6 oz butter	12 tablespoons (1½ sticks) butter
175 g/6 oz caster sugar	¾ cup sugar
3 eggs	3 eggs
75 g/3 oz plain flour	¾ cup all-purpose flour
75 g/3 oz self-raising flour	¾ cup self-rising flour
3–4 tablespoons milk	3–4 tablespoons milk
100 g/4 oz glacé cherries, quartered	⅔ cup quartered candied cherries
halved glacé cherries to decorate	halved candied cherries to decorate
Icing:	**Icing:**
275 g/10 oz icing sugar, sifted	2½ cups confectioners' sugar, sifted
1 teaspoon butter, softened	1 teaspoon butter, softened
¼ teaspoon vanilla essence	¼ teaspoon vanilla extract
2–3 tablespoons milk	2–3 tablespoons milk

Cream the butter with the sugar until light and fluffy. Beat in the eggs one at a time, adding a tablespoon of flour with each one. Sift in the remaining flour and fold in with the milk. Fold in the cherries. Pour into a greased and floured 20 cm/8 inch round deep cake pan, or a baba or ring mould.

Bake in a preheated moderate oven (180°C/350°F, Gas Mark 4) for about 1 hour or until a skewer inserted into the centre of the cake comes out clean. Cool on a wire rack.

For the icing, mix together all the ingredients until smooth and of a coating consistency. Spread the icing over the cake, or warm it and trickle it over the top and down the sides. Decorate with halved cherries.

Hazelnut Cake

Metric/Imperial	American
4 eggs	4 eggs
175 g/6 oz caster sugar	¾ cup sugar
few drops of vanilla essence	few drops of vanilla extract
100 g/4 oz self-raising flour, sifted	1 cup self-rising flour, sifted
100 g/4 oz hazelnuts, finely chopped	1 cup finely chopped hazelnuts
1 quantity glacé icing (see page 42) made with lemon juice instead of water	1 quantity glacé icing (see page 42) made with lemon juice instead of water

Beat the eggs, sugar and vanilla together until the mixture is pale and very thick and will make a ribbon trail on itself when the beater is lifted. Fold in the flour and nuts. Pour into a greased 20 cm/8 inch round deep cake pan.

Bake in a preheated moderate oven (180°C/350°F, Gas Mark 4) for 1 hour. Cool slightly, then spread over the icing and leave to set.

Honey Sponge Cake

Metric/Imperial	American
75 g/3 oz self-raising flour	¾ cup self-rising flour
3 tablespoons arrowroot	3 tablespoons arrowroot
pinch of salt	pinch of salt
3 eggs, separated	3 eggs, separated
100 g/4 oz caster sugar	½ cup sugar
½ teaspoon vanilla essence	½ teaspoon vanilla extract
1½ tablespoons clear honey	1½ tablespoons clear honey
1 tablespoon butter	1 tablespoon butter
3 tablespoons hot milk	3 tablespoons hot milk

Sift the flour, arrowroot and salt together three times. Beat the egg whites until stiff, then gradually beat in the sugar. Add the vanilla and egg yolks and beat until stiff again. Fold in the flour mixture, followed by the honey and the butter melted in the milk. Divide the batter between two greased and floured 18 cm/7 inch sandwich tins (layer cake pans).

Bake in a preheated moderate oven (180°C/350°F, Gas Mark 4) for 20 to 25 minutes. Cool on a wire rack. Sandwich the cakes with jam.

Ginger Fluff Sponge Cake

Metric/Imperial	American
2 tablespoons plain flour	2 tablespoons all-purpose flour
50 g/2 oz arrowroot	½ cup arrowroot
2 teaspoons ground ginger	2 teaspoons ground ginger
2 teaspoons ground cinnamon	2 teaspoons ground cinnamon
2 teaspoons cocoa power	2 teaspoons unsweetened cocoa
2 teaspoons cream of tartar	2 teaspoons cream of tartar
1 teaspoon bicarbonate of soda	1 teaspoon baking soda
4 eggs, separated	4 eggs, separated
100 g/4 oz caster sugar	½ cup sugar
1 tablespoon golden syrup, warmed	1 tablespoon light corn syrup,
sweetened whipped cream	warmed
	sweetened whipped cream

Sift together the flour, arrowroot, ginger, cinnamon, cocoa, cream of tartar and bicarbonate of soda (baking soda) four times.

Beat the egg whites until stiff, then gradually beat in the sugar. Beat in the egg yolks, then fold in the sifted dry ingredients followed by the syrup.

Divide the batter between two greased and floured 18 cm/7 inch sandwich tins (layer cake pans). Bake in a preheated moderate oven (180°C/350°F, Gas Mark 4) for 15 to 20 minutes. Cool on a wire rack. Sandwich the layers together with sweetened whipped cream.

Brown Coconut Cake

Metric/Imperial	American
2 × 18 cm/7 inch Victoria sandwich cake layers (see page 16)	2 × 7 inch Victoria layer cake layers (see page 16)
jam	jam
50 g/2 oz butter	4 tablespoons butter
50 g/2 oz brown sugar	⅓ cup brown sugar
grated rind and juice of 1 lemon	grated rind and juice of 1 lemon
3 tablespoons desiccated coconut	3 tablespoons shredded coconut

Spread the bottom cake layer with jam. Cream the butter with the sugar and lemon rind and juice. Beat in the coconut. Spread half the coconut mixture over the jam, then place the second cake layer on top. Spread the rest of the coconut mixture on top. Brown under the grill (broiler) and serve warm.

Variation:
Use orange rind and juice instead of lemon, or diced preserved (candied) ginger and syrup from the jar of ginger.

Pineapple Upside-Down Cake

Metric/Imperial	American
175 g/6 oz plain flour	1½ cups all-purpose flour
1½ teaspoons baking powder	1½ teaspoons baking powder
50 g/2 oz semolina	⅓ cup semolina or cream of wheat
100 g/4 oz butter	8 tablespoons (1 stick) butter
100 g/4 oz caster sugar	½ cup sugar
3 eggs	3 eggs
½ teaspoon vanilla essence	½ teaspoon vanilla extract
little milk	little milk
Topping:	**Topping:**
25 g/1 oz butter	2 tablespoons butter
25 g/1 oz soft brown sugar	2½ tablespoons light brown sugar
1 small can pineapple rings, drained	1 small can pineapple rings, drained
glacé cherries	candied cherries

First make the topping. Melt the butter with the sugar and pour it into an 18 cm/7 inch round cake pan. Arrange the pineapple rings on the bottom of the pan and place a cherry in the centre of each ring.

Sift the flour, baking powder and semolina together. Cream the butter with the sugar until light and fluffy. Beat in the eggs one at a time, adding a tablespoonful of the flour mixture with each egg. Fold in the remaining flour mixture with the vanilla and a little milk. Spread over the fruit in the pan.

Bake in a preheated moderately hot oven (190°C/375°F, Gas Mark 5) for about 20 minutes. Invert onto a serving plate to serve, warm or cold.

Coffee Nut Sandwich (Layer) Cake

Metric/Imperial
100 g/4 oz self-raising flour
pinch of salt
100 g/4 oz butter
100 g/4 oz caster sugar
1 teaspoon vanilla essence
2 eggs
25 g/1 oz walnuts, finely chopped
300 ml/½ pint double cream
icing sugar
coffee essence
walnut halves to decorate

American
1 cup self-rising flour
pinch of salt
8 tablespoons (1 stick) butter
½ cup sugar
1 teaspoon vanilla extract
2 eggs
¼ cup finely chopped walnuts
1¼ cups heavy cream
confectioners' sugar
coffee flavoring
walnut halves to decorate

Sift the flour and salt together. Cream the butter with the sugar and vanilla until light and fluffy. Beat in the eggs, one at a time, adding a tablespoon of flour with each egg. Add the finely chopped walnuts. Fold in the remaining flour.

Divide the batter between two greased and floured or lined 18 cm/7 inch sandwich tins (layer cake pans). Bake in a preheated moderate oven (180°C/350°F, Gas Mark 4) for 25 to 30 minutes or until well risen and golden. Cool in the tins (pans) for 5 minutes, then turn out and cool completely on a wire rack.

When the layers are cold, slice each into two layers, to make 4 in all. Whip the cream until thick and sweeten with the icing (confectioners') sugar. Flavour the cream to taste with the coffee. Use most of the cream to sandwich the cake layers together, and spread the rest over the top. Decorate with walnut halves.

Variation:
Use coffee flavoured buttercream (see page 41) to sandwich the layers together.

Hazelnut and Raspberry Torte

Metric/Imperial
4 eggs, separated
100 g/4 oz soft brown sugar
100 g/4 oz coarsely ground hazelnuts
Filling:
500 g/1 lb cooking apples, peeled,
  cored and sliced
grated rind and juice of ½ lemon
225 g/8 oz raspberries
50 g/2 oz soft brown sugar
To decorate:
whipped cream
few unblanched hazelnuts

American
4 eggs, separated
⅔ cup light brown sugar
1 cup coarsely ground hazelnuts
Filling:
1 lb tart apples, peeled, cored and
  sliced
grated rind and juice of ½ lemon
½ lb raspberries
⅓ cup light brown sugar
To decorate:
whipped cream
few unblanched hazelnuts

Beat the egg yolks and sugar together until pale and thick. Beat the egg whites until stiff, then fold into the egg yolk mixture with the hazelnuts. Divide the batter between two greased and floured 23 cm/9 inch sandwich tins (layer cake pans).

Bake in a preheated moderate oven (180°C/350°F, Gas Mark 4) for about 30 minutes or until firm to the touch. Cool on a wire rack.

For the filling, put all the ingredients in a saucepan and cook gently until pulpy, stirring occasionally. Remove from the heat and beat until smooth, or purée in a sieve (strainer). Cool.

Sandwich together the cake layers with the filling. Pipe rosettes of cream on top and decorate with hazelnuts.

Walnut Spice Sandwich (Layer) Cake

Metric/Imperial
3 eggs
75 g/3 oz caster sugar
25 g/1 oz walnuts, chopped
1 teaspoon ground cinnamon
75 g/3 oz plain flour, sifted
whipped cream or buttercream (see
   page 41) to fill
walnut halves to decorate

American
3 eggs
6 tablespoons sugar
¼ cup chopped walnuts
1 teaspoon ground cinnamon
¾ cup all-purpose flour, sifted
whipped cream or buttercream (see
   page 41) to fill
walnut halves to decorate

Beat the eggs and sugar together until the mixture is pale and very thick and will make a ribbon trail on itself when the beater is lifted. Fold in the chopped walnuts. Sift the cinnamon with the flour and fold into the egg mixture. Pour the mixture into two greased and floured 18 cm/7 inch sandwich tins (layer cake pans) and bake in a preheated moderate oven (180°C/350°F, Gas Mark 4) for 15 to 20 minutes. Turn out and leave to cool on a wire rack. Sandwich with whipped cream or buttercream (see page 41) and decorate.

Continental Fruit Cake

Metric/Imperial
225 g/8 oz butter
175 g/6 oz caster sugar
2 eggs, beaten
275 g/10 oz self-raising flour, sifted
Filling:
50 g/2 oz butter
50 g/2 oz brown sugar
1 cooking apple, peeled, cored and
   grated
50 g/2 oz sultanas
50 g/2 oz raisins
25 g/1 oz currants
1 teaspoon ground cinnamon

American
½ lb (2 sticks) butter
¾ cup sugar
2 eggs, beaten
2½ cups self-rising flour, sifted
Filling:
4 tablespoons butter
⅓ cup brown sugar
1 tart apple, peeled, cored and
   grated
⅓ cup seedless white raisins
⅓ cup raisins
2½ tablespoons currants
1 teaspoon ground cinnamon

Cream the butter with the sugar until light and fluffy. Beat in the eggs, then fold in the flour. Pour into a greased and lined 18 cm/7 inch round deep cake pan. Bake in a moderate oven (180°C/350°F, Gas Mark 4) for 1 hour. Cool.

For the filling, melt the butter with the sugar, stirring to dissolve the sugar. Remove from the heat and mix in the remaining filling ingredients.

Split the cake into two layers and sandwich together with the filling.

Spiced Streusel Cake

Metric/Imperial
175 g/6 oz butter
225 g/8 oz caster sugar
1 teaspoon vanilla essence
3 eggs
150 g/5 oz self-raising flour
75 g/3 oz plain flour
3 tablespoons milk
Topping:
100 g/4 oz plain flour
1 tablespoon ground cinnamon
75 g/3 oz dark brown sugar
75 g/3 oz butter

American
12 tablespoons (1½ sticks) butter
1 cup sugar
1 teaspoon vanilla extract
3 eggs
1¼ cups self-rising flour
¾ cup all-purpose flour
3 tablespoons milk
Topping:
1 cup all-purpose flour
1 tablespoon ground cinnamon
½ cup dark brown sugar
6 tablespoons butter

Cream the butter with the sugar and vanilla until light and fluffy. Beat in the eggs one at a time, adding a tablespoon of flour with each egg. Sift in the flours and fold in with the milk. Pour into a greased and floured 23 cm/9 inch square deep cake pan.

For the topping, sift the flour, cinnamon and sugar into a bowl and rub in the butter. Sprinkle the topping over the cake batter in the pan.

Bake in a preheated moderately hot oven (190°C/375°F, Gas Mark 5) for 35 to 40 minutes or until a skewer inserted into the centre of the cake comes out clean.

French Almond Cake

Metric/Imperial
100 g/4 oz butter
165 g/5½ oz caster sugar
3 large eggs, beaten
75 g/3 oz ground almonds
40 g/1½ oz plain flour, sifted
few drops of almond essence
caster sugar to dredge

American
8 tablespoons (1 stick) butter
11 tablespoons sugar
3 eggs, beaten
¾ cup ground almonds
6 tablespoons all-purpose flour,
  sifted
few drops of almond extract
sugar to dredge

Cream the butter with the sugar until light and fluffy. Beat in the eggs one at a time, adding a little of the ground almonds with each egg. Fold in the remaining ground almonds, the flour and almond essence (extract).

Pour the batter into a greased and lined 18 cm/7 inch round deep cake pan. Bake in a preheated moderate oven (180°C/350°F, Gas Mark 4) for about 50 minutes or until golden brown and firm to the touch. Turn out onto a wire rack, sprinkle with sugar and cool.

Coconut Streusel Cake

Metric/Imperial
350 g/12 oz self-raising flour
pinch of salt
225 g/8 oz butter
175 g/6 oz caster sugar
100 g/4 oz desiccated coconut
3 eggs, beaten
about 75 ml/3 fl oz milk
Topping:
40 g/1½ oz butter
50 g/2 oz plain flour, sifted
50 g/2 oz demerara sugar
desiccated coconut

American
3 cups self-rising flour
pinch of salt
½ lb (2 sticks) butter
¾ cup sugar
1⅓ cups shredded coconut
3 eggs, beaten
about 6 tablespoons milk
Topping:
3 tablespoons butter
½ cup all-purpose flour, sifted
⅓ cup raw brown sugar
shredded coconut

Sift the flour and salt into a bowl. Rub in the butter, then stir in the sugar and coconut. Add the eggs and enough milk to mix to a fairly stiff dropping consistency. Pour into a greased and lined 20 cm/8 inch round or square deep cake pan.

For the topping, rub the butter into the flour and stir in the sugar. Sprinkle this over the top of the cake followed by a little coconut.

Bake in a preheated moderate oven (180°C/350°F, Gas Mark 4) for 1¼ to 1½ hours or until well risen and firm to the touch. Turn out carefully and cool on a wire rack.

Rich Almond Cake

Metric/Imperial
175 g/6 oz butter
175 g/6 oz sugar
3 large eggs, beaten
75 g/3 oz ground almonds
175 g/6 oz self-raising flour
few drops of almond essence
about 1 tablespoon water
2 tablespoons flaked almonds

American
12 tablespoons (1½ sticks) butter
¾ cup sugar
3 eggs, beaten
¾ cup ground almonds
1½ cups self-rising flour
few drops of almond extract
about 1 tablespoon water
2 tablespoons slivered almonds

Cream the butter with the sugar until light and fluffy. Beat in the eggs one at a time, adding a little of the ground almonds with each egg. Fold in the remaining ground almonds, the flour, almond essence (extract) and water.

Pour the batter into a greased and lined 18 cm/7 inch round deep cake pan. Sprinkle the top with the flaked (slivered) almonds and bake in a preheated moderate oven (160°C, 325°F, Gas Mark 3) for 1¼ hours.

CAKES, PASTRIES AND BREADS

Small Cakes

Meringues

Metric/Imperial
2 large egg whites
pinch of cream of tartar
150 g/5 oz caster sugar
2 teaspoons cornflour
150 ml/¼ pint double cream

American
2 egg whites
pinch of cream of tartar
⅔ cup sugar
2 teaspoons cornstarch
⅔ cup heavy cream

Beat the egg whites with the cream of tartar until stiff. Gradually beat in half the sugar and continue beating until the mixture is shiny and holds a firm peak when the beater is lifted out of the bowl. Fold in the cornflour (cornstarch) and the remaining sugar.

Put the meringue into a piping bag fitted with a large meringue tube (nozzle) and pipe in 16 whirls on a baking sheet lined with non-stick silicone paper. Dry out in a preheated very cool oven (100°C/225°F, Gas Mark ¼) for 1½ hours or until the meringues are very pale cream and set.

Turn the meringues upside down and return to the oven for a further 30 minutes to dry out completely. Cool on a wire rack.

Whip the cream until thick and use to sandwich together pairs of meringues.
Makes 8

Butterfly Cakes

Metric/Imperial
1 quantity Victoria sandwich cake
  batter (see page 16)
⅓ quantity simple buttercream,
  flavoured with ½ teaspoon vanilla
  essence (see page 41)
sifted icing sugar

American
1 quantity Victoria layer cake batter
  (see page 16)
⅓ quantity simple buttercream,
  flavored with ½ teaspoon vanilla
  extract (see page 41)
sifted confectioners' sugar

Divide the cake batter between 20 to 24 fluted paper cake cases placed in
bun tins (cup cake pans). Bake in a preheated moderately hot oven (190°C/
375°F, Gas Mark 5) for about 20 minutes or until well risen and golden. Cool
on a wire rack.

Cut a slice off the top of each cake, then cut this slice in half to form two
'wings'. Pipe a heavy line of buttercream down the centre of the top of each
cake and put the wings in the buttercream, at angles. Dust with icing
(confectioners') sugar.
Makes 20–24

Sponge (Lady) Fingers

Metric/Imperial
3 large eggs
75 g/3 oz caster sugar
few drops of vanilla essence
75 g/3 oz plain flour, sifted twice
300 ml/½ pint whipping cream
sifted icing sugar

American
3 eggs
6 tablespoons sugar
few drops of vanilla extract
¾ cup all-purpose flour, sifted twice
1¼ cups whipping cream
sifted confectioners' sugar

Beat the eggs and sugar together until the mixture is very thick and pale and
makes a ribbon trail on itself when the beater is lifted. Add the vanilla, then
fold in the flour.

Put the batter into a piping bag fitted with a 1 cm/½ inch plain tube (nozzle)
and pipe in fingers on a baking sheet lined with non-stick silicone paper.

Bake in a preheated hot oven (220°C/425°F, Gas Mark 7) for 7 minutes or
until pale brown. Cool on a wire rack.

Whip the cream until thick and use to sandwich together pairs of fingers.
Dredge lightly with icing (confectioners') sugar.
Makes about 20 pairs
Variations:
Sandwich together the fingers with buttercream (see page 41) or jam. Drizzle
the tops with melted chocolate if you like.

Hazelnut Meringue Petit Fours

Metric/Imperial
2 egg whites
150 g/5 oz icing sugar, sifted
50 g/2 oz hazelnuts, toasted and
  finely chopped

American
2 egg whites
1¼ cups confectioners' sugar, sifted
½ cup toasted, finely chopped
  hazelnuts

Put the egg whites and sugar in a heatproof mixing bowl. Place the bowl over a pan of gently simmering water and beat the egg whites and sugar until the mixture stands in stiff peaks. Remove from the heat and fold in the hazelnuts. Put teaspoons of the mixture onto baking sheets lined with rice paper. Bake in a cool oven (150°C/300°F, Gas Mark 2) for 20 to 25 minutes. Cool.

Walnut Squares

Metric/Imperial
1 egg
225 g/8 oz brown sugar
75 g/3 oz wholemeal flour
1 teaspoon bicarbonate of soda
¼ teaspoon salt
100 g/4 oz walnuts, finely chopped

American
1 egg
1⅓ cups brown sugar
¾ cup wholewheat flour
1 teaspoon baking soda
¼ teaspoon salt
1 cup finely chopped walnuts

Mix together the egg and sugar, then stir in the remaining ingredients. Pour into a greased 20 cm/8 inch square cake pan.
  Bake in a preheated moderate oven (180°C/350°F, Gas Mark 4) for 20 minutes. Cool in the pan, then cut into squares.
Makes 16

Butterscotch Brownies

Metric/Imperial
100 g/4 oz butter
100 g/4 oz soft brown sugar
2 eggs
1 teaspoon vanilla essence
75 g/3 oz self-raising flour, sifted
50 g/2 oz walnuts, chopped

American
8 tablespoons (1 stick) butter
⅔ cup light brown sugar
2 eggs
1 teaspoon vanilla extract
¾ cup self-rising flour, sifted
½ cup chopped walnuts

Cream the butter with the sugar, then beat in the eggs, vanilla and flour. Fold in the walnuts. Pour into a greased and floured 18 cm/7 inch square cake pan. Bake in a preheated moderate oven (160°C/325°F, Gas Mark 3) for 35 to 45 minutes. Cool, then cut into squares.

Brownies

Metric/Imperial
50 g/2 oz plain chocolate
65 g/2½ oz butter
175 g/6 oz caster sugar
½ teaspoon vanilla essence
65 g/2½ oz self-raising flour
large pinch of salt
50 g/2 oz walnuts, chopped
2 eggs, beaten

American
⅓ cup semi-sweet chocolate chips
5 tablespoons butter
¾ cup sugar
½ teaspoon vanilla extract
½ cup plus 2 tablespoons self-rising
  flour
large pinch of salt
½ cup chopped walnuts
2 eggs, beaten

Melt the chocolate gently with the butter. Remove from the heat and stir in the sugar and vanilla.

Sift the flour and salt into a bowl and stir in the walnuts. Add the chocolate mixture and eggs and mix well together. Pour into a greased and floured 20 cm/8 inch square cake pan.

Bake in a preheated moderate oven (180°C/350°F, Gas Mark 4) for 35 to 40 minutes or until well risen and just beginning to shrink away from the sides of the pan. Cool in the pan, then cut into squares.
Makes 12

Apple Squares

Metric/Imperial
1 quantity Victoria sandwich cake
  batter (see page 16), made with 1
  egg and 1 teaspoon each ground
  cinnamon and mixed spice sifted
  with the flour
300 ml/½ pint stewed apple slices,
  well drained
sifted icing sugar

American
1 quantity Victoria layer cake batter
  (see page 16), made with 1 egg
  and 1 teaspoon each ground
  cinnamon and allspice sifted with
  the flour
1¼ cups stewed apple slices, well
  drained
sifted confectioners' sugar

Spread half the batter over the bottom of a greased and floured 20 cm/8 inch square deep cake pan. Cover with the apple slices, then spread the remaining cake batter over the top.

Bake in a preheated moderate oven (180°C/350°F, Gas Mark 4) for about 45 minutes. Cool, then sprinkle with icing (confectioners') sugar. Cut into squares to serve.

Orange or Lemon Cup Cakes

Metric/Imperial
225 g/8 oz self-raising flour
pinch of salt
100 g/4 oz butter
100 g/4 oz caster sugar
finely grated rind of 1 small orange or
    lemon
1 egg, beaten
1 teaspoon vanilla essence
about 5 tablespoons milk

American
2 cups self-rising flour
pinch of salt
8 tablespoons (1 stick) butter
½ cup sugar
finely grated rind of 1 small orange or
    lemon
1 egg, beaten
1 teaspoon vanilla extract
about 5 tablespoons milk

Place fluted paper cake cases in 16 to 18 bun tins (cup cake pans).

Sift the flour and salt into a bowl. Rub in the butter, then mix in the sugar and orange or lemon rind. Add the egg, vanilla and milk and mix to a softish batter, adding more milk if necessary.

Divide the batter between the paper cases. Bake in a preheated moderately hot oven (190°C/375°F, Gas Mark 5) for 15 to 20 minutes or until well risen, golden and firm. Cool on a wire rack.

Makes 16–18

Variations:

Fruity Cup Cakes: Omit the orange or lemon rind and add 65 g/2½ oz (½ cup) dried fruit.

Coconut Cup Cakes: Omit the orange or lemon rind and reduce the flour to 200 g/7 oz (1¾ cups). Add 40 g/1½ oz desiccated coconut (½ cup shredded coconut) with the sugar and increase the vanilla to 2 teaspoons.

Chocolate Cup Cakes: Omit the orange or lemon rind. Replace 25 g/1 oz (¼ cup) of the flour with half cornflour (cornstarch) and half cocoa powder (unsweetened cocoa). Use 100 g/4 oz (⅔ cup) soft brown sugar instead of caster sugar.

Date and Hazelnut Fingers

Metric/Imperial	American
2 eggs	2 eggs
175 g/6 oz dark brown sugar	1 cup dark brown sugar
75 g/3 oz self-raising wholemeal flour	¾ cup self-rising wholewheat flour
pinch of salt	pinch of salt
50 g/2 oz bran cereal	1 cup bran cereal
50 g/2 oz hazelnuts, chopped	½ cup chopped hazelnuts
100 g/4 oz stoned dates, chopped	⅔ cup chopped pitted dates

Beat the eggs and sugar together until pale and creamy. Stir in the remaining ingredients. Spread the batter in a greased and lined 28 × 18 cm/11 × 7 inch cake pan.

Bake in a preheated moderate oven (180°C/350°F, Gas Mark 4) for 30 minutes. Cool in the pan, then cut into fingers.
Makes 12

Coconut Buns

Metric/Imperial	American
100 g/4 oz self-raising flour	1 cup self-rising flour
50 g/2 oz butter	4 tablespoons butter
50 g/2 oz caster sugar	¼ cup sugar
50 g/2 oz desiccated coconut	⅔ cup shredded coconut
1 egg, beaten	1 egg, beaten
little milk	little milk

Sift the flour into a bowl and rub in the butter. Stir in the sugar and coconut, then bind to a soft dropping consistency with the egg and a little milk. Divide between 10 greased bun (muffin) tins.

Bake in a preheated moderately hot oven (190°C/375°F, Gas Mark 5) for 20 minutes. Cool on a wire rack.
Makes about 10

CAKES, PASTRIES

Icings, Frostings and Fillings

AND BREADS

Chocolate Buttercream 1

Metric/Imperial
50 g/2 oz butter
75 g/3 oz icing sugar
1½ tablespoons cocoa powder
½ teaspoon vanilla essence
1 tablespoon hot water

American
4 tablespoons butter
¾ cup confectioners' sugar
1½ tablespoons unsweetened cocoa
½ teaspoon vanilla extract
1 tablespoon hot water

Cream the butter until very soft. Sift together the sugar and cocoa and beat into the butter. Add the vanilla essence (extract) and the hot water and mix well.

Chocolate Buttercream 2

Metric/Imperial
50 g/2 oz butter
100 g/4 oz icing sugar, sifted
50 g/2 oz plain chocolate, melted
1 teaspoon vanilla essence

American
4 tablespoons butter
1 cup confectioners' sugar, sifted
⅓ cup semi-sweet chocolate chips,
  melted
1 teaspoon vanilla extract

Beat the butter until it is very soft, then gradually beat in the sugar. Beat the melted chocolate and vanilla essence (extract) into the buttercream.

Classic Buttercream

Metric/Imperial	American
225 g/8 oz sugar	1 cup sugar
4 tablespoons water	¼ cup water
2 egg yolks	2 egg yolks
225 g/8 oz butter, softened	½ lb (2 sticks) butter, softened
flavouring	flavoring

Dissolve the sugar in the water in a saucepan, then bring to the boil and boil until the syrup reaches a temperature of 116°C/240°F. Remove from the heat. Beat the egg yolks in a bowl and gradually beat in the hot syrup. Continue beating until the mixture is cool and thick. Gradually beat the egg syrup into the butter.

Flavour to taste.

Variations:
Vanilla Buttercream: Add 1 teaspoon vanilla essence (extract).
Coffee Buttercream: Add 2 to 3 teaspoons coffee essence (flavoring).

Simple Buttercream

Metric/Imperial	American
175 g/6 oz butter	12 tablespoons butter
350 g/12 oz icing sugar, sifted	3 cups confectioners' sugar, sifted
flavouring	flavoring

Beat the butter until it is very soft, then gradually beat in the sugar. Flavour the buttercream as suggested in the classic buttercream recipe (above).

Variation:
Orange or Lemon Buttercream: Flavour the buttercream with the grated rind of 2 large oranges (or 1 lemon), creamed in well while adding the sugar.

Butterscotch Buttercream

Metric/Imperial	American
75 g/3 oz butter	6 tablespoons butter
1½ tablespoons black treacle	1½ tablespoons molasses
2 teaspoons lemon juice	2 teaspoons lemon juice
225 g/8 oz icing sugar, sifted	2 cups confectioners' sugar, sifted
water	water

Cream the butter with the treacle (molasses) until soft. Beat in the lemon juice, then gradually beat in the sugar. Add a little water if necessary to give a spreading consistency.

Crème Pâtissière

Metric/Imperial
550 ml/18 fl oz milk
1 vanilla pod or few drops of vanilla
   essence
115 g/4½ oz sugar
3 egg yolks
25 g/1 oz plain flour
25 g/1 oz cornflour

American
2¼ cups milk
1 vanilla bean or few drops of vanilla
   extract
½ cup plus 1 tablespoon sugar
3 egg yolks
¼ cup all-purpose flour
¼ cup cornstarch

Put the milk, vanilla pod (bean) and 50 g/2 oz (¼ cup) of the sugar in a saucepan and bring slowly to the boil, stirring to dissolve the sugar. Remove from the heat and leave to infuse.

Beat the remaining sugar with the egg yolks. Sift in the flour and cornflour (cornstarch) and beat until smooth. Gradually strain in the hot milk, beating well. Add the vanilla essence (extract), if using.

Pour the mixture into the saucepan and bring to the boil, stirring. Cook gently for 1 minute. Use hot or cold.

Almond Paste

Metric/Imperial
500 g/1 lb ground almonds
225 g/8 oz icing sugar, sifted
225 g/8 oz caster sugar
1½ teaspoons lemon juice
3 drops of almond essence
1 egg

American
4 cups ground almonds
2 cups confectioners' sugar, sifted
1 cup granulated sugar
1½ teaspoons lemon juice
3 drops of almond extract
1 egg

Put all the ingredients in a bowl and mix well together to form a stiff paste. Knead until smooth.

Glacé Icing

Metric/Imperial
100 g/4 oz icing sugar
1–2 tablespoons warm water
food colouring and/or flavouring
   (optional)

American
1 cup confectioners' sugar
1–2 tablespoons warm water
food coloring and/or flavoring
   (optional)

Sift the sugar into a bowl and gradually beat in enough water to give a smooth icing that is thick enough to coat the back of the spoon. Add food colouring and/or flavouring and use at once.

Royal Icing

Metric/Imperial
4 egg whites
1 kg/2 lb icing sugar, sifted
2 teaspoons glycerine

American
4 egg whites
2 lb (16 cups) confectioners' sugar,
  sifted
2 teaspoons glycerine

Beat the egg whites until frothy. Gradually beat in the sugar and continue beating until the icing stands in peaks when the beater is lifted out of the bowl. Beat in the glycerine.

Keep the bowl of icing covered with a damp cloth to prevent it hardening while icing the cake.

Boiled White Frosting

Metric/Imperial
500 g/1 lb sugar
150 ml/¼ pint water
1 teaspoon vanilla, almond or rum
  essence (optional)
2 egg whites

American
2 cups sugar
⅔ cup water
1 teaspoon vanilla, almond or rum
  extract (optional)
2 egg whites

Put the sugar and water in a saucepan and heat, stirring to dissolve the sugar. Bring to the boil and boil briskly until the syrup reaches 120°C/250°F on a sugar thermometer. Remove from the heat and stir in the flavouring.

Beat the egg whites until stiff. Gradually add the syrup in a slow steady stream, beating constantly, and continue beating until the frosting is cool and thick enough to spread. Swirl over the top and sides of the cake and leave for 3 to 4 hours to set.

Rich Buttercream

Metric/Imperial
75 g/3 oz butter
1 egg yolk
225 g/8 oz icing sugar
1 tablespoon milk, or orange juice,
  or lemon juice, or strong black
  coffee, depending on flavouring
  required

American
6 tablespoons butter
1 egg yolk
2 cups confectioners' sugar
1 tablespoon milk, or orange juice,
  or lemon juice, or strong black
  coffee depending on flavoring
  required

Melt the butter in a saucepan, remove from the heat and beat in the egg yolk. Gradually beat in the sugar alternately with the tablespoon of flavouring.

Orange Chocolate Frosting

Metric/Imperial
50 g/2 oz butter
175 g/6 oz soft brown sugar
grated rind and juice of 1 medium
  orange
25 g/1 oz plain chocolate, chopped
175 g/6 oz icing sugar, sifted

American
4 tablespoons butter
1 cup light brown sugar
grated rind and juice of 1 medium
  orange
1 square semi-sweet chocolate,
  chopped
1½ cups confectioners' sugar, sifted

Put the butter, brown sugar and orange rind and juice into a saucepan and
heat, stirring to dissolve the sugar. Remove from the heat, add the chocolate
and stir until melted. Gradually stir in the icing (confectioners') sugar and
beat until the frosting is smooth and of a spreading consistency.

Mocha Frosting

Metric/Imperial
50 g/2 oz butter
100 g/4 oz soft brown sugar
3 tablespoons coffee essence
1 tablespoon evaporated milk
500 g/1 lb icing sugar, sifted

American
4 tablespoons butter
⅔ cup light brown sugar
3 tablespoons coffee flavoring
1 tablespoon evaporated milk
4 cups confectioners' sugar, sifted

Put the butter, brown sugar, coffee essence (flavoring) and evaporated milk
in a saucepan and heat, stirring to dissolve the sugar. Bring to the boil and
boil for 3 minutes. Remove from the heat and gradually beat in the icing
(confectioners') sugar. Continue beating until the frosting is beginning to
thicken. Quickly spread it over the cake.

Chocolate Frosting

Metric/Imperial
100 g/4 oz plain chocolate, broken
  up
50 g/2 oz butter
2 egg yolks
about 100 g/4 oz icing sugar, sifted

American
⅔ cup semi-sweet chocolate chips
4 tablespoons butter
2 egg yolks
about 1 cup confectioners' sugar,
  sifted

Melt the chocolate gently with the butter. Remove from the heat and beat in
the egg yolks and enough sugar to give a thick, smooth spreading
consistency. Cool slightly before using.

Seven Minute Frosting

Metric/Imperial
1 egg white
175 g/6 oz caster sugar
pinch of salt
2 tablespoons water
pinch of cream of tartar

American
1 egg white
¾ cup sugar
pinch of salt
2 tablespoons water
pinch of cream of tartar

Put all the ingredients into a heatproof bowl placed over a saucepan of gently simmering water. Beat hard, preferably with a hand-held electric mixer, until the mixture is thick and stiff and will stand in peaks. Remove from the heat and spread immediately over the cake, pulling the frosting up into peaks. Leave to set before serving.

Variation:

For a butterscotch flavour, use soft brown sugar (1 cup light brown sugar) instead of the caster (granulated) sugar.

Sour Cream Chocolate Frosting

Metric/Imperial
100 g/4 oz plain chocolate
150 ml/¼ pint soured cream
pinch of salt
4–5 tablespoons sifted icing sugar

American
⅔ cup semi-sweet chocolate chips
⅔ cup sour cream
pinch of salt
4–5 tablespoons sifted
    confectioners' sugar

Melt the chocolate gently. Remove from the heat and cool slightly, then beat in the remaining ingredients to make a spreading consistency.

Peanut Butter Frosting

Metric/Imperial
100 g/4 oz peanut butter
75 g/3 oz butter
275 g/10 oz icing sugar, sifted
1 tablespoon coffee essence
1 tablespoon milk

American
½ cup peanut butter
6 tablespoons butter
2½ cups confectioners' sugar, sifted
1 tablespoon coffee flavoring
1 tablespoon milk

Beat the peanut butter with the butter, then gradually beat in the sugar. Beat in the coffee essence (flavoring) and milk.

CAKES, PASTRIES AND BREADS

Fruit Cakes and Teabreads

Family Fruit Cake

Metric/Imperial
225 g/8 oz self-raising flour
pinch of salt
100 g/4 oz butter
100 g/4 oz sugar
150 g/5 oz mixed dried fruit
1 teaspoon grated orange rind
1 egg, beaten
about 6 tablespoons milk

American
2 cups self-rising flour
pinch of salt
8 tablespoons (1 stick) butter
½ cup sugar
1 cup mixed dried fruit
1 teaspoon grated orange rind
1 egg, beaten
about 6 tablespoons milk

Sift the flour and salt into a bowl. Rub in the butter, then stir in the sugar, fruit and orange rind. Mix to a semi-stiff batter with the egg and milk, adding more milk if necessary.

Pour the batter into a greased and lined or floured 500 g/1 lb (4½ × 2½ × 1½ inch) loaf pan or a 15 cm/6 inch round deep cake pan. Bake in a preheated moderate oven (180°C/350°F, Gas Mark 4) for 1 to 1¼ hours or until a skewer inserted into the centre of the cake comes out clean.

Cool in the pan for 20 minutes, then turn out and cool completely on a wire rack.

Variations:

Farmhouse Cake: Add 12 chopped glacé (candied) cherries and 50 g/2 oz (⅓ cup) chopped mixed candied peel with the other fruit.

Date and Walnut Cake: Omit the dried fruit and add the same amount of chopped stoned (pitted) dates plus 50 g/2 oz (½ cup) chopped walnuts.

Spicy Fruit Cake: Add ½ teaspoon ground cinnamon, ½ teaspoon ground cloves and ½ teaspoon grated nutmeg with the salt.

Raisin Orange Cake: Use raisins instead of the mixed dried fruit and increase the orange rind to 1 tablespoon. Substitute 3 tablespoons of the milk with orange juice.

Barmitzvah Cake

Metric/Imperial
225 g/8 oz margarine
225 g/8 oz caster or soft brown sugar
pinch of salt
grated rind of ½ lemon
grated rind of ½ orange
½ teaspoon vanilla essence
½ teaspoon almond essence
½ teaspoon ground cinnamon
½ teaspoon ground mixed spice
pinch of grated nutmeg
5 eggs, beaten
250 g/9 oz plain flour, sifted
250 g/9 oz sultanas
175 g/6 oz currants
150 g/5 oz raisins
75 g/3 oz ground almonds
100 g/4 oz glacé cherries, quartered
75 g/3 oz chopped mixed peel
pinch of bicarbonate of soda
1 teaspoon brandy

American
½ lb (2 sticks) margarine
1 cup sugar, or 1⅓ cups light brown
  sugar
pinch of salt
grated rind of ½ lemon
grated rind of ½ orange
½ teaspoon vanilla extract
½ teaspoon almond extract
½ teaspoon ground cinnamon
½ teaspoon ground allspice
pinch of grated nutmeg
5 eggs, beaten
2¼ cups all-purpose flour, sifted
1½ cups seedless white raisins
1 cup currants
1 cup raisins
¾ cup ground almonds
⅔ cup quartered candied cherries
½ cup chopped mixed candied peel
pinch of baking soda
1 teaspoon brandy

Cream the margarine with the sugar, salt, fruit rinds, vanilla and almond essences (extracts) and spices until light and fluffy. Gradually beat in the eggs, then fold in the flour. Add the fruit, nuts and peel and mix thoroughly. Dissolve the soda in the brandy and stir into the fruit mixture. Pour into a greased and lined 20 cm/8 inch round deep cake pan and smooth the top.

Tie a double thickness of brown paper around the pan and place it on a baking sheet. Bake in a preheated cool oven (150°C/300°F, Gas Mark 2) for about 4 hours. Cool completely, then wrap in foil and store for at least 1 week before serving.

If you like, cover the cake with almond paste (see page 42) and then with royal icing (see page 43), following the instructions given in the recipe for rich fruit cake (see page 48).

Rich Fruit Cake 1

Metric/Imperial
225 g/8 oz butter
225 g/8 oz soft brown sugar
5 eggs
grated rind of 1 lemon
2 tablespoons brandy (optional)
1 tablespoon black treacle
250 g/9 oz plain flour
2 teaspoons baking powder
1 teaspoon grated nutmeg
1 teaspoon ground mixed spice
750 g/1½ lb mixed dried fruit
4 tablespoons glacé cherries,
    quartered
100 g/4 oz chopped mixed peel
50 g/2 oz blanched almonds,
    chopped
1 quantity almond paste (see page 42)
apricot jam, melted
1 quantity royal icing (see page 43)

American
½ lb (2 sticks) butter
1⅓ cups light brown sugar
5 eggs
grated rind of 1 lemon
2 tablespoons brandy (optional)
1 tablespoon molasses
2¼ cups all-purpose flour
2 teaspoons baking powder
1 teaspoon grated nutmeg
1 teaspoon ground allspice
4 cups mixed dried fruit
¼ cup quartered candied cherries
⅔ cup chopped mixed candied peel
½ cup chopped blanched almonds
1 quantity almond paste (see page 42)
apricot jam, melted
1 quantity royal icing (see page 43)

Grease and line a 23 cm/9 inch round deep cake pan and tie a strip of folded brown paper around the outside of the pan to prevent the outer edges of the cake burning during the long baking.

Cream the butter with the sugar until light and fluffy. Beat in the eggs, lemon rind, brandy, if used, and treacle (molasses). Sift in the flour, baking powder and spices, then fold in the dried fruit, cherries, peel and nuts.

Pour the batter into the pan and smooth the top level. Place the pan on a baking sheet lined with brown paper or newspaper and bake in a preheated very cool oven (120°C/250°F, Gas Mark ½) for 4½ to 5 hours.

Leave in the pan to cool for 15 to 20 minutes, then turn out onto a wire rack to cool completely. Wrap in foil and store for at least 1 week before covering with almond paste.

Roll out one-third of the almond paste on a work surface dusted with caster sugar to a round large enough to cover the top of the cake. Brush the cake with the apricot jam, then place the almond paste round on top. Trim edges.

Roll out the remaining almond paste to a long strip the length and width of the sides of the cake. Brush the sides with apricot jam and press on the almond paste strip. Seal the join. Leave to dry for 3 to 4 days before icing.

Place the cake on a board. Spread about two-thirds of the icing smoothly over the top and sides of the cake, using a large flat-bladed knife (spatula) dipped in hot water. Leave the icing to dry before decorating.

Colour the remaining icing with food colouring, if you like, then pipe on the decoration of your choice, depending on the occasion.

Rich Fruit Cake 2

Metric/Imperial
2 eggs
175 g/6 oz soft brown sugar
150 ml/¼ pint corn oil
275 g/10 oz plain flour
1½ teaspoons baking powder
pinch of salt
3 tablespoons sweet sherry or port
750 g/1½ lb mixed dried fruit
100 g/4 oz mixed candied peel, chopped
75 g/3 oz blanched almonds, chopped
3 tablespoons chopped glacé cherries
1 quantity almond paste (see page 42)
1 quantity royal icing (see page 43)

American
2 eggs
1 cup light brown sugar
⅔ cup corn oil
2½ cups all-purpose flour
1½ teaspoons baking powder
pinch of salt
3 tablespoons sweet sherry or port
4 cups mixed dried fruit
⅔ cup chopped mixed candied peel
¾ cup chopped blanched almonds
3 tablespoons chopped candied cherries
1 quantity almond paste (see page 42)
1 quantity royal icing (see page 43)

Beat together the eggs, sugar and corn oil. Sift in the flour, baking powder and salt. Add the rest of the ingredients and mix together well.

Transfer to a greased and lined 20 cm/8 inch round deep cake pan and bake in a preheated cool oven (150°C/300°F, Gas Mark 2) for 2½ to 3 hours. Cool and leave to mature for 1 week before covering with almond paste and icing. For instructions on how to do this, see Rich Fruit Cake 1 (page 48).

Cider Loaf Cake

Metric/Imperial
350 g/12 oz mixed dried fruit
300 ml/½ pint sweet cider
275 g/10 oz self-raising flour, sifted
50 g/2 oz nuts, chopped
175 g/6 oz soft brown sugar
grated rind of 1 orange
2 large eggs, beaten

American
2 cups mixed dried fruit
1¼ cups hard sweet cider
2½ cups self-rising flour, sifted
½ cup chopped nuts
1 cup light brown sugar
grated rind of 1 orange
2 eggs, beaten

Put the fruit in a bowl with the cider and leave to soak for at least 3 hours. Pour into a saucepan and bring to the boil. Cool.

Mix together the flour, nuts, sugar and orange rind. Add the fruit mixture and eggs and mix well. Pour into a greased and lined 1 kg/2 lb (9 × 5 × 3 inch) loaf pan.

Bake in a preheated moderate oven (160°C/325°F, Gas Mark 3) for 1½ to 1¾ hours or until well risen and firm to the touch. Cool on a wire rack.

Boiled Fruit Cake

Metric/Imperial
300 ml/½ pint water
100 g/4 oz margarine
150 g/5 oz soft brown sugar
350 g/12 oz mixed dried fruit
2 teaspoons ground mixed spice
½ teaspoon grated nutmeg
275 g/10 oz plain flour
2 teaspoons bicarbonate of soda
1 teaspoon baking powder
1 egg, beaten
grated rind of 1 orange

American
1¼ cups water
8 tablespoons (1 stick) margarine
¾ cup plus 1½ tablespoons light
  brown sugar
2 cups mixed dried fruit
2 teaspoons apple pie spice
½ teaspoon grated nutmeg
2½ cups all-purpose flour
2 teaspoons baking soda
1 teaspoon baking powder
1 egg, beaten
grated rind of 1 orange

Put the water in a saucepan with the margarine, sugar, fruit and spices and bring to the boil, stirring to dissolve the sugar. Simmer gently for 20 minutes, then cool.

Sift the flour with the soda and baking powder. Fold into the fruit mixture with the egg and orange rind. Pour into a greased and lined 20 cm/8 inch round deep cake pan.

Bake in a preheated moderate oven (180°C/350°F, Gas Mark 4) for about 1¼ hours or until a skewer inserted into the centre of the cake comes out clean. Cool on a wire rack.

Dripping Gingerbread

Metric/Imperial
100 g/4 oz beef dripping
75 g/3 oz soft brown sugar
100 g/4 oz black treacle
100 g/4 oz golden syrup
1 teaspoon bicarbonate of soda
150 ml/¼ pint milk, warmed
350 g/12 oz wholemeal flour
pinch of salt
2 teaspoons ground ginger

American
½ cup beef drippings
½ cup light brown sugar
⅓ cup molasses
⅓ cup light corn syrup
1 teaspoon baking soda
⅔ cup milk, warmed
3 cups wholewheat flour
pinch of salt
2 teaspoons ground ginger

Melt the beef dripping with the sugar, treacle (molasses), and syrup. Dissolve the bicarbonate of soda (baking soda) in the milk and add to the melted mixture. Sift the flour with the salt and ground ginger. Add to the liquids and mix thoroughly.

Pour the mixture into a greased and lined 25 × 20 cm/10 × 8 inch cake pan. Bake in a preheated cool oven (150°C/300°F, Gas Mark 2) for 1 hour.

Gingerbread

Metric/Imperial	American
100 g/4 oz butter	8 tablespoons (1 stick) butter
50 g/2 oz soft brown sugar	⅓ cup light brown sugar
175 g/6 oz black treacle	½ cup molasses
50 g/2 oz golden syrup	3 tablespoons light corn syrup
150 ml/¼ pint milk	⅔ cup milk
2 eggs, beaten	2 eggs, beaten
225 g/8 oz plain flour	2 cups all-purpose flour
1 teaspoon ground mixed spice	1 teaspoon ground allspice
2 teaspoons ground ginger	2 teaspoons ground ginger
1 teaspoon bicarbonate of soda	1 teaspoon baking soda

Put the butter, sugar, treacle (molasses) and syrup in a saucepan and heat until the butter has melted and the sugar dissolved. Remove from the heat and stir in the milk. Cool, then stir in the eggs.

Sift the flour, spices and soda into a bowl. Add the liquid and stir briskly, but do not beat. Pour into a greased and floured or lined 20 cm/8 inch square cake pan.

Bake in a preheated cool oven (150°C/300°F, Gas Mark 2) for 1¼ to 1½ hours or until a skewer inserted into the centre of the cake comes out clean.

Cool completely, then store in an airtight tin for at least one day before serving.

Variations:

Add 100 g/4 oz (1 cup) chopped stoned (pitted) prunes or figs, with 25 g/1 oz (¼ cup) chopped walnuts if you like.

Add 100 g/4 oz (1 cup) chopped stoned (pitted) dates and 1 teaspoon grated orange rind.

Add 100 g/4 oz (⅔ cup) mixed dried fruit – currants, raisins and sultanas (seedless white raisins).

Parkin

Metric/Imperial	American
225 g/8 oz plain flour	2 cups all-purpose flour
½ teaspoon salt	½ teaspoon salt
1 teaspoon ground cinnamon	1 teaspoon ground cinnamon
1 teaspoon ground mixed spice	1 teaspoon ground allspice
½ teaspoon ground ginger	½ teaspoon ground ginger
225 g/8 oz medium oatmeal	1½ cups medium oatmeal
150 g/5 oz butter	10 tablespoons butter
100 g/4 oz soft brown sugar	⅔ cup light brown sugar
100 g/4 oz golden syrup	⅓ cup light corn syrup
100 g/4 oz black treacle	⅓ cup molasses
1 egg, beaten	1 egg, beaten
150 ml/¼ pint milk	⅔ cup milk

Sift the flour, salt and spices into a bowl and stir in the oatmeal. Put the butter, sugar, syrup and treacle (molasses) in a saucepan and heat until the butter melts and the sugar dissolves. Stir this mixture into the dry ingredients with the egg and milk to make a soft batter. Pour into a greased and lined 23 cm/9 inch square deep cake pan.

Bake in a preheated moderate oven (160°C/325°F, Gas Mark 3) for 1½ to 1¾ hours or until a skewer inserted into the centre of the cake comes out clean. Cool in the pan for 10 minutes, then turn out onto a wire rack to cool completely. Store in an airtight container for at least one day before serving.

Variation:

Wholemeal (Wholewheat) Parkin: Make the batter as above, using 100 g/ 4 oz wholemeal flour (1 cup wholewheat flour), 1 teaspoon ground ginger, 350 g/12 oz (2 cups) medium oatmeal, 100 g/4 oz (8 tablespoons) butter, 100 g/4 oz (⅓ cup) honey, 100 g/4 oz black treacle (⅓ cup molasses) and ½ teaspoon bicarbonate of soda (baking soda) dissolved in 4 tablespoons warm milk. Pour into a greased 28 × 18 cm/11 × 7 inch cake pan and bake as above.

Cherry and Walnut Loaf

Metric/Imperial	American
175 g/6 oz soft margarine	¾ cup soft margarine
175 g/6 oz caster sugar	¾ cup sugar
3 eggs, beaten	3 eggs, beaten
75 g/3 oz glacé cherries, quartered, rinsed and dried	½ cup quartered candied cherries, rinsed and dried
225 g/8 oz plain flour, sifted	2 cups all-purpose flour, sifted
½ teaspoon baking powder	½ teaspoon baking powder
40 g/1½ oz walnuts, chopped	⅓ cup chopped walnuts
Topping:	**Topping:**
100 g/4 oz glacé cherries, halved	⅔ cup halved candied cherries
3 tablespoons apricot jam	3 tablespoons apricot jam

Put all the ingredients for the cake in a mixing bowl and beat well with a wooden spoon for 4 to 5 minutes or until well mixed. Pour into a greased and lined 1 kg/2 lb (9 × 5 × 3 inch) loaf pan. Arrange the halved cherries on top.

Bake in a preheated moderate oven (160°C/325°F, Gas Mark 3) for 1½ to 1¾ hours or until well risen and firm to the touch. Cool in the pan for 5 minutes, then turn out onto a wire rack.

Heat the jam, then sieve (strain) it. Brush over the cherry topping and cool.

Variations:

Quick Mixed Fruit Cake: Replace the quartered cherries with 275 g/10 oz (1⅔ cups) mixed dried fruit, 50 g/2 oz (⅓ cup) chopped mixed candied peel and 50 g/2 oz chopped glacé cherries (⅓ cup chopped candied cherries). Bake in a greased and lined 18 cm/7 inch round deep cake pan for 1¾ to 2 hours.

Apple and Raisin Loaf: Beat together 100 g/4 oz (½ cup) soft margarine, 100 g/4 oz (½ cup) sugar, 2 large eggs, 1 tablespoon clear honey, 175 g/6 oz (1 cup) raisins, 225 g/8 oz sifted self-raising flour (2 cups sifted self-rising flour), a pinch of salt, 1 teaspoon ground mixed spice (apple pie spice) and 1 large cooking (tart) apple, peeled, cored and grated. Bake as above. Brush the top with 1 to 2 tablespoons clear honey and cool.

Glacé Fruit Cake

Metric/Imperial
250 g/9 oz self-raising flour
25 g/1 oz cornflour
225 g/8 oz butter
225 g/8 oz caster sugar
4 eggs
2 tablespoons quartered glacé
  cherries
1 tablespoon chopped candied
  angelica
40 g/1½ oz crystallized orange slices,
  chopped
40 g/1½ oz crystallized pineapple,
  chopped
1 tablespoon chopped pistachio nuts
  or blanched almonds
finely grated rind and juice of ½
  lemon
boiled white frosting (see page 43)
glacé fruit to decorate

American
2¼ cups self-rising flour
¼ cup cornstarch
½ lb (2 sticks) butter
1 cup sugar
4 eggs
2 tablespoons quartered candied
  cherries
1 tablespoon chopped candied
  angelica
¼ cup chopped candied orange
  slices
¼ cup chopped candied pineapple
1 tablespoon chopped pistachio nuts
  or blanched almonds
finely grated rind and juice of ½
  lemon
boiled white frosting (see page 43)
candied fruit to decorate

Sift together the flour and cornflour (cornstarch). Cream the butter with the sugar until light and fluffy. Beat in the eggs one at a time, adding a tablespoon of the flour mixture after each egg. Stir in the fruits, nuts and lemon rind and juice, then fold in the rest of the flour mixture. Pour into a greased and lined 18 cm/7 inch round deep cake pan.

Bake in a preheated moderate oven (160°C/325°F, Gas Mark 3) for 1¼ to 1½ hours or until a skewer inserted into the centre of the cake comes out clean. Cool in the pan for 5 minutes, then turn out onto a wire rack to cool completely.

Cover the cake with the frosting and swirl it decoratively. Decorate with glacé (candied) fruit.

Ginger Fruit Cake

Metric/Imperial
225 g/8 oz self-raising flour
½ teaspoon salt
2 teaspoons ground ginger
1 teaspoon ground cinnamon
100 g/4 oz butter
100 g/4 oz caster sugar
1 egg, beaten
2 tablespoons black treacle
¼ teaspoon bicarbonate of soda
275 ml/9 fl oz buttermilk
175 g/6 oz sultanas or raisins

American
2 cups self-rising flour
½ teaspoon salt
2 teaspoons ground ginger
1 teaspoon ground cinnamon
8 tablespoons (1 stick) butter
½ cup sugar
1 egg, beaten
2 tablespoons molasses
¼ teaspoon baking soda
1 cup plus 2 tablespoons buttermilk
1 cup seedless white raisins

Sift together the flour, salt and spices. Cream the butter with the sugar until light and fluffy. Beat in the egg and treacle (molasses), then fold in about one-quarter of the flour mixture. Dissolve the soda in the buttermilk and stir a little of this liquid into the batter. Add the fruit, the remaining flour mixture and the rest of the liquid and mix well.

Pour into a greased and floured or lined 28 × 18 cm/11 × 7 inch cake pan and level the top. Bake in a preheated moderate oven (180°C/350°F, Gas Mark 4) for 45 minutes.

Cool in the pan for 10 minutes, then turn out onto a wire rack to cool completely. Cut into fingers to serve.

Farmhouse Cherry Cake

Metric/Imperial
100 g/4 oz glacé cherries, chopped
275 g/10 oz self-raising flour
pinch of salt
100 g/4 oz butter
2 teaspoons grated lemon rind
100 g/4 oz caster sugar
2 eggs, beaten
3 tablespoons milk

American
⅔ cup candied cherries, chopped
2½ cups self-rising flour
pinch of salt
8 tablespoons (1 stick) butter
2 teaspoons grated lemon rind
½ cup sugar
2 eggs, beaten
3 tablespoons milk

Rinse the cherries and dry thoroughly. Sift the flour and salt into a bowl. Rub in the butter, then stir in the lemon rind, sugar and cherries. Add the eggs and milk and mix well. Pour into a greased and lined 15 cm/6 inch round deep cake pan.

Bake in a preheated moderately hot oven (190°C/375°F, Gas Mark 5) for about 1 hour or until well risen and firm to the touch. Cool on a wire rack.

Dundee Cake

Metric/Imperial
225 g/8 oz plain flour
½ teaspoon baking powder
¼ teaspoon salt
225 g/8 oz butter, softened
225 g/8 oz caster sugar
grated rind of 1 small orange
1 teaspoon vanilla essence
4 eggs
50 g/2 oz ground almonds
350 g/12 oz mixed dried fruit
50 g/2 oz chopped mixed peel
blanched split almonds

American
2 cups all-purpose flour
½ teaspoon baking powder
¼ teaspoon salt
½ lb (2 sticks) butter, softened
1 cup sugar
grated rind of 1 small orange
1 teaspoon vanilla extract
4 eggs
½ cup ground almonds
2 cups mixed dried fruit
⅓ cup chopped mixed candied peel
blanched split almonds

Sift together the flour, baking powder and salt. Cream the butter with the sugar, orange rind and vanilla until light and fluffy. Beat in the eggs one at a time, adding a tablespoon of flour with each egg. Fold in the remaining flour with the ground almonds, fruit and peel.

Pour the batter into a greased and lined 18 cm/7 inch round deep cake pan. Cover the top with rings of split almonds.

Bake in a preheated cool oven (150°C/300°F, Gas Mark 2) for 2 to 2½ hours or until a skewer inserted into the centre of the cake comes out clean. Cool in the pan for 15 minutes before turning out onto a wire rack to cool.

Simnel Cake

Metric/Imperial
1 quantity rich fruit cake batter (see
 page 48)
½ quantity almond paste (see page
 42)
apricot jam

American
1 quantity rich fruit cake batter (see
 page 48)
½ quantity almond paste (see page
 42)
apricot jam

Put half the cake batter in a greased and lined 20 cm/8 inch round deep cake pan. Smooth the surface. Roll out about one-third of the almond paste to a round the same diameter as the pan and place it on top of the cake batter. Cover with the remaining cake batter and bake in a preheated cool oven (150°C/300°F, Gas Mark 2) for 2½ to 3 hours. Cool.

Roll half the remaining almond paste into a round the same diameter as the top of the cake, and form the remaining almond paste into 11 small balls. Brush the top of the cooled cake with apricot jam and place the almond paste round in position on top. Put the balls around the top edge of the cake, fixing them with a little jam. Tie a wide yellow ribbon around the sides of the cake.

Sherried Spice Cake

Metric/Imperial
225 g/8 oz sultanas
150 ml/¼ pint water
100 g/4 oz butter
150 g/5 oz soft brown sugar
1 large egg, beaten
175 g/6 oz plain flour
1 teaspoon bicarbonate of soda
½ teaspoon ground cloves
½ teaspoon grated nutmeg
¼ teaspoon ground cinnamon
75 g/3 oz walnuts, chopped
3 tablespoons sherry
1 quantity rich buttercream (see
 page 43)
walnut halves to decorate

American
1⅓ cups seedless white raisins
⅔ cup water
8 tablespoons (1 stick) butter
¾ cup plus 1½ tablespoons light
 brown sugar
1 egg, beaten
1½ cups all-purpose flour
1 teaspoon baking soda
½ teaspoon ground cloves
½ teaspoon grated nutmeg
¼ teaspoon ground cinnamon
¾ cup chopped walnuts
3 tablespoons sherry
1 quantity rich buttercream (see
 page 43)
walnut halves to decorate

Put the sultanas (raisins) and water in a saucepan and bring to the boil. Simmer gently for 15 minutes. Strain off the water and make it up to 120 ml/ 4 fl oz (½ cup). Cool.

Cream the butter with the sugar until pale and fluffy. Beat in the egg. Sift the flour with the soda and spices and fold into the butter mixture with the sultana (raisin) liquid. Add the walnuts, sultanas (raisins) and 2 tablespoons of the sherry and mix evenly. Divide between two greased and floured 20 cm/ 8 inch round deep cake pans.

Bake in a preheated moderate oven (180°C/350°F, Gas Mark 4) for 30 to 35 minutes or until firm. Cool in the pans for 5 minutes, then turn out onto a wire rack to cool completely.

Beat the remaining sherry into the buttercream. Use half to sandwich together the cake layers and spread the rest over the top of the cake. Decorate with walnut halves.

Malted Tea Loaf

Metric/Imperial
50 g/2 oz butter
100 g/4 oz golden syrup
100 g/4 oz malt extract
4 tablespoons milk
225 g/8 oz self-raising flour
pinch of salt
100 g/4 oz sultanas
50 g/2 oz chopped mixed peel
1 egg, beaten

American
4 tablespoons butter
⅓ cup light corn syrup
⅓ cup malt extract or molasses
¼ cup milk
2 cups self-rising flour
pinch of salt
⅔ cup seedless white raisins
⅓ cup chopped mixed candied peel
1 egg, beaten

Put the butter, syrup, malt extract (or molasses) and milk in a saucepan and heat gently until melted. Remove from the heat. Sift the flour and salt into a bowl and stir in the sultanas (seedless white raisins) and peel. Add the melted mixture and the egg and beat until smooth. Pour into a greased and lined 1 kg/2 lb (9 × 5 × 3 inch) loaf pan.

Bake in a preheated moderate oven (160°C/325°F, Gas Mark 3) for 1 to 1¼ hours or until well risen and firm to the touch. Cool on a wire rack. When cold, wrap in foil and store for 1 to 2 days before serving.

Date and Nut Loaf

Metric/Imperial
350 g/12 oz plain flour
1 teaspoon salt
175 g/6 oz caster sugar
50 g/2 oz walnuts, chopped
225 g/8 oz stoned dates, chopped
2 tablespoons corn oil
1 egg
1 teaspoon bicarbonate of soda
300 ml/½ pint boiling water

American
3 cups all-purpose flour
1 teaspoon salt
¾ cup sugar
½ cup chopped walnuts
1½ cups chopped pitted dates
2 tablespoons corn oil
1 egg
1 teaspoon baking soda
1¼ cups boiling water

Sift the flour, salt and sugar into a bowl and stir in the nuts and dates. Beat together the oil and egg. Dissolve the soda in the water. Add the two liquid mixtures to the flour mixture and stir briskly to form a smooth batter.

Pour into a greased and floured or lined 1 kg/2 lb (9 × 5 × 3 inch) loaf pan. Bake in a preheated moderate oven (180°C/350°F, Gas Mark 4) for 1¼ to 1½ hours or until well risen and firm. Cool in the pan for 5 minutes, then turn out onto a wire rack to cool completely.

Cut into slices to serve.

Variation:
Substitute cashew nuts or peanuts for the walnuts and dried figs for dates.

Seeded Fruit Ring

Metric/Imperial
175 g/6 oz butter
175 g/6 oz caster sugar
3 large eggs, beaten
225 g/8 oz self-raising flour, sifted
100 g/4 oz glacé cherries, quartered,
  rinsed and dried
75 g/3 oz chopped mixed peel
2–3 teaspoons caraway or sesame
  seeds
1–2 tablespoons milk
Topping:
50 g/2 oz glacé cherries, halved
½ quantity glacé icing (see page 42)

American
12 tablespoons (1½ sticks) butter
¾ cup sugar
3 eggs, beaten
2 cups self-rising flour, sifted
⅔ cup quartered candied cherries,
  rinsed and dried
½ cup chopped mixed candied peel
2–3 teaspoons caraway or sesame
  seeds
1–2 tablespoons milk
Topping:
⅓ cup halved candied cherries
½ quantity glacé icing (see page 42)

Cream the butter with the sugar until light and fluffy. Beat in the eggs one at a time, adding a tablespoon of the flour with each egg. Fold in the remaining flour followed by the cherries, peel, seeds and enough milk to give a dropping consistency. Pour into a greased 1 litre/2 pint (1 quart capacity) ring mould and smooth the top.

Bake in a preheated moderate oven (180°C/350°F, Gas Mark 4) for 30 minutes. Reduce the temperature to 160°C/325°F, Gas Mark 3 and continue baking for 30 to 35 minutes or until firm to the touch. Turn out onto a wire rack and cool.

For the topping, stir the cherries into the icing. As it begins to thicken, spoon it over the top of the ring and let it run down the sides. Leave to set.

Orange Loaf Cake

Metric/Imperial
100 g/4 oz caster sugar
120 ml/4 fl oz milk
100 g/4 oz butter
1 tablespoon grated orange rind
2 eggs
225 g/8 oz self-raising flour

American
½ cup sugar
½ cup milk
8 tablespoons (1 stick) butter
1 tablespoon grated orange rind
2 eggs
2 cups self-rising flour

Dissolve the sugar in half the milk. Cream in the butter and orange rind. Beat in the eggs. Sift in the flour and fold in with the remaining milk. Pour into a greased and floured or lined 1 kg/2 lb (9 × 5 × 3 inch) loaf pan.

Bake in a preheated moderate oven (180°C/350°F, Gas Mark 4) for 40 minutes.

Golden Ginger Cake

Metric/Imperial
275 g/10 oz plain flour
1 teaspoon bicarbonate of soda
½ teaspoon ground ginger
175 g/6 oz plus 1½ tablespoons clear honey
100 g/4 oz butter
175 g/6 oz sugar
2 tablespoons ginger syrup (from preserved ginger)
1½ tablespoons milk
2 eggs, beaten

American
2½ cups all-purpose flour
1 teaspoon baking soda
½ teaspoon ground ginger
½ cup plus 1½ tablespoons clear honey
8 tablespoons (1 stick) butter
¾ cup sugar
2 tablespoons ginger syrup (from candied ginger)
1½ tablespoons milk
2 eggs, beaten

Sift together the flour, soda and ginger. Put the 175 g/6 oz (½ cup) of honey in a saucepan with the butter and sugar and heat gently until the butter melts and the sugar dissolves. Stir into the flour mixture.

Warm the ginger syrup and milk in the saucepan and add to the flour mixture with the eggs. Beat well until smooth, then pour into a greased 1 kg/2 lb (9 × 5 × 3 inch) loaf pan.

Bake in a preheated moderate oven (160°C/325°F, Gas Mark 3) for 1 to 1¼ hours or until just firm to the touch. Cool in the pan for 15 minutes, then turn out onto a wire rack. Brush the top with the remaining honey and leave to cool.

Variation:

For a darker, stronger-flavoured cake, use golden syrup (light corn syrup) or black treacle (molasses) or a mixture of the two, in place of the honey. The ground ginger may also be increased to 2 teaspoons.

Buttermilk Fruit Cake

Metric/Imperial
350 g/12 oz self-raising flour
1 teaspoon ground mixed spice
175 g/6 oz butter
175 g/6 oz brown sugar
1 tablespoon black treacle
2 eggs, beaten
150 ml/¼ pint buttermilk
350 g/12 oz mixed dried fruit

American
3 cups self-rising flour
1 teaspoon ground allspice
12 tablespoons (1½ sticks) butter
1 cup brown sugar
1 tablespoon molasses
2 eggs, beaten
⅔ cup buttermilk
2 cups mixed dried fruit

Sift the flour and spice into a bowl and rub in the butter. Stir in the sugar, treacle (molasses) and eggs. Add the buttermilk and fruit and mix well. Pour into a greased and floured 20 cm/8 inch round deep cake pan. Bake in a preheated moderate oven (160°C/325°F, Gas Mark 3) for 1¼ to 1½ hours.

Buttermilk Raisin Bread

Metric/Imperial
225 g/8 oz self-raising flour
pinch of salt
50 g/2 oz butter
50 g/2 oz sugar
100 g/4 oz raisins
100 g/4 oz walnuts, chopped
1 egg, beaten
1 tablespoon golden syrup
7 tablespoons buttermilk
Topping:
1 tablespoon sugar
2 tablespoons chopped walnuts
little buttermilk

American
2 cups self-rising flour
pinch of salt
4 tablespoons butter
¼ cup sugar
⅔ cup raisins
1 cup chopped walnuts
1 egg, beaten
1 tablespoon light corn syrup
7 tablespoons buttermilk
Topping:
1 tablespoon sugar
2 tablespoons chopped walnuts
little buttermilk

Sift the flour and salt into a bowl and rub in the butter. Stir in the sugar, raisins, walnuts and egg. Mix the syrup with the buttermilk, then add to the fruit mixture and combine thoroughly. Pour into a greased and floured 1 kg/ 2 lb (9 × 5 × 3 inch) loaf pan.

Mix together the sugar and nuts for the topping. Brush the top of the bread with a little buttermilk, then sprinkle over the sugar and nuts. Press in gently.

Bake in a preheated moderate oven (180°C/350°F, Gas Mark 4) for 45 to 50 minutes or until firm to the touch. Cool on a wire rack.

Variation:
Use chopped stoned (pitted) dates instead of raisins.

Barm Brack

Metric/Imperial
450 ml/¾ pint cold strained tea
200 g/7 oz soft brown sugar
350 g/12 oz mixed dried fruit
275 g/10 oz self-raising flour
1 egg, beaten

American
2 cups cold strained tea
1 cup plus 2½ tablespoons light
   brown sugar
2 cups mixed dried fruit
2½ cups self-rising flour
1 egg, beaten

Put the tea, sugar and fruit in a bowl, cover and leave to soak overnight.

The next day, sift the flour into a bowl. Stir in the egg, then gradually stir in the fruit and tea mixture.

Pour into a greased and lined 1 kg/2 lb (9 × 5 × 3 inch) loaf pan. Bake in a preheated moderate oven (180°C/350°F, Gas Mark 4) for about 1¾ hours. Cool until lukewarm, then turn out onto a wire rack to cool completely.

Cut into slices to serve.

Chocolate Fruit Cake

Metric/Imperial

500 g/1 lb sultanas
225 g/8 oz raisins
100 g/4 oz currants
100 g/4 oz glacé cherries, quartered
75 g/3 oz chopped mixed peel
50 g/2 oz glacé pineapple, chopped
50 g/2 oz glacé apricots, chopped
50 g/2 oz stoned dates, chopped
25 g/1 oz dried apricots, chopped
6 tablespoons brandy
225 g/8 oz butter
250 g/9 oz dark brown sugar
1 teaspoon grated orange rind
1 teaspoon grated lemon rind
1 teaspoon vanilla essence
¼ teaspoon almond essence
2 tablespoons marmalade
100 g/4 oz plain chocolate, melted
4 eggs
275 g/10 oz plain flour
1 teaspoon ground mixed spice
¼ teaspoon grated nutmeg
1 teaspoon ground cinnamon
pinch of salt

American

2⅔ cups seedless white raisins
1⅓ cups raisins
⅔ cup currants
⅔ cup quartered candied cherries
½ cup chopped mixed candied peel
⅓ cup chopped candied pineapple
⅓ cup chopped candied apricots
⅓ cup chopped pitted dates
2½ tablespoons chopped dried
  apricots
6 tablespoons brandy
½ lb (2 sticks) butter
1½ cups dark brown sugar
1 teaspoon grated orange rind
1 teaspoon grated lemon rind
1 teaspoon vanilla extract
¼ teaspoon almond extract
2 tablespoons marmalade
⅔ cup semi-sweet chocolate chips,
  melted
4 eggs
2½ cups all-purpose flour
1 teaspoon ground allspice
¼ teaspoon grated nutmeg
1 teaspoon ground cinnamon
pinch of salt

Put all the fruit in a bowl, sprinkle over the brandy and stir well. Cover and leave overnight.

The next day, cream the butter with the sugar until fluffy. Beat in the fruit rinds, vanilla, almond essence (extract), marmalade and chocolate. Sift the flour with the spices and salt and fold into the creamed mixture. Fold in the fruit mixture.

Pour into a greased and lined 23 cm/9 inch round deep cake pan. Tie a double thickness of brown paper around the outside of the pan.

Bake in a preheated cool oven (140°C/275°F, Gas Mark 1) for about 4 hours or until a skewer inserted into the centre of the cake comes out clean. Cool in the pan.

Pineapple Teacake

Metric/Imperial
175 g/6 oz self-raising flour
pinch of salt
100 g/4 oz sugar
50 g/2 oz butter, melted
1 egg, beaten
150 ml/¼ pint milk
425 g/15 oz can crushed pineapple
Topping:
50 g/2 oz butter
100 g/4 oz honey
25 g/1 oz desiccated coconut
sifted icing sugar

American
1½ cups self-rising flour
pinch of salt
½ cup sugar
4 tablespoons butter, melted
1 egg, beaten
⅔ cup milk
1 × 15 oz can crushed pineapple
Topping:
4 tablespoons butter
⅓ cup honey
⅓ cup shredded coconut
sifted confectioners' sugar

Sift the flour and salt into a bowl. Stir in the sugar, melted butter, beaten egg and milk to make a smooth batter. Pour into a greased and floured 20 cm/ 8 inch round deep cake pan. Spread the crushed pineapple over the batter.

Cream together the butter and honey for the topping and spread over the pineapple. Sprinkle the coconut over the top and bake in a preheated moderate oven (180°C/350°F, Gas Mark 4) for 35 to 40 minutes. Cool, then sprinkle with the icing (confectioners') sugar.

Ginger Honey Cake

Metric/Imperial
75 g/3 oz butter
50 g/2 oz brown sugar
1 egg, beaten
1 egg yolk
2 tablespoons honey
175 g/6 oz self-raising wholemeal
   flour
pinch of salt
1 teaspoon ground ginger
1 teaspoon ground cinnamon
6 tablespoons milk

American
6 tablespoons butter
⅓ cup brown sugar
1 egg, beaten
1 egg yolk
2 tablespoons honey
1½ cups self-rising wholewheat flour
pinch of salt
1 teaspoon ground ginger
1 teaspoon ground cinnamon
6 tablespoons milk

Cream the butter and sugar together until light and fluffy. Beat in the egg, egg yolk and honey, then fold in the flour, salt, ginger and cinnamon. Mix to a dropping consistency with the milk.

Pour into a greased and floured 18 cm/7 inch round deep cake pan and bake in a preheated moderate oven (180°C/350°F, Gas Mark 4) for 50 minutes.

Banana Bread

Metric/Imperial
75 g/3 oz butter
75 g/3 oz caster sugar
75 g/3 oz soft brown sugar
2 eggs, beaten
3 ripe bananas
grated rind of ½ lemon
1 teaspoon lemon juice
40 g/1½ oz walnuts, chopped
(optional)
200 g/7 oz self-raising flour
pinch of salt
¼ teaspoon bicarbonate of soda

American
6 tablespoons butter
6 tablespoons sugar
½ cup light brown sugar
2 eggs, beaten
3 ripe bananas
grated rind of ½ lemon
1 teaspoon lemon juice
⅓ cup chopped walnuts (optional)
1¾ cups self-rising flour
pinch of salt
¼ teaspoon baking soda

Cream the butter with the sugars until light and fluffy. Beat in the eggs. Mash the bananas with the lemon rind and juice and beat into the creamed mixture until smooth. Fold in the nuts, if used. Sift the flour with the salt and soda and mix into the banana mixture. Pour into a greased and lined 1 kg/2 lb (9 × 5 × 3 inch) loaf pan.

Bake in a preheated moderate oven (180°C/350°F, Gas Mark 4) for 1 hour or until firm to the touch. Cool on a wire rack. When cold, wrap in foil and store for 24 hours before serving.

Honey Fruit Loaf

Metric/Imperial
75 g/3 oz butter
75 g/3 oz brown sugar
1 egg, beaten
2 tablespoons honey
225 g/8 oz self-raising wholemeal
flour
¼ teaspoon salt
1 teaspoon ground mixed spice
175 g/6 oz mixed dried fruit
4 tablespoons milk

American
6 tablespoons butter
½ cup brown sugar
1 egg, beaten
2 tablespoons honey
2 cups self-rising wholewheat flour
¼ teaspoon salt
1 teaspoon ground allspice
1 cup mixed dried fruit
¼ cup milk

Cream the butter and sugar together until light and fluffy. Beat in the egg and honey, then fold in the flour, salt, spice and fruit. Mix to a dropping consistency with the milk.

Pour into a greased 750 g/1½ lb loaf pan. Bake in a preheated moderately hot oven (190°C/375°F, Gas Mark 5) for 45 minutes.

Apricot Tea Bread

Metric/Imperial
100 g/4 oz dried apricots, chopped
150 ml/¼ pint water
25 g/1 oz butter
225 g/8 oz sugar
½ teaspoon salt
275 g/10 oz plain flour
1 teaspoon bicarbonate of soda
1 egg, beaten
1 teaspoon orange juice
50 g/2 oz almonds, chopped and
   blanched

American
⅔ cup chopped dried apricots
⅔ cup water
2 tablespoons butter
1 cup sugar
½ teaspoon salt
2½ cups all-purpose flour
1 teaspoon baking soda
1 egg, beaten
1 teaspoon orange juice
½ cup chopped blanched almonds

Put the apricots in a saucepan with the water, butter, sugar and salt. Bring to the boil, stirring to dissolve the sugar, then simmer for 5 minutes. Cool.

Sift the flour into a bowl with the bicarbonate of soda (baking soda). Stir in the apricot mixture, the egg, orange juice and almonds and beat well.

Pour into a greased and lined 1 kg/2 lb (9 × 5 × 3 inch) loaf pan. Bake in a preheated moderate oven (180°C/350°F, Gas Mark 4) for 1 to 1¼ hours or until well risen and firm to the touch. Cool on a wire rack.

Pineapple Fruit Cake

Metric/Imperial
225 g/8 oz sugar
425 g/15 oz can crushed pineapple
500 g/1 lb mixed dried fruit
1 teaspoon bicarbonate of soda
1 teaspoon ground mixed spice
100 g/4 oz butter
100 g/4 oz plain flour
100 g/4 oz self-raising flour
2 eggs, beaten

American
1 cup sugar
1 × 15 oz can crushed pineapple
2⅔ cups mixed dried fruit
1 teaspoon baking soda
1 teaspoon apple pie spice
8 tablespoons (1 stick) butter
1 cup all-purpose flour
1 cup self-rising flour
2 eggs, beaten

Put the sugar, pineapple and can syrup, fruit, soda, spice and butter into a saucepan and bring to the boil, stirring to dissolve the sugar. Boil for 3 minutes, then cool.

Sift the flours into a bowl. Add the fruit mixture and eggs and mix well. Pour into a greased and lined 20 cm/8 inch round deep cake pan.

Bake in a preheated moderate oven (180°C/350°F, Gas Mark 4) for 1½ hours, then reduce the temperature to cool (150°C/300°F, Gas Mark 2) and continue baking for 20 to 30 minutes or until a skewer inserted into the centre of the cake comes out clean.

Sultana (Raisin) Cake

Metric/Imperial
750 g/1½ lb sultanas
225 g/8 oz butter
225 g/8 oz caster sugar
5 eggs
275 g/10 oz plain flour
25 g/1 oz self-raising flour
pinch of salt
100 g/4 oz blanched almonds,
    chopped
2–3 tablespoons brandy
½ teaspoon vanilla essence

American
3 cups seedless white raisins
½ lb (2 sticks) butter
1 cup sugar
5 eggs
2½ cups all-purpose flour
¼ cup self-rising flour
pinch of salt
1 cup chopped blanched almonds
2–3 tablespoons brandy
½ teaspoon vanilla extract

Soak the sultanas (seedless white raisins) in warm water for 2 hours, then drain and let dry overnight.

The next day, cream the butter with the sugar until light and fluffy. Beat in the eggs one at a time, adding a tablespoon of flour with each egg. Sift over the remaining flour and the salt and fold into the creamed mixture with the sultanas (raisins), almonds, brandy and vanilla. Pour into a greased and lined 20 cm/8 inch square deep cake pan.

Bake in a preheated moderate oven (160°C/325°F, Gas Mark 3) for about 1¾ hours.

Rich Bran Fruit Loaf

Metric/Imperial
225 g/8 oz soft brown sugar
100 g/4 oz All Bran
225 g/8 oz mixed dried fruit
1 tablespoon grated orange rind
1 tablespoon golden syrup
250 ml/8 fl oz milk
1 egg, beaten
1 large banana, mashed
100 g/4 oz self-raising flour, sifted

American
1⅓ cups light brown sugar
2 cups All Bran
1⅓ cups mixed dried fruit
1 tablespoon grated orange rind
1 tablespoon light corn syrup
1 cup milk
1 egg, beaten
1 large banana, mashed
1 cup self-rising flour, sifted

Put the sugar, All Bran, fruit, orange rind, syrup and milk in a bowl and stir well. Leave to soak overnight.

The next day, add the remaining ingredients and combine thoroughly. Pour into a greased 1 kg/2 lb (9 × 5 × 3 inch) loaf pan.

Bake in a preheated moderate oven (180°C/350°F, Gas Mark 4) for about 1 hour or until a skewer inserted into the centre of the loaf comes out clean. Cool on a wire rack and serve warm.

Honey Almond Cake

Metric/Imperial
100 g/4 oz butter
50 g/2 oz brown sugar
2 eggs, beaten
3 tablespoons honey
225 g/8 oz wholemeal flour
1 tablespoon baking powder
1 teaspoon ground cinnamon
120 ml/4 fl oz milk
25 g/1 oz flaked almonds

American
8 tablespoons butter
1/3 cup brown sugar
2 eggs, beaten
3 tablespoons honey
2 cups wholewheat flour
1 tablespoon baking powder
1 teaspoon ground cinnamon
1/2 cup milk
1/4 cup slivered almonds

Cream the butter and sugar together until light and fluffy. Beat in the eggs and honey, then fold in the flour, baking powder and cinnamon. Mix to a dropping consistency with the milk.

Scatter the almonds over the bottom of a greased 18 cm/7 inch square cake pan and spoon over the batter. Bake in a preheated moderate oven (180°C/350°F, Gas Mark 4) for 1 hour.

Orange Date Tea Bread

Metric/Imperial
500 g/1 lb dates, stoned and
   chopped
150 ml/1/4 pint orange juice
550 g/1 lb 2 oz self-raising flour
pinch of salt
225 g/8 oz butter
500 g/1 lb sugar
75 g/3 oz mixed candied peel,
   chopped
3 eggs
450 ml/3/4 pint milk, warmed
1/2 teaspoon vanilla essence

American
about 3 cups chopped, pitted dates
2/3 cup orange juice
4 1/2 cups self-rising flour
pinch of salt
1/2 lb (2 sticks) butter
2 cups sugar
1/2 cup chopped mixed candied peel
3 eggs
2 cups milk, warmed
1/2 teaspoon vanilla extract

Soak the dates overnight in the orange juice. Sift the flour and salt into a bowl. Rub in the butter, then stir in the sugar, orange juice mixture and peel.

Mix together the eggs, 300 ml/1/2 pint (1 1/4 cups) of the milk and the vanilla essence (extract). Add the liquid to the fruit mixture. Combine thoroughly, adding more milk (up to 150 ml/1/4 pint (2/3 cup)) if necessary. Pour into a greased and lined 25 cm/10 inch square deep cake pan. Bake in a preheated moderate oven (180°C/350°F, Gas Mark 4) for 30 minutes, then reduce the heat to cool (150°C/300°F, Gas Mark 2) and continue baking for 1 1/2 hours. Cool in the pan.

Orange and Almond Tea Bread

Metric/Imperial
350 g/12 oz self-raising flour
½ teaspoon salt
1 teaspoon ground cinnamon
50 g/2 oz blanched almonds,
  chopped
finely grated rind of 1 orange
75 g/3 oz caster sugar
2 eggs, beaten
300 ml/½ pint milk
50 g/2 oz butter, melted

American
3 cups self-rising flour
½ teaspoon salt
1 teaspoon ground cinnamon
½ cup chopped blanched almonds
finely grated rind of 1 orange
6 tablespoons sugar
2 eggs, beaten
1¼ cups milk
4 tablespoons butter, melted

Sift the flour, salt and cinnamon into a bowl. Stir in the almonds, orange rind and sugar, then mix in the eggs, milk and butter to make a soft batter.

Pour into a greased and floured 1 kg/2 lb (9 × 5 × 3 inch) loaf pan. Bake in a preheated moderate oven (180°C/350°F, Gas Mark 4) for 1 hour or until a skewer inserted into the centre of the loaf comes out clean. Cool in the pan for 5 minutes, then turn out onto a wire rack to cool completely.

Cut into slices to serve.

Variations:

Lemon and Raisin Tea Bread: Substitute 50 g/2 oz sultanas (⅓ cup seedless white raisins) for the almonds and 1 to 2 teaspoons grated lemon rind for the orange rind.

Apricot Tea Bread: Omit the cinnamon and reduce the milk to 150 ml/¼ pint (⅔ cup). Add 175 g/6 oz (1 cup) chopped dried apricots that have been soaked overnight. The batter will have a soft dropping consistency. Bake in a preheated moderate oven (160°C/325°F, Gas Mark 3) for 1½ hours.

Cranberry Tea Bread

Metric/Imperial
225 g/8 oz plain flour
1½ teaspoons baking powder
½ teaspoon bicarbonate of soda
large pinch of salt
50 g/2 oz butter
175 g/6 oz soft brown sugar
grated rind of 1 orange
75 g/3 oz walnuts, chopped
50 g/2 oz raisins
4 tablespoons cranberry sauce
4 tablespoons orange juice
1 large egg, beaten

American
2 cups all-purpose flour
1½ teaspoons baking powder
½ teaspoon baking soda
large pinch of salt
4 tablespoons butter
1 cup light brown sugar
grated rind of 1 orange
¾ cup chopped walnuts
⅓ cup raisins
¼ cup cranberry sauce
¼ cup orange juice
1 egg, beaten

Sift the flour, baking powder, soda and salt into a bowl. Rub in the butter, then stir in the sugar, orange rind, walnuts and raisins. Mix together the cranberry sauce, orange juice and egg and add to the dry ingredients. Mix lightly, then pour into a greased and lined 1 kg/2 lb (9 × 5 × 3 inch) loaf pan.

Bake in a preheated moderate oven (180°C/350°F, Gas Mark 4) for 1 to 1¼ hours or until well risen and firm to the touch. Cool on a wire rack.

Ginger and Peanut Loaf

Metric/Imperial
350 g/12 oz self-raising flour
½ teaspoon salt
1 teaspoon ground ginger
50 g/2 oz soft brown sugar
75 g/3 oz sultanas
50 g/2 oz preserved ginger, chopped
75 g/3 oz unsalted peanuts
2 eggs
150 ml/¼ pint milk
75 g/3 oz butter, melted
4 tablespoons black treacle

American
3 cups self-rising flour
½ teaspoon salt
1 teaspoon ground ginger
½ cup light brown sugar
½ cup seedless white raisins
⅓ cup chopped candied ginger
¾ cup unsalted peanuts
2 eggs
⅔ cup milk
6 tablespoons melted butter
4 tablespoons molasses

Sift the flour, salt and ginger into a bowl. Stir in the sugar, sultanas (seedless white raisins), preserved ginger (candied ginger) and peanuts. Then beat in the eggs, milk, melted butter and black treacle (molasses).

Pour into a greased and floured 1 kg/2 lb (9 × 5 × 3 inch) loaf pan. Bake in a preheated moderate oven (180°C/350°F, Gas Mark 4) for 1 hour or until a skewer inserted into the centre of the loaf comes out clean. Cool in the pan for 5 minutes, then turn out onto a wire rack to cool. Cut into slices to serve.

CAKES, PASTRIES

Biscuits and Cookies

AND BREADS

Sweetmeal Biscuits (Cookies)

Metric/Imperial
75 g/3 oz wholemeal flour
15 g/½ oz plain flour
pinch of salt
½ teaspoon baking powder
15 g/½ oz fine oatmeal
40 g/1½ oz butter
40 g/1½ oz caster sugar
about 2 tablespoons milk

American
¾ cup wholewheat flour
2 tablespoons all-purpose flour
pinch of salt
½ teaspoon baking powder
1 tablespoon fine oatmeal
3 tablespoons butter
3 tablespoons sugar
about 2 tablespoons milk

Sift the flours, salt and baking powder into a bowl and stir in the oatmeal. Rub in the butter. Stir in the sugar with enough milk to make a stiff paste. Knead.

Roll out thinly and cut into 5 to 6 cm/2 to 2½ inch rounds. Place on greased baking sheets and prick all over.

Bake in a preheated moderately hot oven (190°C/375°F, Gas Mark 5) for 15 to 20 minutes or until light golden brown. Cool on a wire rack.

Makes 16–18
Variation:
Digestive Biscuits (Cookies): Make the dough using 350 g/12 oz wholemeal flour (3 cups wholewheat flour), 2 teaspoons salt, 150 g/5 oz (10 tablespoons) butter, 50 g/2 oz (⅓ cup) brown sugar and 1 egg beaten with 4 tablespoons water. Cut into rounds as above, then bake in a preheated moderate oven (180°C/350°F, Gas Mark 4) for 25 minutes.

Hazelnut Cinnamon Shorties

Metric/Imperial
100 g/4 oz butter
75 g/3 oz caster sugar
1 egg yolk
1 teaspoon ground cinnamon
150 g/5 oz self-raising flour, sifted
50 g/2 oz hazelnuts, toasted and
  chopped

American
8 tablespoons (1 stick) butter
6 tablespoons sugar
1 egg yolk
1 teaspoon ground cinnamon
1¼ cups self-rising flour, sifted
½ cup toasted chopped hazelnuts

Cream the butter with the sugar until pale and fluffy. Beat in the egg yolk and cinnamon, then fold in the flour to make a smooth dough. Shape into a roll and cut into 24 slices. Flatten each slice slightly and coat in chopped nuts. Place on greased baking sheets, allowing room for spreading.

Bake in a preheated moderately hot oven (190°C/375°F, Gas Mark 5) for 15 to 20 minutes or until lightly browned. Cool on a wire rack.

Makes 24

Variations:

Hazelnut Chocolate Biscuits (Cookies): Make up the dough as above, using 175 g/6 oz (12 tablespoons) butter, 225 g/8 oz (1 cup) caster sugar, 1 egg, ½ teaspoon vanilla essence (extract) and 225 g/8 oz self-raising flour (2 cups self-rising flour). Fold in 50 g/2 oz (½ cup) chopped hazelnuts, 50 g/2 oz (⅓ cup) chopped plain chocolate (⅓ cup semi-sweet chocolate chips) and 75 g/3 oz desiccated coconut (1 cup shredded coconut). Roll into walnut-sized balls and arrange on greased baking sheets, well apart. Bake in a preheated moderate oven (180°C/350°F, Gas Mark 4) for 15 minutes. If you like, drizzle melted chocolate over the biscuits (cookies).

Makes about 48

Honey Hazelnut Cookies: Make up the dough as above, using 100 g/4 oz (8 tablespoons) butter, 100 g/4 oz demerara sugar (⅔ cup raw brown sugar), 1 beaten egg, 1 tablespoon honey, 225 g/8 oz self-raising flour (2 cups self-rising flour), a pinch of salt and 50 g/2 oz (½ cup) chopped hazelnuts. Divide the dough into 36 walnut-sized pieces and shape into balls. Place on greased baking sheets and flatten each ball with a fork dipped in cold water. Bake in a preheated moderate oven (180°C/350°F, Gas Mark 4) for 12 minutes. Cool on a wire rack.

Makes 36

Hazelnut Balls: Make up the dough as above, substituting 2 to 3 drops of vanilla essence (extract) for the cinnamon, using 100 g/4 oz plain flour (1 cup all-purpose flour) and adding 100 g/4 oz (1 cup) ground hazelnuts. Roll the dough into small balls and flatten them slightly with a fork. Bake in a preheated moderate oven (180°C/350°F, Gas Mark 4) for 20 minutes. Coat with icing (confectioners') sugar and cool.

Makes about 36

Flapjacks

Metric/Imperial	American
100 g/4 oz butter	8 tablespoons (1 stick) butter
25 g/1 oz caster sugar	2 tablespoons sugar
2 tablespoons golden syrup	2 tablespoons light corn syrup
225 g/8 oz rolled oats	2¼ cups rolled oats
pinch of salt	pinch of salt

Cream the butter with the sugar until pale and fluffy. Melt the syrup, then beat into the creamed mixture followed by the oats and salt. Spread out in a greased 20 cm/8 inch square cake pan.

Bake in a preheated moderately hot oven (190°C/375°F, Gas Mark 5) for 30 to 40 minutes or until firm and golden brown. Cut into bars and cool in the pan.

Makes 12

Variation:

Muesli (Granola) Flapjacks: Cream 150 g/5 oz (10 tablespoons) butter with 75 g/3 oz (½ cup) dark brown sugar and 1 tablespoon honey. Beat in 225 g/8 oz muesli (1½ cups granola) and 50 g/2 oz (½ cup) chopped nuts. Press firmly into a greased 18 cm/7 inch square cake pan. Bake as above, allowing 25 minutes.

Makes 9

Melting Moments

Metric/Imperial	American
75 g/3 oz butter	6 tablespoons butter
75 g/3 oz lard	6 tablespoons lard
150 g/5 oz caster sugar	⅔ cup sugar
1 egg, beaten	1 egg, beaten
175 g/10 oz self-raising flour, sifted	2½ cups self-rising flour, sifted
1 teaspoon vanilla essence	1 teaspoon vanilla extract
about 50 g/2 oz cornflakes, crushed	about 2 cups crushed cornflakes
8 glacé cherries, quartered	8 candied cherries, quartered

Beat the butter and lard together, then cream in the sugar until light and fluffy. Beat in the egg. Work in the flour and vanilla to make a fairly stiff dough. Form into 30 balls and roll each ball in crushed cornflakes to coat on all sides. Place on greased baking sheets, allowing room for spreading, and flatten each ball slightly. Press a piece of cherry into the top of each.

Bake in a preheated moderate oven (180°C/350°F, Gas Mark 4) for 15 to 20 minutes or until golden brown. Cool on a wire rack.

Makes 30

Oat Crisps

Metric/Imperial	**American**
150 g/5 oz butter	10 tablespoons butter
50 g/2 oz golden syrup	3 tablespoons light corn syrup
100 g/4 oz demerara sugar	⅔ cup raw brown sugar
75 g/3 oz rolled oats	1 cup rolled oats
50 g/2 oz desiccated coconut	⅔ cup shredded coconut
100 g/4 oz plain flour, sifted	1 cup all-purpose flour, sifted
1 teaspoon bicarbonate of soda	1 teaspoon baking soda
1 teaspoon hot water	1 teaspoon hot water

Put the butter, syrup and sugar into a saucepan and heat gently until the sugar has dissolved and the butter melted. Remove from the heat. Mix together the oats, coconut and flour and stir into the melted mixture. Dissolve the soda in the hot water and add to the oat mixture. Cool slightly, then form into 20 to 25 balls. Place well apart on greased baking sheets.

Bake in a preheated moderate oven (160°C/325°F, Gas Mark 3) for 15 to 20 minutes or until evenly browned. Cool on a wire rack.

Makes 20–25

Variation:

Almond Oat Biscuits (Cookies): Cream 100 g/4 oz (8 tablespoons) butter with 100 g/4 oz (½ cup) caster sugar until light and fluffy. Beat in 1 tablespoon treacle (molasses) or golden syrup (light corn syrup). Fold in 100 g/4 oz sifted self-raising flour (1 cup sifted self-rising flour), 250 g/9 oz (3 cups) rolled oats and 75 g/3 oz flaked almonds (¾ cup slivered almonds). Dissolve 1 teaspoon bicarbonate of soda (baking soda) in 4 tablespoons boiling water and add to the oat mixture. Mix to a stiff dough. Form the dough into small balls and arrange on greased baking sheets, well apart. Press the balls flat. Bake in a preheated moderate oven (180°C/350°F, Gas Mark 4) for about 15 minutes. Cool on the baking sheets.

Makes about 48

Anzac Biscuits (Cookies): Make up the mixture as above, using 100 g/4 oz (8 tablespoons) butter, 1 tablespoon golden syrup (light corn syrup), 225 g/8 oz (1 cup) sugar, 100 g/4 oz (1⅓ cups) rolled oats, 100 g/4 oz desiccated coconut (1⅓ cups shredded coconut), 100 g/4 oz plain flour (1 cup all-purpose flour), 1½ teaspoons bicarbonate of soda (baking soda) and 2 tablespoons hot water. Drop in tablespoons onto greased baking sheets, then bake in a preheated cool oven (150°C/300°F, Gas Mark 2) for about 30 minutes.

Makes about 36

Walnut Bars

Metric/Imperial
225 g/8 oz plain flour
175 g/6 oz butter
100 g/4 oz icing sugar
100 g/4 oz walnuts, chopped finely
1 egg white
2 teaspoons coffee essence

American
2 cups all-purpose flour
12 tablespoons (1½ sticks) butter
1 cup confectioners' sugar
1 cup finely chopped walnuts
1 egg white
2 teaspoons coffee flavoring

Sift the flour onto a working surface and make a well in the centre. Cut the butter into pieces and put into the well with the sugar. Work the butter and sugar together with the fingertips, then gradually work in the flour. Work in the walnuts and knead to a smooth dough. Chill for 20 minutes.

Roll out half the dough to a rectangle about 5 mm/¼ inch thick. Mark with a criss-cross pattern all over. Mix together the egg white and coffee essence (flavoring) and brush half over the dough. Cut into bars about 7.5 × 4 cm/3 × 1½ inches and transfer to a baking sheet. Repeat with the rest of the dough.

Bake in a preheated moderately hot oven (190°C/375°F, Gas Mark 5) for about 15 minutes or until lightly coloured. Cool on a wire rack.

Makes about 30

Variations:

Caramel Shortbread Squares: Make the dough with 100 g/4 oz (1 cup) flour, 100 g/4 oz (8 tablespoons) butter and 75 g/3 oz icing sugar (¾ cup confectioners' sugar), omitting the walnuts. Press the dough into a greased 20 cm/8 inch square cake pan and bake in a preheated moderate oven (180°C/350°F, Gas Mark 4) for 20 to 25 minutes. Cool. For the topping, melt 100 g/4 oz (8 tablespoons) butter with 65 g/2½ oz golden syrup (3½ tablespoons light corn syrup). Stir in 65 g/2½ oz (6 tablespoons) dark brown sugar, 1 teaspoon (unflavoured) gelatine and 250 ml/8 fl oz (1 cup) condensed milk. Stir until the sugar dissolves, then bring to the boil and boil for 4 minutes, stirring. Pour over the shortbread base and chill until firm. Cut into small squares to serve.

Makes about 25

Butterscotch Bars: Make the dough with 100 g/4 oz (1 cup) flour, 65 g/2½ oz (6 tablespoons) dark brown sugar and 75 g/3 oz (6 tablespoons) butter. Press onto the bottom of a greased and lined 20 cm/8 inch square cake pan and bake as above, allowing 10 to 12 minutes. For the topping, put 175 g/6 oz butterscotch toffees in a saucepan with 1 tablespoon golden (light corn) syrup, 1 tablespoon water, 25 g/1 oz (2 tablespoons) butter and a pinch of salt. Cook gently, stirring, until the butterscotch has melted. Stir in 100 g/4 oz (1 cup) chopped walnuts. Spread over the shortbread base. Return to the oven and bake for a further 8 to 10 minutes. Cool on a wire rack, then cut into squares.

Makes about 16

Almond Fingers

Metric/Imperial
150 g/5 oz butter
75 g/3 oz sugar
175 g/3 oz plain flour
Filling:
150 ml/¼ pint whipping cream
65 g/2½ oz ground almonds
1 teaspoon ground cinnamon
brown sugar to taste
1 egg yolk, beaten
Icing:
75 g/3 oz icing sugar, sifted
lemon juice

American
10 tablespoons butter
6 tablespoons sugar
¾ cup all-purpose flour
Filling:
⅔ cup whipping cream
½ cup plus 2 tablespoons ground
  almonds
1 teaspoon ground cinnamon
brown sugar to taste
1 egg yolk, beaten
Icing:
¾ cup confectioners' sugar, sifted
lemon juice

Cream the butter with the sugar until light and fluffy. Sift over the flour, then mix to a dough. Press the dough onto the bottom of a greased 28 × 18 cm/ 11 × 7 inch cake pan. Bake blind (unfilled) in a preheated moderate oven (160°C/325°F, Gas Mark 3) for 20 minutes. Cool.

For the filling, whip the cream until thick. Fold in the almonds, cinnamon and sugar to taste. Mix in the egg yolk. Spread the filling over the pastry base and return to the oven. Bake for a further 40 minutes. Cool, then chill. For the icing, mix the sugar with enough lemon juice to make a spreading consistency. Spread the icing over the filling and chill until set. Cut into fingers.
Makes about 24

Australian Honey Raisin Bars

Metric/Imperial
75 g/3 oz butter
175 g/6 oz honey
3 eggs
175 g/6 oz plain flour
1 teaspoon baking powder
175 g/6 oz raisins
100 g/4 oz nuts, chopped

American
6 tablespoons butter
½ cup honey
3 eggs
1½ cups all-purpose flour
1 teaspoon baking powder
1 cup raisins
1 cup chopped nuts

Cream the butter with the honey until light and fluffy. Beat in the eggs one at a time. Sift in the flour and baking powder, then fold in with the raisins and nuts. Spread in a greased 23 × 30 cm/9 × 12 inch baking pan.

Bake in a preheated moderate oven (180°C/350°F, Gas Mark 4) for about 30 minutes. Cool in the pan, then cut into bars.
Makes 16–20

Shortbread

Metric/Imperial	American
100 g/4 oz plain flour	1 cup all-purpose flour
pinch of salt	pinch of salt
4 tablespoons fine semolina	¼ cup fine semolina or cream of
50 g/2 oz sugar	wheat
100 g/4 oz butter	¼ cup sugar
sugar for sprinkling	8 tablespoons (1 stick) butter
	sugar for sprinkling

Sift the flour, salt and semolina into a bowl and stir in the sugar. Rub in the butter to make a crumbly mixture. Knead lightly, then press into an 18 cm/ 7 inch sandwich tin (layer cake pan). Prick all over with a fork.

Bake in a preheated moderate oven (160°C/325°F, Gas Mark 3) for 35 to 45 minutes or until the colour of pale straw. Cool in the tin (pan) for 5 minutes, then cut into eight wedges. Transfer to a wire rack to cool, and sprinkle with sugar when cold.

Variations:

Rich Shortbread: Cream 100 g/4 oz (8 tablespoons or 1 stick) butter with 50 g/2 oz (¼ cup) sugar. Sift in 50 g/2 oz cornflour (½ cup cornstarch) and 100 g/4 oz plain flour (1 cup all-purpose flour) and work in lightly to form a soft, smooth dough. Roll out to a 20 cm/8 inch round about 1 cm/½ inch thick and cut with a large shortbread cutter. Place the round on a baking sheet, prick it all over with a fork and mark it into eight sections with a knife. Bake in a preheated moderate oven (160°C/325°F, Gas Mark 3) for 35 to 40 minutes or until a pale biscuit colour. Sprinkle with more sugar and break into sections to serve.

Shortbread Flapjacks: Make the shortbread as for rich shortbread above, using 50 g/2 oz (4 tablespoons) butter, 25 g/1 oz (2 tablespoons) sugar, 100 g/4 oz plain flour (1 cup all-purpose flour) and as little milk as possible to bind. Press out to a 20 cm/8 inch round and place on a baking sheet. For the flapjack topping, melt 40 g/1½ oz (3 tablespoons) butter with 25 g/1 oz (2½ tablespoons) brown sugar and 1 tablespoon golden (light corn) syrup. Stir in 100 g/4 oz (1⅓ cups) rolled oats. Spread the flapjack mixture over the shortbread round. Bake as above, allowing about 30 minutes. Mark into wedges while warm.

Fruit Slices

Metric/Imperial
Shortbread:
175 g/6 oz self-raising flour
40 g/1½ oz ground rice
2½ tablespoons cornflour
50 g/2 oz sugar
100 g/4 oz butter
1 egg
Filling:
225 g/8 oz dates, chopped and
 stoned
grated rind and juice of 1 lemon
100 g/4 oz sultanas
100 g/4 oz raisins
2½ tablespoons mixed candied peel
50 g/2 oz chopped glacé cherries
1 tablespoon sugar
25 g/1 oz butter
1 teaspoon ground allspice
150 ml/¼ pint water
1 tablespoon arrowroot
1 tablespoon rum or orange juice
sugar to sprinkle

American
Shortbread:
1½ cups self-rising flour
⅓ cup ground rice
2½ tablespoons cornstarch
¼ cup sugar
8 tablespoons butter
1 egg
Filling:
1⅓ cups chopped and pitted dates
grated rind and juice of 1 lemon
⅔ cup seedless white raisins
⅔ cup raisins
2½ tablespoons chopped mixed
 candied peel
⅓ cup chopped candied cherries
1 tablespoon sugar
2 tablespoons butter
1 teaspoon ground allspice
⅔ cup water
1 tablespoon arrowroot
1 tablespoon rum or orange juice
sugar to sprinkle

Sift the flour and add the ground rice, cornflour (cornstarch) and sugar. Rub in the butter and mix in the egg. Divide the dough in half and roll out half to line a greased and lined 28 × 18 cm/11 × 7 inch cake pan.

For the filling, mix together the dates, lemon juice and rind, the sultanas, raisins, candied peel, cherries, sugar, butter, allspice and water in a saucepan. Cook gently, stirring, until thick. Dissolve the arrowroot in the rum or orange juice and add to the fruit mixture. Simmer, stirring, for 3 minutes. Cool, then spread the fruit mixture over the dough in the pan. Roll out the remaining dough and lay over the fruit filling. Brush with water and sprinkle with sugar. Bake in a preheated hot oven (220°C/425°F, Gas Mark 7) for 25 to 30 minutes. Cool, then cut into slices.

Lunch-box Cookies

Metric/Imperial
75 g/3 oz butter
65 g/2½ oz dark brown sugar
100 g/4 oz caster sugar
1 teaspoon vanilla essence
1 egg
175 g/6 oz plain flour
½ teaspoon baking powder
½ teaspoon bicarbonate of soda
½ teaspoon salt
½ teaspoon ground ginger
½ teaspoon ground cinnamon
175 g/6 oz rolled oats
50 g/2 oz marmalade
100 g/4 oz raisins

American
6 tablespoons butter
⅓ cup dark brown sugar
½ cup granulated sugar
1 teaspoon vanilla extract
1 egg
1½ cups all-purpose flour
½ teaspoon baking powder
½ teaspoon baking soda
½ teaspoon salt
½ teaspoon ground ginger
½ teaspoon ground cinnamon
2 cups rolled oats
2½ tablespoons marmalade
⅔ cup raisins

Cream the butter with the sugars until light and fluffy. Beat in the vanilla and egg. Sift the flour with the baking powder, soda, salt and spices and fold into the creamed mixture with the oats, marmalade and raisins. Drop in teaspoons onto greased baking sheets.

Bake in a preheated moderately hot oven (190°C/375°F, Gas Mark 5) for about 15 minutes.

Makes about 36

Chocolate Cherry Bars

Metric/Imperial
225 g/8 oz plain chocolate
2 eggs
100 g/4 oz caster sugar
175 g/6 oz desiccated coconut
50–75 g/2–3 oz glacé cherries,
    chopped
sifted icing sugar

American
1⅓ cups semi-sweet chocolate chips
2 eggs
½ cup sugar
2 cups shredded coconut
½ cup chopped candied cherries
sifted confectioners' sugar

Melt the chocolate gently, then spread it over the bottom of a greased 28 × 18 cm/11 × 7 inch cake pan. Chill until set.

Beat the eggs and sugar together until light and frothy. Fold in the coconut and cherries. Spread over the chocolate base.

Bake in a preheated moderate oven (180°C/350°F, Gas Mark 4) for 10 to 15 minutes or until firm to the touch. Cool, then chill.

Sprinkle with icing (confectioners') sugar, then cut into bars.

Makes about 24

Chocolate Caramels

Metric/Imperial	American
150 g/5 oz plain flour	1¼ cups all-purpose flour
½ teaspoon salt	½ teaspoon salt
50 g/2 oz caster sugar	¼ cup sugar
100 g/4 oz butter	8 tablespoons (1 stick) butter
Filling:	**Filling:**
100 g/4 oz butter	8 tablespoons (1 stick) butter
100 g/4 oz soft brown sugar	⅔ cup light brown sugar
2 tablespoons golden syrup	2 tablespoons light corn syrup
1 small can condensed milk	1 small can condensed milk
few drops of vanilla essence	few drops of vanilla extract
100 g/4 oz plain chocolate,	4 oz dark sweet chocolate,
broken up	broken up

Sift the flour and salt into a bowl and stir in the sugar. Rub in the butter, then knead to a smooth dough. Press evenly over the bottom of a greased 18 cm/7 inch square cake pan.

Bake in a preheated moderate oven (180°C/350°F, Gas Mark 4) for about 25 minutes or until pale golden brown and just firm. Cool.

For the filling, put the butter, sugar, syrup and condensed milk in a saucepan and heat gently until the butter has melted and the sugar has dissolved. Bring to the boil and boil gently for 7 to 8 minutes, stirring occasionally. Add the vanilla and beat until smooth and beginning to thicken. Pour over the shortbread base in the pan. Cool, then chill.

Melt the chocolate gently and pour it over the caramel filling. Spread evenly. As the chocolate sets, mark it into swirls with a knife. Chill until set, then cut into squares.

Makes 16

Florentines

Metric/Imperial	American
75 g/3 oz butter	6 tablespoons butter
100 g/4 oz caster sugar	½ cup sugar
100 g/4 oz flaked almonds, chopped	1 cup chopped slivered almonds
25 g/1 oz raisins, chopped	2½ tablespoons chopped raisins
40 g/1½ oz chopped mixed peel	¼ cup chopped mixed candied peel
40 g/1½ oz glacé cherries, chopped	¼ cup chopped candied cherries
grated rind of ¼ lemon	grated rind of ¼ lemon
175 g/6 oz plain chocolate	6 oz dark sweet chocolate

Melt the butter with the sugar in a saucepan, stirring to dissolve the sugar. Bring to the boil and boil for 1 minute. Remove from the heat and stir in the remaining ingredients except the chocolate. Cool.

Put teaspoons of the mixture, well spaced apart, on baking sheets lined with non-stick silicone paper – four or five spoons per sheet.

Bake in a preheated moderate oven (180°C/350°F, Gas Mark 4) for 10 to 12 minutes or until golden brown. Cool on the baking sheets until firm, pressing the edges back to make neat shapes, then transfer to a wire rack to cool completely.

Melt the chocolate gently. Spread it over the smooth side of each florentine. As the chocolate sets, mark it into wavy lines with a fork. Leave to harden.

Makes 24–30

Variation:

Easy Florentines: Mix together 75 g/3 oz sultanas (½ cup seedless white raisins), 100 to 175 g/4 to 6 oz (1 to 1½ cups) crushed cornflakes, 75 g/3 oz (½ cup) raw peanuts, 50 g/2 oz chopped glacé cherries (⅓ cup chopped candied cherries) and 175 ml/6 fl oz (¾ cup) condensed milk. Drop tablespoons of the mixture in heaps onto baking sheets lined with greased and floured greaseproof (wax) paper. Bake as above, allowing 15 to 20 minutes.

Cool on the baking sheets, then spread 75 g/3 oz melted plain (dark sweet) chocolate over the bases of the biscuits (cookies). Mark with a fork and leave to harden.

Makes about 24

Coconut Rings

Metric/Imperial
100 g/4 oz plain flour
100 g/4 oz caster sugar
100 g/4 oz butter
100 g/4 oz desiccated coconut
1 egg, beaten
raspberry jam or bramble jelly

American
1 cup all-purpose flour
½ cup sugar
8 tablespoons (1 stick) butter
1⅓ cups shredded coconut
1 egg, beaten
raspberry jam or blackberry jelly

Sift the flour into a bowl and stir in the sugar. Rub in the butter then stir in the coconut. Bind to a soft dough with the egg. Roll out the dough thinly and cut into 6 cm/2½ inch rounds. Stamp out the centres with a 2.5 cm/1 inch cutter. Put the rings on greased baking sheets.

Bake in a preheated moderately hot oven (190°C/375°F, Gas Mark 5) for about 15 minutes or until lightly browned. Cool on a wire rack, then sandwich together pairs of rings with jam or jelly.

Makes 16–18

Variation:

Butter Coconut Crisps: Sift 175 g/6 oz self-raising flour (1½ cups self-rising flour) and 225 g/8 oz (1 cup) caster sugar into a bowl. Stir in 1 beaten egg and 100 g/4 oz (8 tablespoons) melted butter. Form into walnut-sized balls and coat in desiccated (shredded) coconut. Place on greased baking sheets, well apart, and bake in a preheated moderate oven (180°C/350°F, Gas Mark 4) for 10 to 15 minutes. Cool on the baking sheets.

Makes about 30

Walnut and Cherry Squares

Metric/Imperial
150 g/5 oz butter
75 g/3 oz sugar
1 egg, beaten
200 g/7 oz self-raising flour, sifted
100 g/4 oz glacé cherries, chopped
50 g/2 oz walnuts, chopped
sugar to dredge

American
10 tablespoons butter
6 tablespoons sugar
1 egg, beaten
1¾ cups self-rising flour, sifted
⅔ cup chopped candied cherries
½ cup chopped walnuts
sugar to dredge

Cream the butter with the sugar until light and fluffy. Beat in the egg, then fold in the flour to make a dough. Work in the cherries and walnuts.

Spread the dough over the bottom of a greased 18 cm/7 inch square cake tin and sprinkle with sugar. Bake in a preheated moderate oven (160°C/325°F, Gas Mark 3) for 1 hour. Cut into squares to serve.

Ginger Nuts (Snaps)

Metric/Imperial	American
75 g/3 oz butter	6 tablespoons butter
75 g/3 oz soft brown sugar	½ cup light brown sugar
75 g/3 oz golden syrup	¼ cup light corn syrup
225 g/8 oz plain flour	2 cups all-purpose flour
2 teaspoons ground ginger	2 teaspoons ground ginger
½ teaspoon ground cinnamon	½ teaspoon ground cinnamon
½ teaspoon ground mixed spice	½ teaspoon ground allspice
¼ teaspoon salt	¼ teaspoon salt
1 teaspoon bicarbonate of soda	1 teaspoon baking soda
1 tablespoon warm water	1 tablespoon warm water

Put the butter, sugar and syrup in a saucepan and heat until the butter has melted and the sugar has dissolved. Remove from the heat.

Sift the flour, spices and salt into a bowl. Make a well in the centre and add the butter mixture. Dissolve the soda in the water and add to the bowl. Mix thoroughly with a fork, then form into 24 balls. Place the balls on greased baking sheets, leaving space between them for spreading.

Bake in a preheated moderate oven (160°C/325°F, Gas Mark 3) for 16 to 18 minutes. Cool on a wire rack.

Makes 24

Variation:

Ginger Crunchies: Cream 100 g/4 oz (8 tablespoons) butter with 50 g/2 oz (¼ cup) sugar until light and fluffy. Sift together 100 g/4 oz plain flour (1 cup all-purpose flour), 1 teaspoon baking powder and 1 teaspoon ground ginger and fold into the creamed mixture. Spread in a greased 28 × 18 cm/11 × 7 inch cake pan. Bake in a preheated moderate oven (180°C/350°F, Gas Mark 4) for 15 to 20 minutes. For the topping, put 50 g/2 oz sifted icing sugar (½ cup sifted confectioners' sugar) in a saucepan with 50 g/2 oz (4 tablespoons) butter, 1 teaspoon ground ginger and 1 tablespoon golden (light corn) syrup. Heat gently, stirring, until well mixed. Pour over the base in the pan and cool. Cut into fingers to serve.

Makes about 18

Currant Crisps

Metric/Imperial
100 g/4 oz butter
100 g/4 oz caster sugar
1 egg yolk
100 g/4 oz currants
225 g/8 oz plain flour, sifted

American
8 tablespoons (1 stick) butter
½ cup sugar
1 egg yolk
⅔ cup currants
2 cups all-purpose flour, sifted

Cream the butter with the sugar until pale and fluffy. Beat in the egg yolk, then fold in the currants and flour. Knead well.

Roll out the dough to 3 mm/⅛ inch thick and cut into hearts or other shapes. Place them on a greased baking sheet.

Bake in a preheated moderate oven (160°C/325°F, Gas Mark 3) for 10 to 12 minutes. Cool on the baking sheet.

Makes 20–24

Variations:

Sift ¼ teaspoon ground mixed spice (apple pie spice) with the flour and substitute chopped glacé (candied) cherries or raisins for the currants.

Zebra Biscuits (Cookies): Omit the currants and add 1 teaspoon instant coffee powder with the egg yolk. Add a few drops of water with the flour if necessary to bind the dough. Roll out and bake as above, on ungreased baking sheets. Cool, then pipe lines of melted plain (dark sweet) chocolate across the biscuits (cookies).

Traffic Lights: Omit the currants. Roll out the dough and cut it into fingers. Make three small holes in half the fingers (use a thimble), then bake as above. When cold, sandwich together plain fingers and those with holes using a little jam. Put half a glacé (candied) cherry or a little raspberry jam in one hole of each biscuit (cookie), lemon curd or marmalade in the next and greengage jam in the third.

Makes 10–12

Coconut Crisps: Increase the sugar to 225 g/8 oz (1 cup), use 1 egg instead of the egg yolk, omit the currants, and use self-raising flour. Fold in a pinch of salt and 175 g/6 oz desiccated coconut (2 cups shredded coconut) with the flour. Roll into balls and press flat with the hands, then dip one side into sugar. Bake in a preheated moderately hot oven (190°C/375°F, Gas Mark 5) for 10 to 15 minutes.

Makes about 24

Macaroons

Metric/Imperial	American
1 egg white	1 egg white
75 g/3 oz ground almonds	¾ cup ground almonds
90 g/3½ oz caster sugar	7 tablespoons sugar
¼–½ teaspoon almond essence	¼–½ teaspoon almond extract
few split blanched almonds	few split blanched almonds
(optional)	(optional)

Beat the egg white until stiff, then fold in the ground almonds, sugar and almond essence (extract). Put the mixture into a piping bag fitted with a plain vegetable tube (nozzle) and pipe small dots on baking sheets lined with rice paper. Top each with a piece of almond, if liked.

Bake in a preheated moderate oven (180°C/350°F, Gas Mark 4) for 20 to 25 minutes or until lightly coloured. Cool on a wire rack, then cut off the surplus rice paper before serving.

Makes about 15

Variations:

Coconut Macaroons: Substitute desiccated coconut (1 cup shredded coconut) for the ground almonds and omit the almond essence (extract) and blanched almonds. Roll into 5 to 6 balls and press half a glacé (candied) cherry into the top of each. Bake as above.

Oatmeal Macaroons: Substitute rolled oats for half the ground almonds, or use half rolled oats and half desiccated (shredded) coconut. Top with almonds or glacé (candied) cherries.

Almond Snaps: Make the macaroon mixture as above, using 2 large egg whites, 100 g/4 oz (1 cup) ground almonds, 100 g/4 oz (½ cup) caster sugar and 2 to 3 drops of almond essence (extract). Divide into 18 balls and arrange on greased baking sheets, allowing room for spreading. Flatten the balls with your fingers. Bake as above for about 12 minutes, baking one batch at a time. Cool for about 1 minute, then roll each biscuit (cookie) around the greased handle of a wooden spoon. Cool on a wire rack.

Easy Ratafias: Beat 2 egg whites with a pinch of salt until stiff. Gradually beat in 225 g/8 oz (1 cup) caster sugar, then fold in 175 g/6 oz (½ cup) instant mashed potato flakes, 175 g/6 oz desiccated coconut (2 cups shredded coconut) and a few drops of almond essence (extract). Drop in teaspoons onto a greased baking sheet and top with flaked (slivered) almonds. Bake as above, allowing 15 to 20 minutes.

Makes about 36

Viennese Biscuits (Cookies)

Metric/Imperial
225 g/8 oz plain flour
pinch of salt
225 g/8 oz butter
50 g/2 oz caster sugar
few drops of vanilla essence
icing sugar to dredge
1–2 tablespoons seedless
raspberry jam

American
2 cups all-purpose flour
pinch of salt
½ lb (2 sticks) butter
¼ cup sugar
few drops of vanilla extract
confectioners' sugar to dredge
1–2 tablespoons raspberry jelly

Sift the flour and salt together. Cream the butter with the sugar until light and fluffy. Work the flour into the creamed mixture with the vanilla. Put into a piping bag fitted with a star vegetable tube (nozzle) and pipe in a whirl in 16 paper (cup) cake cases in patty (cup cake) tins. Alternatively, pipe in whirls, stars, figure-of-eights or fingers on greased baking sheets.

Bake in a preheated moderate oven (180°C/350°F, Gas Mark 4) for 15 to 25 minutes or until pale golden brown and firm. Cool on a wire rack.

Sprinkle with icing (confectioners') sugar and put a dot of jam (jelly) in the centre of each biscuit (cookie).

Makes 16

Variations:

Place a small piece of glacé (candied) cherry in the centre of each biscuit (cookie) before baking and omit the jam (jelly). Dip half of each biscuit (cookie) into melted chocolate instead of adding jam (jelly) and sprinkling with sugar.

Orange Viennese Stars: Substitute 100 g/4 oz cornflour (1 cup cornstarch) for half the flour. Reduce the butter to 175 g/6 oz (12 tablespoons) and substitute 100 g/4 oz icing sugar (1 cup confectioners' sugar) for the caster (granulated) sugar. Replace the vanilla with the grated rind of 1 large orange. Put the mixture into a piping bag fitted with a 1 cm/½ inch rose tube (nozzle) and pipe 14 to 16 neat rose shapes on a baking sheet. Sandwich together pairs of biscuits (cookies) with ½ quantity orange buttercream (see page 41) and dust with icing (confectioners') sugar.

Makes 7–8

Cherry Ginger Biscuits (Cookies): Make the mixture as for orange Viennese stars above, substituting 1 teaspoon ground ginger for the orange rind. Roll into 14 to 16 balls and flatten into rounds. Bake as above and cool. Top with glacé icing (see page 42) and a glacé (candied) cherry.

Makes 14–16

Orange Biscuits (Cookies)

Metric/Imperial
225 g/8 oz plain flour
150 g/5 oz butter
100 g/4 oz caster sugar
grated rind of 1 or 2 oranges
few drops of orange juice if
   necessary

American
2 cups all-purpose flour
10 tablespoons butter
½ cup sugar
grated rind of 1 or 2 oranges
few drops of orange juice if
   necessary

Sift the flour into a bowl and rub in the butter. Stir in the sugar and orange rind, then knead to a smooth dough, adding a little orange juice if necessary.

Roll out the dough to 3 mm/⅛ inch thick and cut it into 5 cm/2 inch rounds or other shapes. Place them on a baking sheet and prick lightly with a fork.

Bake in a preheated moderate oven (160°C/325°F, Gas Mark 3) for 10 to 12 minutes. Cool on the baking sheet.
Makes 14–18

Variations:

Sugar Rings: Omit the orange rind and juice (use water if necessary). Cut the dough into rings and bake them for 8 to 9 minutes or until well set and nearly cooked. Beat 1 egg white until it begins to hold its shape (not as stiff as for meringue) and fold in 3½ tablespoons caster sugar and a few drops of vanilla essence (extract). Spread this mixture over the rings and dredge with ½ to 1 tablespoon caster sugar. Reduce the oven temperature to very cool (120°C/250°F, Gas Mark ½) and bake for a further 40 minutes or until the topping is very crisp but still white.
Makes 18–20

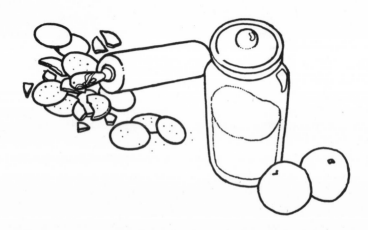

Brandy Snaps

Metric/Imperial
50 g/2 oz butter
50 g/2 oz sugar
65 g/2½ oz golden syrup
50 g/2 oz plain flour
1 teaspoon ground ginger
½ teaspoon ground mixed spice
2 teaspoons lemon juice
whipped cream

American
4 tablespoons butter
¼ cup sugar
¼ cup light corn syrup
½ cup all-purpose flour
1 teaspoon ground ginger
½ teaspoon ground allspice
2 teaspoons lemon juice
whipped cream

Put the butter, sugar and syrup in a saucepan and heat until the butter has melted and the sugar has dissolved. Remove from the heat.

Sift together the flour and spices. Add to the butter mixture with the lemon juice and stir to combine well.

Drop 8 teaspoons of the batter onto a greased baking sheet, spacing them well apart as they spread. Bake in a preheated moderate oven (160°C/325°F, Gas Mark 3) for 8 minutes.

Remove the baking sheet from the oven and leave for about 30 seconds, then lift off each biscuit (cookie) and wrap it fairly quickly around the greased handle of a wooden spoon. Slide the biscuits (cookies) off the handle and cool on a wire rack. Make the remaining brandy snaps in the same way. When they are cool, fill them with whipped cream.
Makes 16

Peanut Butter Cookies

Metric/Imperial
50 g/2 oz peanut butter
50 g/2 oz butter
grated rind of ½ orange
50 g/2 oz caster sugar
40 g/1½ oz soft brown sugar
½ egg, beaten
40 g/1½ oz raisins, chopped
100 g/4 oz self-raising flour, sifted

American
¼ cup peanut butter
4 tablespoons butter
grated rind of ½ orange
¼ cup sugar
¼ cup light brown sugar
½ egg, beaten
¼ cup chopped raisins
1 cup self-rising flour, sifted

Beat together the peanut butter, butter, orange rind and sugars until light and fluffy. Beat in the egg, then fold in the raisins and flour. Roll into walnut-sized balls and place well apart on baking sheets. Slightly flatten the balls and mark with a criss-cross pattern using a fork.

Bake in a preheated moderate oven (180°C/350°F, Gas Mark 4) for about 25 minutes or until well risen and golden brown. Cool on a wire rack.
Makes 16–20

Orange Creams

Metric/Imperial
100 g/4 oz butter
100 g/4 oz caster sugar
2 teaspoons golden syrup
grated rind of 1 small orange
1 egg yolk
175 g/6 oz plain flour
25 g/1 oz custard powder
¼ teaspoon salt
½ teaspoon cream of tartar
½ teaspoon bicarbonate of soda
Filling:
40 g/1½ oz butter
75 g/3 oz icing sugar, sifted
little grated orange rind
about 1 teaspoon orange juice

American
8 tablespoons (1 stick) butter
½ cup sugar
2 teaspoons light corn syrup
grated rind of 1 small orange
1 egg yolk
1½ cups all-purpose flour
¼ cup custard powder
¼ teaspoon salt
½ teaspoon cream of tartar
½ teaspoon baking soda
Filling:
3 tablespoons butter
¾ cup confectioners' sugar, sifted
little grated orange rind
about 1 teaspoon orange juice

Cream the butter with the sugar until pale and fluffy. Beat in the syrup, orange rind and egg yolk. Sift together the flour, custard powder, salt, cream of tartar and soda and fold into the creamed mixture. Roll into walnut-sized balls and place on greased baking sheets, allowing room for spreading.

Bake in a preheated moderately hot oven (190°C/375°F, Gas Mark 5) for about 20 minutes or until golden brown. Cool on a wire rack.

For the filling, cream the butter with the sugar, then beat in the orange rind and juice to make a thick spreading consistency. Use this filling to sandwich together pairs of biscuits (cookies).
Makes about 12

Almond Bread

Metric/Imperial
3 egg whites
100 g/4 oz caster sugar
100 g/4 oz plain flour, sifted
100 g/4 oz whole unblanched
　almonds

American
3 egg whites
½ cup sugar
1 cup all-purpose flour, sifted
1 cup whole unblanched almonds

Beat the egg whites until stiff, then gradually beat in the sugar. Fold in the flour and almonds. Spoon into a greased 1 kg/2 lb (9 × 5 × 3 inch) loaf pan.

Bake in a preheated moderate oven (180°C/350°F, Gas Mark 4) for 30 to 40 minutes. Cool in the pan, then wrap in foil and keep for 1 to 2 days before serving

To serve, cut into wafer-thin slices and place on a baking sheet. Dry out in a preheated cool oven (150°C/300°F, Gas Mark 2) for 45 minutes. Serve with ice cream.

Sugar Biscuits (Cookies)

Metric/Imperial
200 g/7 oz self-raising flour
pinch of salt
25 g/1 oz cornflour
100 g/4 oz butter
100 g/4 oz caster sugar
1 egg or 2 egg yolks
¼ teaspoon vanilla essence
little milk
caster sugar to dredge

American
1¾ cups self-rising flour
pinch of salt
¼ cup cornstarch
8 tablespoons (1 stick) butter
½ cup sugar
1 egg or 2 egg yolks
¼ teaspoon vanilla extract
little milk
sugar to dredge

Sift the flour, salt and cornflour (cornstarch) into a bowl. Rub in the butter, then stir in the sugar. Beat in the egg or egg yolks and vanilla with a little milk if necessary to make a fairly soft dough. Knead lightly, then chill for 30 minutes.

Roll out the dough to about 5 mm/¼ inch thick. Cut into rounds or other shapes and place on greased baking sheets. Bake in a preheated moderately hot oven (200°C/400°F, Gas Mark 6) for 8 to 10 minutes or until light golden brown. Dredge with sugar, then cool on a wire rack.
Makes 30–40
Variations:
Add 25 to 40 g/1 to 1½ oz (¼ to ⅓ cup) finely chopped nuts to the dry ingredients.
Add 25 g/1 oz desiccated coconut (⅓ cup shredded coconut) to the dry ingredients.

Grantham Gingerbreads

Metric/Imperial
100 g/4 oz butter
350 g/12 oz caster sugar
1 large egg, beaten
250 g/9 oz self-raising flour
1–1½ teaspoons ground ginger
little granulated sugar to dredge

American
8 tablespoons (1 stick) butter
1½ cups sugar
1 egg, beaten
2¼ cups self-rising flour
1–1½ teaspoons ground ginger
little sugar to dredge

Cream the butter with the sugar until pale and fluffy, then beat in the egg. Sift the flour and ginger together and add to the creamed mixture. Work to a pliable dough. Roll into walnut-sized balls and place on greased baking sheets, allowing space for spreading. Sprinkle each ball with a little sugar.

Bake in a preheated cool oven (150°C/300°F, Gas Mark 2) for about 40 minutes or until puffed up and lightly browned. Cool on a wire rack.

Makes 25–30
Variation:
Add a little finely grated lemon or orange rind. Use ground cinnamon or mixed spice (apple pie spice) instead of the ginger.

Gingerbread Men

Metric/Imperial
225 g/8 oz plain flour
1 teaspoon baking powder
½ teaspoon bicarbonate of soda
1–2 teaspoons ground ginger
75 g/3 oz butter
75 g/3 oz soft brown sugar
75 g/3 oz golden syrup
To decorate:
currants
glacé cherries
glacé icing (see page 42)

American
2 cups all-purpose flour
1 teaspoon baking powder
½ teaspoon baking soda
1–2 teaspoons ground ginger
6 tablespoons butter
½ cup light brown sugar
¼ cup light corn syrup
To decorate:
currants
candied cherries
glacé icing (see page 42)

Sift the flour with the baking powder, soda and ginger. Cream the butter with the sugar and syrup until fluffy. Add the dry ingredients and knead well to a smooth dough. Roll out the dough to about 5 mm/¼ inch thick and cut out men (or boys and girls). Place them on lightly greased baking sheets.

Press in currants for the eyes and pieces of cherry for the mouths. Bake in a preheated hot oven (220°C/425°F, Gas Mark 7) for about 10 minutes.

Cool on the baking sheets, then decorate with the glacé icing, piping in hair, clothes, etc.

Makes 8–12

Chocolate Chip Cookies

Metric/Imperial
100 g/4 oz butter
100 g/4 oz soft brown sugar
75 g/3 oz golden syrup
1 egg
225 g/8 oz plain flour, sifted
½ teaspoon bicarbonate of soda
1 tablespoon hot water
½ teaspoon vanilla essence
100 g/4 oz chocolate dots or chips

American
8 tablespoons (1 stick) butter
⅔ cup light brown sugar
¼ cup light corn syrup
1 egg
2 cups all-purpose flour, sifted
½ teaspoon baking soda
1 tablespoon hot water
½ teaspoon vanilla extract
½ cup chocolate chips

Cream the butter with the sugar and syrup until fluffy. Beat in the egg, then fold in the flour. Dissolve the soda in the water and add to the mixture with the vanilla. Mix well. Stir in the chocolate dots or chips.

Drop spoonsful of the mixture onto greased baking sheets, allowing plenty of space for them to spread. Bake in a preheated moderate oven (160°C/325°F, Gas Mark 3) for about 20 minutes. Cool on the baking sheets.

Makes 36

Variation:

Add 2 to 3 tablespoons chopped walnuts or pecans with the chocolate dots or chips.

Peanut and Raisin Biscuits (Cookies)

Metric/Imperial
275 g/10 oz self-raising flour
½ teaspoon ground cinnamon
275 g/10 oz butter
225 g/8 oz soft brown sugar
100 g/4 oz salted peanuts, finely chopped
100 g/4 oz raisins
1–2 tablespoons milk

American
2½ cups self-raising flour
½ teaspoon ground cinnamon
2¼ sticks butter
1⅓ cups light brown sugar
1 cup finely chopped salted peanuts
⅔ cup raisins
1–2 tablespoons milk

Sift the flour and cinnamon together. Cream the butter with the sugar until light and fluffy. Fold in the flour mixture with the peanuts, raisins and enough milk to make a soft dough.

Drop teaspoons of the dough onto baking sheets, well spaced. Bake in a preheated moderate oven (180°C/350°F, Gas Mark 4) for 10 minutes. Cool on a wire rack.

Makes about 48

Bourbon Biscuits (Cookies)

Metric/Imperial
100 g/4 oz butter
100 g/4 oz caster sugar
175 g/6 oz plain flour
50 g/2 oz custard powder
2 tablespoons cocoa powder
½ teaspoon baking powder
1 egg
caster sugar to dredge
Filling:
50 g/2 oz butter
65 g/2½ oz icing sugar, sifted
4 teaspoons drinking chocolate
  powder
1 teaspoon coffee essence

American
8 tablespoons (1 stick) butter
½ cup sugar
1½ cups all-purpose flour
½ cup custard powder
2 tablespoons unsweetened cocoa
½ teaspoon baking powder
1 egg
sugar to dredge
Filling:
4 tablespoons butter
½ cup plus 2 tablespoons
  confectioners' sugar, sifted
4 teaspoons hot chocolate powder
1 teaspoon coffee flavoring

Cream the butter with the sugar until pale and fluffy. Sift the flour with the custard powder, cocoa and baking powder. Beat the egg into the creamed mixture, then work in the flour mixture to make a fairly stiff dough.

Roll out the dough to about 3 mm/⅛ inch thick and cut into 7.5 × 2.5 cm/ 3 × 1 inch bars. Prick all over and dredge with sugar. Place on greased baking sheets.

Bake in a preheated moderate oven (180°C/350°F, Gas Mark 4) for 15 to 20 minutes or until just firm. Cool on a wire rack.

For the filling, cream the butter with the sugar, then beat in the chocolate powder and coffee essence (flavoring). Sandwich together pairs of biscuits (cookies) with the filling.
Makes 22–24

Wholemeal (Wholewheat) Fruit Slices

Metric/Imperial
1 quantity wholemeal pastry (see page 107)
100 g/4 oz currants
100 g/4 oz sultanas
1 large cooking apple, peeled, cored and grated
finely grated rind of 1 orange
juice of ½ lemon
50 g/2 oz demerara sugar
Topping:
1 egg white, lightly beaten
little demerara sugar

American
1 quantity wholewheat pastry (see page 107)
⅔ cup currants
⅔ cup seedless white raisins
1 large tart apple, peeled, cored and grated
finely grated rind of 1 orange
juice of ½ lemon
⅓ cup raw brown sugar
Topping:
1 egg white, lightly beaten
little raw brown sugar

Divide the dough in half and roll out one portion to line the bottom of a 28 × 18 cm/11 × 7 inch cake pan.

Mix together the dried fruit, apple, orange rind, lemon juice and sugar and spread over the dough in the pan. Roll out the rest of the dough and lay over the fruit mixture. Brush with the egg white and sprinkle with sugar. Bake in a preheated hot oven (220°C/425°F, Gas Mark 7) for 25 minutes. Cool in the pan, then cut into slices.
Makes 16

Wine Biscuits (Cookies)

Metric/Imperial
150 g/5 oz butter
75 g/3 oz sugar
1 egg, beaten
2 teaspoons red wine
275 g/10 oz self-raising flour, sifted
jam
sugar to dredge

American
10 tablespoons butter
6 tablespoons sugar
1 egg, beaten
2 teaspoons red wine
2½ cups self-rising flour, sifted
jam
sugar to dredge

Cream the butter with the sugar until light and fluffy. Beat in the egg and wine, then fold in the flour. Form into small balls. Make a depression in each ball with the floured handle of a wooden spoon and fill the depression with jam. Place on greased baking sheets and sprinkle with sugar.

Bake in a preheated moderately hot oven (190°C/375°F, Gas Mark 5) for 15 to 20 minutes.
Makes about 48

Sultana (Raisin) and Nut Crescents

Metric/Imperial
100 g/4 oz plain flour
100 g/4 oz butter
100 g/4 oz curd cheese
sifted icing sugar to dredge
Filling:
25 g/1 oz sultanas
1 tablespoon sugar
25 g/1 oz nuts, chopped
¼ teaspoon ground cinnamon
   (optional)

American
1 cup all-purpose flour
8 tablespoons (1 stick) butter
½ cup small-curd cottage cheese
sifted confectioners' sugar to dredge
Filling:
2½ tablespoons seedless white
   raisins
1 tablespoon sugar
¼ cup chopped nuts
¼ teaspoon ground cinnamon
   (optional)

Sift the flour into a bowl and rub in the butter. Add the cheese and mix to a dough. Chill.

Roll out the dough and cut into triangles. Mix together the filling ingredients and put a small spoonful of filling in the centre of each triangle. Roll them up from the wide side, and press to the dampened point to seal. Arrange on a greased baking sheet, curving slightly into crescents.

Bake in a preheated hot oven (220°C/425°F, Gas Mark 7) for 15 minutes. Sprinkle with icing (confectioners') sugar and cool.

Makes about 24

Variation:

Kasse Strudel: Roll out the chilled dough into an oblong. Beat together 225 g/8 oz curd cheese (1 cup small-curd cottage cheese), 1 egg, 50 g/2 oz (¼ cup) sugar and 50 g/2 oz sultanas (⅓ cup seedless white raisins). Spread this filling over the dough to within 1 cm/½ inch of the edges. Dampen the edges, then roll up tightly like a Swiss (jelly) roll. Bake in a preheated hot oven (220°C/425°F, Gas Mark 7) and continue baking for 15 minutes. Cool, then sprinkle with icing (confectioners') sugar.

Jam and Cheese Turnovers

Metric/Imperial	American
100 g/4 oz plain flour	1 cup all-purpose flour
100 g/4 oz butter	8 tablespoons (1 stick) butter
100 g/4 oz cheese, grated	1 cup grated cheese
jam	jam
sifted icing sugar to dredge	sifted confectioners' sugar to dredge

Sift the flour into a bowl and rub in the butter. Work in the cheese to make a dough. Chill.

Roll out the dough and cut into rounds. Dampen the edges, then put a little jam in the centre of each round. Fold them over and press to seal. Place on a greased baking sheet.

Bake in a preheated hot oven (220°C/425°F, Gas Mark 7) for 15 minutes. Sprinkle with icing (confectioners') sugar and cool.

Makes about 24

Apricot Squares

Metric/Imperial	American
150 g/5 oz butter	10 tablespoons butter
75 g/3 oz plus 1 teaspoon sugar	6 tablespoons plus 1 teaspoon sugar
1 egg, beaten	1 egg, beaten
225 g/8 oz self-raising flour, sifted	2 cups self-rising flour, sifted
500 g/1 lb apricots, halved and stoned	1 lb apricots, halved and pitted
1 teaspoon lemon juice	1 teaspoon lemon juice
Crumble topping:	**Crumble topping:**
40 g/1½ oz butter	3 tablespoons butter
75 g/3 oz plain flour, sifted	¾ cup all-purpose flour, sifted
50 g/2 oz sugar	¼ cup sugar
25 g/1 oz ground almonds	¼ cup ground almonds

Cream the butter with 75 g/3 oz (6 tablespoons) of the sugar until light and fluffy. Beat in the egg, then fold in the flour. Press over the bottom of a greased 20 cm/8 inch square cake pan. Arrange the apricot halves on the dough, cut sides down, and sprinkle with the lemon juice.

For the topping, rub the butter into the flour, then stir in the sugar and almonds. Sprinkle the topping over the apricots, then sprinkle with the remaining 1 teaspoon sugar.

Bake in a preheated moderate oven (180°C/350°F, Gas Mark 4) for 1 hour. Cool, then cut into squares.

Makes about 16

Cherry Slices

Metric/Imperial	American
100 g/4 oz self-raising flour	1 cup self-rising flour
65 g/2½ oz butter	5 tablespoons butter
25 g/1 oz sugar	2 tablespoons sugar
1 egg, beaten	1 egg, beaten
Topping:	**Topping:**
500 g/1 lb stoned cherries	1 lb pitted cherries
75 g/3 oz sugar	6 tablespoons sugar
25 g/1 oz plain flour, sifted	¼ cup all-purpose flour, sifted
½ teaspoon ground cinnamon	½ teaspoon ground cinnamon
25 g/1 oz butter	2 tablespoons butter

Sift the flour into a bowl and rub in the butter. Stir in the sugar, then bind to a dough with the egg. Press the dough into the bottom of a greased 18 cm/7 inch square cake pan. Cover with the cherries.

Mix together the sugar, flour and cinnamon and sprinkle over the cherries. Dot with the butter.

Bake in a preheated moderate oven (180°C/350°F, Gas Mark 4) for 1 hour. Cut into squares or slices to serve.

Variations:
Other fruit, such as apricots, plums and apples, can be used instead of cherries.

Clover Leaf Cookies

Metric/Imperial	American
50 g/2 oz butter	4 tablespoons butter
50 g/2 oz sugar	¼ cup sugar
1 egg	1 egg
100 g/4 oz plain flour, sifted	1 cup all-purpose flour, sifted
few caraway seeds	few caraway seeds
½ teaspoon ground ginger	½ teaspoon ground ginger
1 teaspoon grated lemon rind	1 teaspoon grated lemon rind

Cream the butter with the sugar until light and fluffy. Beat in the egg, followed by the flour. Divide the dough into three portions. Work the caraway seeds into one portion, the ginger into the second, and the lemon rind into the third.

Roll the three portions into small balls and arrange in groups of three (one ball of each flavour) on greased baking sheets. Press flat to form clover leaf shapes.

Bake in a preheated moderately hot oven (190°C/375°F, Gas Mark 5) for 10 to 15 minutes. Cool on a wire rack.

Makes about 15

Hazelnut Bars

Metric/Imperial	American
175 g/6 oz plain flour	*1½ cups all-purpose flour*
100 g/4 oz butter	*8 tablespoons (1 stick) butter*
about 2 tablespoons water	*about 2 tablespoons water*
sifted icing sugar to dredge	*sifted confectioners' sugar to dredge*
Filling:	**Filling:**
3 tablespoons apricot jam	*3 tablespoons apricot jam*
100 g/4 oz butter	*8 tablespoons (1 stick) butter*
175 g/6 oz caster sugar	*¾ cup sugar*
few drops of vanilla essence	*few drops of vanilla extract*
½ teaspoon lemon juice	*½ teaspoon lemon juice*
2 eggs, beaten	*2 eggs, beaten*
50 g/2 oz self-raising flour, sifted	*½ cup self-rising flour, sifted*
225 g/8 oz ground hazelnuts	*2 cups ground hazelnuts*

Sift the flour into a bowl and rub in the butter. Bind to a dough with the water. Roll out the dough and use to line the bottom of a 30 × 20 cm/12 × 8 inch cake pan. Bake blind (unfilled) in a preheated hot oven (220°C/425°F, Gas Mark 7) for 10 minutes.

Spread the jam over the pastry.

Cream the butter with the sugar until light and fluffy. Beat in the vanilla, lemon juice and eggs, then fold in the flour and nuts. Spread over the jam.

Return to the oven, reduce the temperature to moderate (180°C/350°F, Gas Mark 4) and bake for a further 30 to 40 minutes.

Sprinkle with icing (confectioners') sugar and cut into bars to serve.

Almond Biscuits (Cookies)

Metric/Imperial
150 g/5 oz butter
150 g/5 oz sugar
1 egg, beaten
few drops of almond essence
225 g/8 oz plain flour, sifted
75 g/3 oz ground almonds
To finish:
2 tablespoons sugar
2 tablespoons chopped almonds
blanched almonds or glacé cherries

American
10 tablespoons butter
⅔ cup sugar
1 egg, beaten
few drops of almond extract
2 cups all-purpose flour, sifted
¾ cup ground almonds
To finish:
2 tablespoons sugar
2 tablespoons chopped almonds
blanched almonds or candied
 cherries

Cream the butter with the sugar until light and fluffy. Beat in the egg and almond essence (extract), then fold in the flour and ground almonds to make a dough.

Roll the dough into small balls. Mix the sugar with the chopped almonds and use to coat the balls. Press them flat and top each with a blanched almond or a piece of cherry. Arrange on greased baking sheets.

Bake in a preheated moderately hot oven (200°C/400°F, Gas Mark 6) for 15 to 20 minutes.
Makes about 50

Oatmeal Crunchies

Metric/Imperial
225 g/8 oz wholemeal flour
75 g/3 oz medium oatmeal
75 g/3 oz bran
150 g/5 oz dark brown sugar
½ teaspoon ground ginger
½ teaspoon ground mixed spice
100 g/4 oz butter
about 150 ml/¼ pint water

American
2 cups wholewheat flour
½ cup medium oatmeal
1½ cups bran
¾ cup dark brown sugar
½ teaspoon ground ginger
½ teaspoon ground allspice
8 tablespoons (1 stick) butter
about ⅔ cup water

Mix together the flour, oatmeal, bran, sugar and spices and rub in the butter. Mix in enough water to make a stiff dough.

Roll out the dough to 1 cm/½ inch thick and cut out 6 cm/2½ inch rounds. Place them on greased baking sheets.

Bake in a preheated oven (180°C/350°F, Gas Mark 4) for 25 minutes. Cool on a wire rack.
Makes 48

Cinnamon Biscuits (Cookies)

Metric/Imperial	American
225 g/8 oz self-raising flour	2 cups self-rising flour
½ teaspoon bicarbonate of soda	½ teaspoon baking soda
1 teaspoon ground cinnamon	1 teaspoon ground cinnamon
100 g/4 oz butter	8 tablespoons (1 stick) butter
100 g/4 oz soft brown sugar	⅔ cup light brown sugar
1 teaspoon lemon juice	1 teaspoon lemon juice
1 teaspoon orange juice	1 teaspoon orange juice
1 egg, separated	1 egg, separated
2 tablespoons caster sugar	2 tablespoons granulated sugar

Sift the flour, soda and ½ teaspoon of the cinnamon into a bowl. Rub in the butter, then stir in the brown sugar. Add the juices, egg yolk and enough of the egg white to make a dough.

Roll out the dough thinly and cut into 5 cm/2 inch rounds. Place on greased baking sheets. Brush with the rest of the egg white, lightly beaten. Mix the white sugar with the remaining cinnamon and sprinkle on top.

Bake in a preheated moderately hot oven (190°C/375°F, Gas Mark 5) for 15 to 20 minutes.

Makes about 50

Icebox Cookies

Metric/Imperial	American
225 g/8 oz plain flour	2 cups all-purpose flour
4 tablespoons semolina	¼ cup semolina or cream of wheat
175 g/6 oz butter	12 tablespoons (1½ sticks) butter
150 g/5 oz sugar	⅔ cup sugar
1 egg, separated	1 egg, separated
2 tablespoons water	2 tablespoons water
walnut halves to decorate	walnut halves to decorate

Sift the flour into a bowl. Stir in the semolina. Rub in the butter, then stir in the sugar. Mix the egg yolk with the water and use to bind the dry ingredients to a stiff dough. Divide the dough in half and shape each half into a roll about 5 cm/2 inches in diameter. Chill for 3 hours.

Cut off as many thin slices from a roll as you wish to make biscuits (cookies). Return any remaining dough to the refrigerator and store until required. Arrange the slices on greased baking sheets and brush with the lightly beaten egg white. Top each with a walnut half.

Bake in a preheated moderately hot oven (200°C/400°F, Gas Mark 6) for 8 to 10 minutes or until golden. Cool on a wire rack.

Makes about 60

Cheese and Sesame Wafers

Metric/Imperial	American
100 g/4 oz plain flour	1 cup all-purpose flour
½ teaspoon salt	½ teaspoon salt
pinch of cayenne pepper	pinch of cayenne pepper
½ teaspoon dry mustard	½ teaspoon dry mustard
½ teaspoon ground ginger	½ teaspoon ground ginger
½ teaspoon caster sugar	½ teaspoon sugar
50 g/2 oz Cheddar cheese, grated	½ cup grated Cheddar cheese
2–3 tablespoons toasted sesame seeds	2–3 tablespoons toasted sesame seeds
1 egg yolk	1 egg yolk
50 g/2 oz butter, melted	4 tablespoons butter, melted
1 tablespoon water	1 tablespoon water

Sift the flour, salt, spices and sugar into a bowl. Stir in the cheese and sesame seeds. Mix together the egg yolk, butter and water and use to bind the dry ingredients. Chill for 30 minutes.

Roll out the dough to 3 mm/⅛ inch thick and cut into 5 cm/2 inch squares. Place on a baking sheet. Bake in a preheated moderate oven (180°C/350°F, Gas Mark 4) for 15 minutes. Cool on the baking sheet.

Makes about 50

Herb Cheese Biscuits (Crackers)

Metric/Imperial	American
25 g/1 oz butter	2 tablespoons butter
50 g/2 oz Cheddar cheese, grated	½ cup grated Cheddar cheese
1 egg yolk	1 egg yolk
50 g/2 oz plain flour	½ cup all-purpose flour
pinch of salt	pinch of salt
pinch of cayenne pepper	pinch of cayenne pepper
½ teaspoon caraway seeds or dried dill seed	½ teaspoon caraway seeds or dried dill seed
½ teaspoon Dijon mustard	½ teaspoon Dijon mustard
1 tablespoon water	1 tablespoon water

Cream together the butter, cheese and egg yolk. Work in the flour, salt, cayenne pepper, caraway seeds or dill seed and the mustard. Bind to a soft but firm dough with the water.

Roll out to 3 mm/⅛ inch thick and cut into small rounds. Bake in a preheated moderately hot oven (200°C/400°F, Gas Mark 6) for 7 minutes or until golden brown. Serve hot.

Makes about 20

Wholemeal (Wholewheat) Cheese Biscuits (Crackers)

Metric/Imperial
25g/1 oz butter
225 g/8 oz Cheddar cheese, grated
100 g/4 oz wholemeal flour
½ teaspoon salt
1 teaspoon dry mustard
2 tablespoons water

American
2 tablespoons butter
2 cups grated Cheddar cheese
1 cup wholewheat flour
½ teaspoon salt
1 teaspoon dry mustard
2 tablespoons water

Cream together the butter and the cheese. Work in the flour, salt and mustard. Bind to a firm dough with the water.

Roll out the dough to 5 mm/¼ inch thick and cut into 5 cm/2 inch rounds. Bake in a preheated very hot oven (230°C/450°F, Gas Mark 8) for 6 minutes.
Makes about 30

Flaky Cheese Biscuits (Crackers)

Metric/Imperial
50 g/2 oz butter
50 g/2 oz Cheddar cheese, grated
½ egg yolk
salt
large pinch of paprika
50 g/2 oz plain flour, sifted

American
4 tablespoons butter
½ cup grated Cheddar cheese
½ egg yolk
salt
large pinch of paprika
½ cup all-purpose flour, sifted

Cream together the butter, cheese and egg yolk. Beat in salt to taste and the paprika, then work in the flour. Chill for 1 hour.

Roll out the dough to 5 mm/¼ inch thick and cut into 2.5 cm/1 inch rounds. Arrange on greased baking sheets.

Bake in a preheated hot oven (220°C/425°F, Gas Mark 7) for 10 minutes.
Makes about 30

Variation:
Paprika Biscuits (Crackers): Cream together 75 g/3 oz (6 tablespoons) butter and 75 g/3 oz (¾ cup) grated Cheddar cheese. Sift 100 g/4 oz plain flour (1 cup all-purpose flour) with 1 teaspoon paprika, ½ teaspoon salt and ½ teaspoon dry mustard and work into the creamed mixture. Roll into small balls, place on greased baking sheets and flatten slightly. Sprinkle with poppy or caraway seeds. Bake in a preheated moderate oven (180°C/350°F, Gas Mark 4) for 15 to 20 minutes. Cool on the baking sheets.
Makes about 18

Onion Biscuits (Crackers)

Metric/Imperial
225 g/8 oz plain flour
pinch of salt
pinch of pepper
150 g/5 oz butter
1 onion, finely grated
1 egg, beaten
beaten egg to glaze
poppy seeds (optional)

American
2 cups all-purpose flour
pinch of salt
pinch of pepper
10 tablespoons butter
1 onion, finely grated
1 egg, beaten
beaten egg to glaze
poppy seeds (optional)

Sift the flour, salt and pepper into a bowl and rub in the butter. Add the onion and egg and mix to a stiff dough. Roll out the dough and cut into 5 cm/2 inch squares. Place on greased baking sheets and brush with beaten egg. Sprinkle with poppy seeds, if liked.

Bake in a preheated moderately hot oven (200°C/400°F, Gas Mark 6) for 15 to 20 minutes.
Makes about 24

Cottage Cheese Biscuits (Crackers)

Metric/Imperial
100 g/4 oz plain flour
pinch of salt
100 g/4 oz butter
100 g/4 oz curd or sieved cottage
  cheese
beaten egg to glaze
paprika

American
1 cup all-purpose flour
pinch of salt
8 tablespoons (1 stick) butter
½ cup small-curd cottage cheese
beaten egg to glaze
paprika

Sift the flour and salt into a bowl and rub in the butter. Work in the cheese, then chill.

Roll out the dough thickly and cut into 5 cm/2 inch rounds. Place on greased baking sheets and brush with beaten egg.

Bake in a preheated hot oven (220°C/425°F, Gas Mark 7) for 10 to 15 minutes. Serve hot, sprinkled with paprika.
Makes about 30

Puff Pastry

Metric/Imperial
225 g/8 oz plain flour
1 teaspoon salt
225 g/8 oz butter
150 ml/¼ pint iced water
½ teaspoon lemon juice

American
2 cups all-purpose flour
1 teaspoon salt
½ lb (2 sticks) butter
⅔ cup iced water
½ teaspoon lemon juice

Sift the flour and salt into a bowl. Add 50 g/2 oz (4 tablespoons) of the butter and rub into the flour. Bind to a firm dough with the water and lemon juice.

Roll out the dough to an 18 cm/7 inch square. Flatten the remaining butter into a slab and place it in the centre of the dough square. Fold the dough over to enclose the butter completely. Roll out to a rectangle about 30 × 18 cm/ 12 × 7 inches. Fold into three and press the edges together to seal. Chill for 20 minutes.

Roll out the dough again, with the raw edges to one side. Fold and chill as before. Repeat the rolling, folding and chilling four times.

Variation:

Rough Puff Pastry: Sift the flour with ¼ teaspoon salt and 1 teaspoon baking powder. Reduce the butter to 175 g/6 oz (12 tablespoons) and cut it into small nut-sized pieces. Add to the flour all at once, then mix to a stiff, lumpy dough with the water and lemon juice. Roll, fold and chill as above.

Rich Shortcrust (Pie) Pastry

Metric/Imperial
250 g/9 oz plain flour
½ teaspoon salt
115 g/4½ oz butter
1 egg yolk
about 2 tablespoons water

American
2¼ cups all-purpose flour
½ teaspoon salt
9 tablespoons butter
1 egg yolk
about 2 tablespoons water

Sift the flour and salt into a bowl and rub in the butter until the mixture resembles breadcrumbs. Bind to a smooth dough with the egg yolk and water, adding more water if necessary.

Rich Sweet Shortcrust (Pie) Pastry

Metric/Imperial
350 g/12 oz self-raising flour
225 g/8 oz butter
100 g/4 oz sugar
1 egg plus 1 egg yolk
1 tablespoon water

American
3 cups self-rising flour
½ lb (2 sticks) butter
½ cup sugar
1 egg plus 1 egg yolk
1 tablespoon water

Sift the flour into a bowl. Rub in the butter until the mixture resembles breadcrumbs. Mix in the sugar. Bind to a smooth dough with the egg and egg yolk and water. Add more water if necessary.

Choux Pastry

Metric/Imperial
100 g/4 oz butter, cut into pieces
pinch of salt
pinch of sugar
250 ml/8 fl oz water
115 g/4½ oz plain flour, sifted
4 eggs, beaten

American
8 tablespoons (1 stick) butter, cut
    into pieces
pinch of salt
pinch of sugar
1 cup water
1 cup plus 2 tablespoons all-purpose
    flour, sifted
4 eggs, beaten

Put the butter, salt, sugar and water in a saucepan and heat gently to melt the butter. Bring to the boil, then add the flour all at once. Beat vigorously until the mixture forms a ball which leaves the sides of the pan clean. Remove from the heat and cool slightly, then gradually beat in the eggs to form a smooth, glossy dough.

Pancakes (Crêpes)

Metric/Imperial
100 g/4 oz plain flour
pinch of salt
1 egg
300 ml/½ pint milk
oil for frying

American
1 cup all-purpose flour
pinch of salt
1 egg
1¼ cups milk
oil for frying

Sift the flour and salt into a bowl and make a well in the centre. Put in the egg and half the milk and gradually mix into the flour. Beat until smooth, then beat in enough of the remaining milk to make a thin batter.

Lightly oil a 12 to 18 cm/5 to 7 inch heavy pancake (crêpe) pan. Pour in a little of the batter and tilt the pan to spread it out over the bottom in a thin layer. Cook until the underside is browned, then turn or toss and lightly brown the other side.

Slide the pancake (crêpe) onto a plate. Make the remaining pancakes (crêpes) in the same way, and stack them up, interleaved with grease-proof (wax) paper.
Makes 8–12

Flaky Pastry

Metric/Imperial
350 g/12 oz plain flour
½ teaspoon salt
175 g/6 oz butter
6 tablespoons iced water
1 teaspoon lemon juice

American
3 cups all-purpose flour
½ teaspoon salt
12 tablespoons (1½ sticks) butter
6 tablespoons iced water
1 teaspoon lemon juice

Sift the flour and salt into a bowl. Divide the butter into four portions and rub one portion into the flour. Bind to a soft dough with the water and lemon juice. Chill for 30 minutes.

Roll out the dough on a floured surface to a 45 × 18 cm/18 × 7 inch rectangle. Cut another portion of the butter into small pieces and dot these over the top two-thirds of the dough rectangle. Fold the unbuttered bottom third up over the butter and the top third down. Press the edges together to seal. Chill for 30 minutes.

Roll out the dough to a rectangle again, with the raw edges of the dough to one side. Dot with another portion of the butter as before, then fold and chill. Repeat the rolling, buttering, folding and chilling once more.

Shortcrust (Pie) Pastry

Metric/Imperial
225 g/8 oz plain flour
pinch of salt
75–100 g/3–4 oz butter

American
2 cups all-purpose flour
pinch of salt
6–8 tablespoons butter

Sift the flour and salt into a bowl. Rub in the butter until the mixture resembles breadcrumbs. Bind with water to make a firm dough and knead lightly until smooth.

Variation:
Wholemeal (Wholewheat) Pastry: Use wholemeal (wholewheat) flour, and bind to a dough with 2 egg yolks beaten with 1 tablespoon water.

Sweet Shortcrust (Pie) Pastry

Metric/Imperial
225 g/8 oz plain flour
pinch of salt
75–100 g/3–4 oz butter
2 tablespoons sugar
1 egg, beaten

American
2 cups all-purpose flour
pinch of salt
6–8 tablespoons butter
2 tablespoons sugar
1 egg, beaten

Sift the flour and salt into a bowl. Rub in the butter until the mixture resembles breadcrumbs. Mix in the sugar, then bind to a dough with the beaten egg.

Spiced Wholemeal (Wholewheat) Pastry

Metric/Imperial
175 g/6 oz wholemeal flour
100 g/4 oz butter or margarine
50 g/2 oz brown sugar
1 tablespoon ground mixed spice
1 egg, beaten
2 teaspoons cold water, if necessary

American
1½ cups wholewheat flour
8 tablespoons butter or margarine
⅓ cup brown sugar
1 tablespoon ground apple pie spice
1 egg, beaten
2 teaspoons cold water, if necessary

Put the flour in a bowl and rub in the fat. Stir in the sugar and the spice, then combine with the egg to make a dough. Add the cold water if necessary.

Wholemeal (Wholewheat) Almond Pastry

Metric/Imperial
100 g/4 oz wholemeal flour
75 g/3 oz butter or margarine
75 g/3 oz ground almonds
50 g/2 oz sugar
1 egg yolk
2 teaspoons cold water
few drops of almond essence

American
1 cup wholewheat flour
6 tablespoons butter or margarine
¾ cup ground almonds
¼ cup sugar
1 egg yolk
2 teaspoons cold water
few drops of almond extract

Put the flour in a bowl and rub in the fat. Stir in the ground almonds and sugar. Combine the egg yolk, water and almond essence (extract) and add to the dry mixture. Mix to a firm dough.

Pâte Sucrée

Metric/Imperial
225 g/8 oz plain flour
pinch of salt
4 egg yolks
100 g/4 oz butter, softened
100 g/4 oz sugar

American
2 cups all-purpose flour
pinch of salt
4 egg yolks
8 tablespoons (1 stick) butter, softened
½ cup sugar

Sift the flour and salt onto a working surface and make a well in the centre. Put in the egg yolks, butter and sugar. Using the fingertips of one hand, knead the ingredients in the well together until thoroughly combined. Gradually work in the flour and knead lightly to make a smooth dough. Chill for at least 15 minutes before using.

Variation:

Italian Pasta Frolla: Make the dough as above, using 225 g/8 oz plain flour (2 cups all-purpose flour), a pinch of salt, 2 egg yolks, 100 g/4 oz (8 tablespoons) butter, 75 g/3 oz (6 tablespoons) sugar and the grated rind of ½ lemon.

Custard Tarts

Metric/Imperial
½ quantity shortcrust pastry (see
  page 106)
2 eggs, 1 separated
2 tablespoons fresh white
  breadcrumbs
150 ml/¼ pint single cream
½ teaspoon vanilla essence
2 teaspoons sifted icing sugar
grated nutmeg

American
½ quantity pie pastry (see page 106)
2 eggs, 1 separated
2 tablespoons fresh white
  breadcrumbs
⅔ cup light cream
½ teaspoon vanilla extract
2 teaspoons sifted confectioners'
  sugar
grated nutmeg

Roll out the dough and cut out 12 rounds with a fluted cutter. Use these to line
12 bun tins (tartlet or muffin tins).

Beat the one egg white until frothy and brush over the insides of the pastry
cases. Sprinkle with the breadcrumbs (this helps to prevent sogginess).

Beat together the egg yolk, whole egg, cream, vanilla and sugar and spoon
into the pastry cases. Sprinkle lightly with nutmeg.

Bake in a preheated moderately hot oven (190°C/375°F, Gas Mark 5) for
30 to 35 minutes or until the custard filling is set and the pastry is golden.
Cool on a wire rack.
Makes 12

Variation:

Brandied Custard Tarts: Prepare the pastry cases as above. For the filling, omit the extra egg yolk (use only 1 whole egg), use milk instead of cream, substitute 1 tablespoon brandy for the vanilla and use 1 tablespoon granulated sugar instead of the icing (confectioners') sugar. Pour into the pastry cases, sprinkle with nutmeg and bake as above, for 20 minutes.

Mince Pies

Metric/Imperial
1 quantity shortcrust or rich
  shortcrust pastry (see page 106)
350–550 g/12 oz–1 lb mincemeat
beaten egg
caster sugar

American
1 quantity pie or rich pie pastry (see
  page 106)
¾–1 lb mincemeat (about 1½–2 cups)
beaten egg
sugar

Roll out the dough and cut out 12 rounds about 7.5 cm/3 inches in diameter. Use these to line 12 bun (muffin) tins. Fill with mincemeat and moisten the pastry edges with water.

Roll out the dough trimmings and cut out 12 smaller rounds for the lids. Put these on top of the pies and pinch the edges together to seal. Brush the lids with beaten egg.

Bake in a preheated moderately hot oven (200°C/400°F, Gas Mark 6) for about 20 minutes. Cool in the tins until lukewarm, then sprinkle with sugar.

Makes 12

Variations:

Christmas Star Pie: Roll out half the dough and use to line a 23 cm/9 inch pie pan. Peel, core and grate 1 large cooking (tart) apple and spread in the pastry case. Top with a layer of mincemeat (about 350 g/12 oz or 1½ cups). Roll out the remaining dough to a round for the lid and cut out about 8 small star shapes. Moisten the edges of the pastry case and place the lid on top. Pinch the edges together to seal.

Arrange the cut-out dough stars around the edge of the lid, holding them in place with a little water. Bake in a preheated hot oven (220°C/425°F, Gas Mark 7) for 20 minutes, then reduce the heat to moderate (180°C/350°F, Gas Mark 4) and bake for a further 20 minutes. Dust with sifted icing (confectioners') sugar and serve warm.

Iced Mince Tarts: Prepare the pastry cases as above, using only ½ quantity shortcrust (pie) pastry. Bake blind (unfilled) in a preheated moderately hot oven (200°C/400°F, Gas Mark 6) for 20 minutes or until the pastry is set and golden. Cool, then fill with the mincemeat. For the icing, mix together 2 tablespoons sifted icing (confectioners') sugar and ½ egg white. Tint pink with a few drops of red food colouring. Spread the icing thinly over the mincemeat in each pastry case, then bake in a moderate oven (180°C/350°F, Gas Mark 4) for 5 to 10 minutes or until the icing is set.

Apple Strudel

Metric/Imperial
225 g/8 oz plain flour
pinch of salt
4 tablespoons salad oil
150 ml/¼ pint lukewarm water
Filling:
75 g/3 oz butter, melted
4 tablespoons fresh white
  breadcrumbs
25 g/1 oz ground almonds
1 kg/2 lb cooking apples, peeled,
  cored and very thinly sliced
2 teaspoons ground cinnamon
50 g/2 oz caster sugar
2 tablespoons dark rum (optional)
2½ tablespoons flaked almonds
100 g/4 oz sultanas
sifted icing sugar

American
2 cups all-purpose flour
pinch of salt
¼ cup salad oil
⅔ cup lukewarm water
Filling:
6 tablespoons butter, melted
¼ cup fresh white breadcrumbs
¼ cup ground almonds
2 lb tart apples, peeled, cored and
  very thinly sliced
2 teaspoons ground cinnamon
¼ cup sugar
2 tablespoons dark rum (optional)
2½ tablespoons slivered almonds
⅔ cup seedless white raisins
sifted confectioners' sugar

Sift the flour and salt into a bowl. Make a well in the centre and add the oil and water. Mix to a soft dough, then knead until the dough is smooth, elastic and no longer sticky. This will take about 30 minutes. Cover the dough and leave it to 'relax' for 30 minutes.

Put a patterned tablecloth on a kitchen table or work surface and dredge it heavily with flour. Place the dough in the centre and roll it out in all directions as thin as possible. As soon as the pattern of the cloth starts showing through, start pulling the dough with your fingertips. Pull until the edges of the dough are as paper thin as the centre, taking care not to break the dough or get large holes in it.

Brush the sheet of dough all over with half the melted butter, then sprinkle with half the breadcrumbs and ground almonds. Mix together the apples, cinnamon, sugar and rum, if used, and spread over the dough, leaving a 2.5 cm/1 inch margin uncovered at the edges. Sprinkle with the rest of the breadcrumbs and ground almonds, the flaked (slivered) almonds and sultanas (raisins). Fold over the uncovered edges, then carefully roll up like a Swiss (jelly) roll. Roll from the cloth onto a greased baking sheet and brush with the remaining butter.

Bake in a preheated moderately hot oven (190°C/375°F, Gas Mark 5) for 35 to 45 minutes. Leave on the baking sheet to cool.

When still lukewarm, dredge with icing (confectioners') sugar. Serve slightly warm.

Cheese and Cherry Strudel

Metric/Imperial
1 quantity apple strudel dough (see
  opposite)
75 g/3 oz butter, melted
2 tablespoons fresh white
  breadcrumbs
15 g/½ oz ground almonds
Filling:
500 g/1 lb curd cheese
2 egg yolks
4 tablespoons single cream
3 tablespoons sugar
1 teaspoon vanilla essence
pinch of salt
stewed fresh or canned stoned
  cherries

American
1 quantity apple strudel dough (see
  opposite)
6 tablespoons butter, melted
2 tablespoons fresh white
  breadcrumbs
2 tablespoons ground almonds
Filling:
2 cups small-curd cheese
2 egg yolks
4 tablespoons light cream
3 tablespoons sugar
1 teaspoon vanilla extract
pinch of salt
stewed fresh or canned pitted
  cherries

Roll the dough out following directions for apple strudel (see opposite). Brush the dough sheet with half the melted butter and sprinkle with breadcrumbs and ground almonds.

Mix together the curd cheese, egg yolks, cream, sugar, vanilla essence (extract) and salt. Spread this mixture over the dough, then stud generously with the cherries. Fold over the uncovered edges, then carefully roll up like a Swiss (jelly) roll. Roll from the cloth onto a greased baking sheet and brush with the remaining butter.

Bake in a preheated moderately hot oven (190°C/375°F, Gas Mark 5) for 25 to 35 minutes.

Bakewell Tarts

Metric/Imperial
½ quantity shortcrust pastry (see
  page 106)
raspberry jam
50 g/2 oz butter
50 g/2 oz caster sugar
1 large egg, beaten
few drops of almond essence
40 g/1½ oz self-raising flour, sifted
15 g/½ oz ground almonds
sifted icing sugar

American
½ quantity pie pastry (see page 106)
raspberry jam
4 tablespoons butter
¼ cup sugar
1 egg, beaten
few drops of almond extract
6 tablespoons self-rising flour, sifted
2 tablespoons ground almonds
sifted confectioners' sugar

Roll out the dough and cut 16 to 18 rounds using a 7.5 cm/3 inch cutter. Use
to line greased patty (tartlet or shallow muffin) tins. Put a little jam in each
pastry case.
   Cream the butter with the sugar until light and fluffy. Beat in the egg and
almond essence (extract), then fold in the flour and ground almonds. Spoon
this mixture over the jam.
   Bake in a preheated moderately hot oven (200°C/400°F, Gas Mark 6) for
15 to 20 minutes or until well risen and golden brown. Cool on a wire rack,
then dredge with icing (confectioners') sugar.
Makes 16–18

Treacle Tart

Metric/Imperial
1 quantity shortcrust pastry (see
  page 106)
grated rind of ½ lemon
1 tablespoon lemon juice
4 tablespoons golden syrup
fresh breadcrumbs or crushed
  cornflakes

American
1 quantity pie pastry (see page 106)
grated rind of ½ lemon
1 tablespoon lemon juice
¼ cup light corn syrup
fresh breadcrumbs or crushed
  cornflakes

Roll out the dough and use to line a 20 cm/8 inch flan ring on a baking sheet
or a pie pan. Bake blind (unfilled) in a preheated moderately hot oven (200°C/
400°F, Gas Mark 6) for about 10 minutes or until set.
   Meanwhile, mix together the lemon rind and juice and syrup. Spread this
mixture over the bottom of the pastry case and cover with a good sprinkling
of breadcrumbs or cornflakes. Return to the oven, reduce the heat to
moderate (180°C/350°F, Gas Mark 4) and continue baking for 15 to 20
minutes or until the pastry is crisp.

Variation:

Orange Treacle Tart: Prepare the pastry case as above, but don't bake blind. For the filling, mix together 225 g/8 oz golden syrup (⅔ cup light corn syrup), 100 g/4 oz (⅓ cup) chunky marmalade and 2 tablespoons orange juice. Stir in 225 g/8 oz (4 cups) fresh white breadcrumbs. Spoon into the pastry case. Bake in a preheated moderate oven (180°C/350°F, Gas Mark 4) for 25 to 30 minutes or until golden brown.

Banana Cream Pie

Metric/Imperial	American
1 quantity sweet shortcrust pastry (see page 106)	1 quantity sweet pie pastry (see page 106)
25 g/1 oz butter	2 tablespoons butter
100 g/4 oz brown sugar	⅔ cup brown sugar
150 ml/¼ pint water	⅔ cup water
300 ml/½ pint milk	1¼ cups milk
1 tablespoon gelatine	2 envelopes unflavored gelatin
2 eggs, separated	2 eggs, separated
150 ml/¼ pint whipping cream	⅔ cup whipping cream
3–4 bananas, sliced	3–4 bananas, sliced
lemon juice	lemon juice
whipped cream to decorate	whipped cream to decorate

Roll out the dough and use to line a 23 cm/9 inch pie pan. Bake blind (unfilled) in a preheated moderately hot oven (200°C/400°F, Gas Mark 6) for about 20 minutes. Cool.

Put the butter, brown sugar and half the water in a saucepan and stir to dissolve the sugar. Cool, then stir in the milk. Dissolve the gelatine in the remaining water and add to the mixture in the pan with the egg yolks. Mix well, then chill until beginning to set.

Whip the cream until thick and fold into the custard mixture. Beat the egg whites until stiff and fold in.

Dip the banana slices in lemon juice to prevent discoloration. Arrange most of them on the bottom of the pastry case and pour over the cream mixture. Chill until set.

Decorate with the reserved banana slices and whipped cream.

Variation:

Chocolate Cream Pie: Use the dough to line a 20 cm/8 inch pie pan and bake blind as above. For the filling, melt 100 g/4 oz plain (dark sweet) chocolate. Beat in 3 egg yolks and 2 tablespoons brandy and cool. Beat 3 egg whites until stiff and fold into the chocolate mixture. Pour into the pastry case and chill until set. Whip 150 ml/¼ pint (⅔ cup) whipping cream until thick and spread over the filling. Decorate with grated chocolate.

Strawberry Tarts

Metric/Imperial
½ quantity shortcrust pastry (see page 106)
150 ml/¼ pint double cream
350–500 g/12 oz–1 lb strawberries, hulled and halved
3 tablespoons redcurrant jelly
1 tablespoon water

American
½ quantity pie pastry (see page 106)
⅔ cup heavy cream
¾–1 lb strawberries, hulled and halved
3 tablespoons redcurrant jelly
1 tablespoon water

Roll out the dough and cut out 12 rounds with a fluted cutter. Use these to line 12 bun tins (tartlet or muffin tins). Bake blind (unfilled) in a preheated moderately hot oven (200°C/400°F, Gas Mark 6) for 20 minutes or until the pastry is set and golden. Cool on a wire rack.

Whip the cream until thick. Put a little cream into each tartlet case and pile high with the strawberries.

Melt the jelly with the water and use to glaze the strawberries. Top with another dollop of cream and serve.

Makes 12

Variations:

Apricot Cream Tarts: Bake the tartlet cases as above and cool. For the filling, beat together 1 egg yolk, 1½ tablespoons sugar and ½ teaspoon vanilla essence (extract). Stir in 1 tablespoon plain (all-purpose) flour, then gradually stir in 150 ml/¼ pint (⅔ cup) warmed milk. Pour the mixture into the saucepan and heat, stirring, until it boils and thickens. Cool, then pour into the tartlet cases. Drain a 425 g/15 oz can apricot halves, reserving 150 ml/¼ pint (⅔ cup) of the syrup, and place one half, cut side down, in each tartlet case. Put the reserved syrup in a saucepan with 2 teaspoons arrowroot and bring to the boil, stirring until thickened. Spoon over the apricots and cool.

Butterscotch Meringue Tartlets: Bake the tartlet cases as above and cool. For the filling, put 50 g/2 oz (⅓ cup) brown sugar in a saucepan with 25 g/1 oz plain flour (¼ cup all-purpose flour) and 150 ml/¼ pint (⅔ cup) milk. Bring to the boil, stirring, and simmer for 1 minute. Remove from the heat and beat in 25 g/1 oz (2 tablespoons) butter, 1 egg yolk, 1 teaspoon instant coffee powder and ½ teaspoon vanilla essence (extract). Cool, then pour into the tartlet cases. Beat 1 egg white until fluffy, then gradually beat in 50 g/2 oz (¼ cup) caster sugar until stiff. Pipe or spoon the meringue on top of the filling in the tartlet cases. Bake in a preheated moderate oven (180°C/350°F, Gas Mark 4) for 5 to 10 minutes or until the meringue is lightly browned.

Chocolate Tarts: Bake the tartlet cases as above and cool. For the filling, beat 1 egg yolk with 25 g/1 oz (1 square) melted plain (dark sweet) chocolate until smooth and thick. Whip 4 tablespoons whipping cream until thick and fold into the chocolate mixture with 1 teaspoon brandy or rum. Beat 1 egg white until stiff and fold into the chocolate mixture. Spoon into the tartlet cases and chill until firm. Drizzle over melted chocolate before serving.

Pineapple Cream Cheese Tarts: Bake the tartlet cases as above and cool. For the filling, beat 50 g/2 oz (¼ cup) cream cheese with 2 teaspoons lemon juice until smooth. Drain a small can of crushed pineapple, reserving 150 ml/¼ pint (⅔ cup) of the syrup. Mix the pineapple into the cream cheese and spoon into the tartlet cases. Put the reserved syrup into a saucepan with 1 teaspoon arrowroot and bring to the boil, stirring until thickened. Tint pale yellow with a little food colouring, then spoon this glaze over the cream cheese mixture. Chill until set.

Honeyed Lemon Cheese Tartlets: Bake the tartlet cases as above and cool. Put 2 beaten eggs in the top of a double boiler and add 100 g/4 oz (½ cup) sugar, 75 g/3 oz (¼ cup) honey, 50 g/2 oz (4 tablespoons) butter, 1 tablespoon grated lemon rind and 3 to 4 tablespoons lemon juice. Beat over hot water until thickened. Cool, then spoon into the tartlet cases.

Apricot and Yogurt Tart

Metric/Imperial	American
1 quantity wholemeal almond pastry (see page 107)	1 quantity wholewheat almond pastry (see page 107)
300 ml/½ pint milk	1¼ cups milk
2 eggs	2 eggs
2 tablespoons cornflour	2 tablespoons cornstarch
2 tablespoons caster sugar	2 tablespoons sugar
150 ml/¼ pint plain yogurt	⅔ cup unflavored yogurt
1 tablespoon sherry	1 tablespoon sherry
4 tablespoons apricot jam	¼ cup apricot jam
2 tablespoons orange juice	2 tablespoons orange juice
500 g/1 lb apricots, halved and stoned	1 lb apricots, halved and pitted
25 g/1 oz unblanched almonds	¼ cup unblanched almonds

Roll out the dough and use to line a 20 cm/8 inch flan ring on a baking sheet or a tart pan. Bake blind (unfilled) in a preheated moderately hot oven (200°C/400°F, Gas Mark 6) for 20 to 25 minutes or until set and browned. Cool.

Scald the milk. Beat together the eggs, cornflour (cornstarch) and sugar, then gradually stir in the hot milk. Return to the pan and bring to the boil, stirring, until the custard is thick. Cool.

Stir the yogurt and sherry into the custard. Pour into the pastry case.

Melt the jam with the orange juice in a clean saucepan. Add the apricot halves, cut sides down, and simmer for 5 to 10 minutes or until tender. Place the apricot halves on the custard in the pastry case and decorate with the almonds. Pour over the jam syrup and chill until set.

Lemon Meringue Pie

Metric/Imperial

1 quantity shortcrust pastry (see
page 106)
grated rind and juice of 2 lemons
2½ tablespoons cornflour
175–225 g/6–8 oz caster sugar
15 g/½ oz butter
2 eggs, separated

American

1 quantity pie pastry (see page 106)
grated rind and juice of 2 lemons
2½ tablespoons cornstarch
¾–1 cup sugar
1 tablespoon butter
2 eggs, separated

Roll out the dough and use to line a 20 cm/8 inch flan ring on a baking sheet
or a pie pan. Bake blind (unfilled) in a preheated moderately hot oven (200°C/
400°F, Gas Mark 6) for 15 to 20 minutes or until the pastry is golden brown.
Cool.

Make up the lemon juice to 300 ml/½ pint (1¼ cups) with water and pour
into a saucepan. Stir in the cornflour (cornstarch), then add the lemon rind,
50 to 100 g/2 to 4 oz (¼ to ½ cup) of the sugar – depending on how sweet you
want the filling to be – and the butter. Cook gently, stirring, until thickened.

Remove from the heat and stir in the egg yolks. Return to the heat and
cook very gently for 2 to 3 minutes. Taste and add more sugar, if liked. Pour
the lemon filling into the pastry case.

Beat the egg whites until stiff, then gardually beat in 100 g/4 oz (½ cup) of
the remaining sugar. Pile the meringue on top of the lemon filling.

Bake in a preheated moderate oven (180°C/350°F, Gas Mark 4) for 5 to 8
minutes or until the meringue is lightly browned.

Variations:

Lime Meringue Pie: Use bottled or fresh lime juice in place of the lemon
juice. If fresh limes are available, use the grated rind of 2 limes instead of the
lemon rind.

Lemon Apple Meringue Pie: For the filling, peel, core and slice 2 very large
cooking (tart) apples and cook gently with the grated rind and juice of 1
lemon and 50 to 75 g/2 to 3 oz (4 to 6 tablespoons) sugar until thick and
pulpy. Beat or sieve (strain) until smooth, then beat in the egg yolks.

Hazelnut Jam Tart

Metric/Imperial
100 g/4 oz plain flour
1 teaspoon ground cinnamon
pinch of salt
100 g/4 oz ground hazelnuts
100 g/4 oz caster sugar
100 g/4 oz butter, softened
1 egg yolk
raspberry jam
lightly beaten egg white

American
1 cup all-purpose flour
1 teaspoon ground cinnamon
pinch of salt
1 cup ground hazelnuts
½ cup sugar
8 tablespoons (1 stick) butter,
  softened
1 egg yolk
raspberry jam
lightly beaten egg white

Sift the flour, cinnamon and salt into a bowl and stir in the hazelnuts and sugar. Rub in the butter, bind to a dough with the yolk. Chill for 2 hours.

Roll out two-thirds of the dough and use to line an 18 cm/7 inch flan ring on a baking sheet or a tart pan. Fill with jam. Roll out the rest of the dough and cut into strips. Lay these in a lattice over the jam and press the ends to the pastry case. Brush with egg white.

Bake in a preheated moderate oven (160°C/325°F, Gas Mark 3) for 45 minutes to 1 hour or until the pastry is golden. Serve warm.

Almond Slices

Metric/Imperial
¾ quantity shortcrust pastry (see
  page 106)
1 tablespoon jam
100 g/4 oz caster sugar
100 g/4 oz icing sugar, sifted
3 tablespoons semolina
1 egg
1 egg white
1 teaspoon almond essence
2 tablespoons split blanched
  almonds

American
¾ quantity pie pastry (see page 106)
1 tablespoon jam
½ cup sugar
1 cup confectioners' sugar, sifted
3 tablespoons semolina or cream of
  wheat
1 egg
1 egg white
1 teaspoon almond extract
2 tablespoons split blanched
  almonds

Roll out the dough into two strips about 30 × 10 cm/12 × 4 inches. Place them on a greased baking sheet. Spread the dough strips lightly with the jam.

Mix together the sugar and semolina. Stir in the egg, egg white and almond essence (extract) until smooth. Spread this mixture over the jam on the dough strips, then decorate with the split almonds.

Bake in a preheated moderately hot oven (200°C/400°F, Gas Mark 6) for 20 to 25 minutes or until pale gold. Cool, then cut into fingers.

Blackberry Mille Feuilles Gâteau

Metric/Imperial
¾ quantity puff pastry (see page 103)
500 g/1 lb blackberries
sugar to taste
300 ml/½ pint whipping cream

American
¾ quantity puff pastry (see page 103)
1 lb blackberries
sugar to taste
1¼ cups whipping cream

Divide the dough into four portions. Roll out three of the portions thinly into equal rounds and the fourth portion into a wide ring the same diameter as the rounds. Place the rounds and ring on baking sheets.

Bake in a preheated very hot oven (230°C/450°F, Gas Mark 8) for 5 minutes, then reduce the heat to moderately hot (200°C/400°F, Gas Mark 6) and bake for a further 10 minutes or until the pastry is golden brown. Cool. Mash about half the blackberries with sugar to taste. Whip the cream until thick.

Place one of the pastry rounds on a serving plate and spread it with a layer of half the mashed fruit and one-third of the cream. Cover with the second round and spread with the remaining mashed fruit and another third of the cream. Add the top round and spread with the remaining cream. Place the pastry ring on top and fill the centre with the whole blackberries.

Cream Horns

Metric/Imperial
½ quantity puff pastry (see page 103)
egg white
little caster sugar
jam
150–300 ml/¼–½ pint double cream

American
½ quantity puff pastry (see page 103)
egg white
little sugar
jam
⅔–1¼ cups heavy cream

Roll out the dough very thinly and cut into 12 2.5 cm/1 inch wide strips. Lightly grease 12 cream horn tins, then wind a dough strip around each, starting from the bottom of the tin and allowing each round to overlap the previous one. Do not pull the dough. Place on a baking sheet and brush with lightly beaten egg white. Sprinkle with sugar.

Bake in a preheated very hot oven (230°C/450°F, Gas Mark 8) for 8 to 10 minutes or until set and golden brown. Cool for a few minutes, then carefully pull out the tins. Leave to cool completely.

Put a little jam in each pastry horn. Whip the cream until thick and use to fill the horns.
Makes 12

Variations:

Raspberry Cream Horns: Make the pastry horns as above, omitting the sprinkling with sugar before baking. Cool. Crush 100 g/4 oz raspberries and sweeten to taste. Whip 300 ml/½ pint double cream (1¼ cups heavy cream) until thick and fold the raspberry mixture into half the cream. Use this mixture to fill the pastry horns. Decorate with the remaining whipped cream and another 50 to 100 g/2 to 4 oz raspberries. Dust with icing (confectioners') sugar.

Chocolate and Rum Horns: Make the pastry horns as above and cool. Whip 300 ml/½ pint double cream (1¼ cups heavy cream) with sifted icing (confectioners') sugar to taste and 1 to 2 tablespoons rum until thick. Fold in 50 to 75 g/2 to 3 oz (½ cup) chopped plain (dark sweet) chocolate. Use this mixture to fill the horns.

Apple Crunch

Metric/Imperial	American
175 g/6 oz self-raising flour	1½ cups self-rising flour
pinch of salt	pinch of salt
1 tablespoon caster sugar	1 tablespoon sugar
75 g/3 oz butter	6 tablespoons butter
2 large eggs	2 eggs
75 g/3 oz ground almonds	¾ cup ground almonds
75 g/3 oz demerara sugar	½ cup raw brown sugar
1½ teaspoons ground mixed spice or cinnamon	1½ teaspoons ground cinnamon
3 apples, peeled, cored and sliced	3 apples, peeled, cored and sliced
2 tablespoons apricot jam	2 tablespoons apricot jam
1 teaspoon water	1 teaspoon water

Sift together the flour, salt and sugar. Rub in the butter, then bind to a firm, pliable dough with one of the eggs. Press over the bottom of a greased 28 × 18 cm/11 × 7 inch cake pan in an even layer. Beat the other egg lightly and use all of it to glaze the dough layer.

Mix together the almonds, demerara (brown) sugar and spice and sprinkle over the dough. Arrange the apple slices in overlapping rows across the sugar topping, leaving about 1 cm/½ inch between each row. Heat the jam with the water and brush carefully over the apple slices.

Bake in a preheated moderate oven (180°C/350°F, Gas Mark 4) for about 1 hour. Cool in the pan for 10 minutes, then cut into squares. Leave in the pan to cool completely.

Makes about 18

Cream Slices

Metric/Imperial
½ quantity puff pastry (see page 103)
6–8 tablespoons raspberry jam
½ quantity crème pâtissière (see
  page 42)
1 quantity glacé icing (see page 42)
yellow or pink food colouring

American
½ quantity puff pastry (see page 103)
6–8 tablespoons raspberry jam
½ quantity crème pâtissière (see
  page 42)
1 quantity glacé icing (see page 42)
yellow or pink food coloring

Roll out the dough to a rectangle about 30 × 25 cm/12 × 10 inches and trim the edges. Cut the rectangle in half lengthways and transfer the two dough strips to a dampened baking sheet. Leave for 20 minutes, then bake in a preheated very hot oven (230°C/450°F, Gas Mark 8) for 15 to 20 minutes or until well risen and golden. Cool on a wire rack.

Spread one pastry strip with half the jam and then with all the crème pâtissière. Spread the remaining jam over the second pastry strip and place it, jam side down, on the crème pâtissière.

Put 1 tablespoon of the glacé icing in a bowl and colour it yellow or pink with food colouring. Spread the remaining icing over the top of the pastry strip. Pipe the coloured icing in lines across the top. Quickly draw a skewer down the length of the iced strip to make a feathered effect. Leave to set before cutting into slices.

Makes 6

Deep Fruit Pie

Metric/Imperial
750 g–1 kg/1 ½–2 lb fruit such as
  plums, greengages, mangoes or
  gooseberries, stoned if necessary
sugar to taste
1 quantity shortcrust pastry (see
  page 106), or ½–⅔ quantity flaky
  pastry (see page 105)
caster or sifted icing sugar

American
1 ½–2 lb fruit such as plums,
  greengages, mangoes or
  gooseberries, pitted if necessary
sugar to taste
1 quantity pie pastry (see page 106),
  or ½–⅔ quantity flaky pastry (see
  page 105)
granulated or sifted confectioners'
  sugar

Put the fruit in a pie dish with a very little water and sugar to taste. Roll out the pastry dough to a round slightly larger than the diameter of the pie dish and lay over the top. Press the dough to the rim of the dish to seal.

Bake in a preheated moderately hot oven (200°C/400°F, Gas Mark 6) for 40 to 45 minutes or until the pastry is crisp and brown and the fruit is soft (test with a skewer). If the pastry is browning too quickly, cover with foil and reduce the oven temperature. Sprinkle with sugar and serve warm.

Profiteroles

Metric/Imperial
1 quantity choux pastry (see page 104)
vanilla ice cream
Sauce:
175 g/6 oz plain chocolate, broken into pieces
3 tablespoons water
40 g/1½ oz butter

American
1 quantity choux pastry (see page 104)
vanilla ice cream
Sauce:
6 oz (6 squares) bittersweet dark chocolate, broken into pieces
3 tablespoons water
3 tablespoons butter

Spoon the choux pastry into a forcing bag fitted with a plain 1 cm/½ inch tube (nozzle) and pipe small buns, spaced well apart, on greased baking sheets. Bake in a preheated hot oven (220°C/425°F, Gas Mark 7) and continue baking for 5 to 10 minutes or until well puffed up and crisp. Make a slit in the side of each profiterole and transfer to a wire rack to cool.

To make the sauce, melt the chocolate with the water in a heatproof bowl over a pan of hot water, or in a double boiler. Beat in the butter. Cool.

To serve, fill the profiteroles with ice cream. Arrange about four profiteroles on each serving plate and pour over the sauce.

Serves 6–8

Variations:

Apple and Blackberry Profiteroles: Fill the profiteroles with a mixture of 1 × 75 g/3 oz packet cream cheese, 3 tablespoons plain yogurt and sugar to taste. Make the sauce by cooking 225 g/8 oz cooking (tart) apples, peeled, cored and chopped, with 225 g/8 oz blackberries until tender. Beat the fruit until it forms a smooth sauce and sweeten to taste.

Coffee Cream Profiteroles: Fill the profiteroles with a mixture of 300 ml/½ pint (1¼ cups) whipping cream, whipped until thick with 2 tablespoons icing sugar. For the coffee icing, mix 250 g/9 oz icing sugar (2¼ cups confectioners' sugar) with 3 to 4 tablespoons very strong black coffee until smooth. Dip the tops of the profiteroles in the icing, or spread it on with a knife.

Profiterole Gâteau: Pipe the choux pastry in walnut-sized balls onto the baking sheets and bake as above. Cool. Whip 600 ml/1 pint double cream (2½ cups heavy cream) with 2 tablespoons icing (confectioners') sugar until thick. Use about one-third of the cream to fill the profiteroles. Coarsely grate 50 g/2 oz (2 squares) plain (dark sweet) chocolate and fold into the remaining cream with 1 tablespoon rum. Make a layer of profiteroles on an 18 cm/7 inch serving plate. Spoon the chocolate cream on top and pile it up into a pyramid. Stick the remaining profiteroles in circles all around the cream pyramid, finishing with one on the top. Dissolve 225 g/8 oz (1 cup) sugar in 150 ml/¼ pint (⅔ cup) water and boil until straw-coloured. Cool slightly, until the caramel begins to thicken, then drizzle it all over the pyramid of profiteroles. Leave to set.

Nougat Tarts

Metric/Imperial
½ quantity shortcrust pastry (see
   page 106)
raspberry jam
1 egg white
100 g/4 oz caster sugar
50 g/2 oz ground almonds
100 g/4 oz desiccated coconut
1 tablespoon milk
few drops of almond essence
quartered glacé cherries

American
½ quantity pie pastry (see page 106)
raspberry jam
1 egg white
½ cup sugar
½ cup ground almonds
1¼ cups shredded coconut
1 tablespoon milk
few drops of almond extract
quartered candied cherries

Roll out the dough and cut out 12 rounds with a fluted cutter. Use these to line
12 bun tins (tartlet or muffin tins). Put a little jam in each pastry case.

Beat the egg white until stiff, then fold in the sugar, almonds, coconut, milk
and almond essence (extract). Spoon into the cases and top with cherries.

Bake in a preheated moderate oven (180°C/350°F, Gas Mark 4) for 20 to
25 minutes or until golden brown.

Makes 12

Maids of Honour

Metric/Imperial
½ quantity puff pastry (see page 103)
100 g/4 oz curd cheese
75 g/3 oz butter, softened
2 egg yolks
1 tablespoon brandy
75 g/3 oz sugar
40 g/1½ oz cold mashed potato
40 g/1½ oz ground almonds
grated rind of ½ lemon
1 tablespoon lemon juice
¼ teaspoon grated nutmeg

American
½ quantity puff pastry (see page 103)
½ cup small-curd cottage cheese
6 tablespoons butter, softened
2 egg yolks
1 tablespoon brandy
6 tablespoons sugar
¼ cup cold mashed potato
6 tablespoons ground almonds
grated rind of ½ lemon
1 tablespoon lemon juice
¼ teaspoon grated nutmeg

Roll out the pastry dough and cut out 16 to 18 rounds using a 7.5 cm/3 inch
cutter. Use to line greased patty (tartlet or shallow muffin) tins.

Beat together the cheese and butter, then gradually beat in the egg yolks,
brandy, sugar, potato, ground almonds, lemon rind and juice and nutmeg.

When the mixture is smooth, divide between the pastry cases. Bake in a
preheated moderately hot oven (190°C/375°F, Gas Mark 5) for about 30
minutes or until well risen and golden brown.

Makes 16–18

Raspberry Coconut Slices

Metric/Imperial
100 g/4 oz self-raising flour
225 g/8 oz caster sugar
1 tablespoon butter
2 eggs
raspberry jam
100 g/4 oz plus 2 tablespoons
   desiccated coconut
few drops of almond essence

American
1 cup self-rising flour
1 cup sugar
1 tablespoon butter
2 eggs
raspberry jam
1¼ cups plus 2 tablespoons
   shredded coconut
few drops of almond extract

Sift the flour and half the sugar into a bowl and rub in the butter. Add one of the eggs and bind to a stiff dough. Roll out to a 20 cm/8 inch square and place in a greased and floured 20 cm/8 inch square cake pan. Spread with a little raspberry jam.

Beat the remaining egg and sugar together until pale and very thick. Fold in 100 g/4 oz (1¼ cups) of the coconut and the almond essence (extract) and spread over the jam. Sprinkle with the remaining coconut.

Bake in a preheated moderate oven (180°C/350°F, Gas Mark 4) for 30 to 35 minutes or until golden. Cut into slices while still warm.

Iced Chocolate Coconut Slices

Metric/Imperial
100 g/4 oz self-raising flour
1 tablespoon cocoa powder
pinch of salt
65 g/2½ oz sugar
25 g/1 oz desiccated coconut
100 g/4 oz butter, melted
Icing:
3 tablespoons condensed milk
1 tablespoon cocoa powder
175 g/6 oz icing sugar, sifted
25 g/1 oz butter
100 g/4 oz desiccated coconut
1 teaspoon vanilla essence

American
1 cup self-rising flour
1 tablespoon unsweetened cocoa
pinch of salt
5 tablespoons sugar
⅓ cup shredded coconut
8 tablespoons melted butter
Frosting:
3 tablespoons condensed milk
1 tablespoon unsweetened cocoa
1½ cups confectioners' sugar, sifted
2 tablespoons butter
1¼ cups shredded coconut
1 teaspoon vanilla extract

Sift the flour into a bowl with the cocoa powder (unsweetened cocoa) and salt. Stir in the sugar, coconut and the melted butter.

Spread in a greased and floured 28 × 18 cm/11 × 7 inch cake pan. Bake in a preheated moderate oven (180°C/350°F, Gas Mark 4) for about 25 minutes or until golden. Cool slightly. For the icing, mix together the icing ingredients and spread over the cake and cool. Cut into slices when cold.

Pear and Walnut Tart

Metric/Imperial
½ quantity pâte sucrée (see page 107)
225 g/8 oz walnut halves
2–3 pears, peeled, cored and sliced
300 ml/½ pint milk
1 egg
1 egg yolk
1 tablespoon sugar
2 tablespoons kirsch or pear brandy

American
½ quantity pâte sucrée (see page 107)
2 cups walnut halves
2–3 pears, peeled, cored and sliced
1¼ cups milk
1 egg
1 egg yolk
1 tablespoon sugar
2 tablespoons kirsch or pear brandy

Roll out the dough and use to line a 20 cm/8 inch flan ring set on a baking sheet or a tart pan. Chill for 15 minutes.

Set aside some of the walnut halves for the decoration and use the rest to cover the bottom of the pastry case. Cover with the pear slices.

Scald the milk. Beat together the egg, egg yolk, sugar and liqueur, then gradually beat in the hot milk. Strain this custard into the pastry case.

Bake in a preheated moderately hot oven (200°C/400°F, Gas Mark 6) for 10 minutes. Reduce the temperature to moderate (180°C/350°F, Gas Mark 4) and continue baking for 20 to 30 minutes or until the custard has set and the pastry is golden.

Decorate with the reserved walnut halves and serve warm or cold.
Serves 6

Peanut Slices

Metric/Imperial
1 quantity shortcrust pastry (see page 106)
raspberry jam
1 egg white
175 g/6 oz caster sugar
50 g/2 oz cake crumbs
1 tablespoon cocoa powder
½ teaspoon vanilla essence
225 g/8 oz roasted peanuts

American
1 quantity pie pastry (see page 106)
raspberry jam
1 egg white
¾ cup sugar
½ cup cake crumbs
1 tablespoon unsweetened cocoa
½ teaspoon vanilla extract
½ lb roasted peanuts

Roll out the dough and use to line a greased 28 × 18 cm/11 × 7 inch cake pan. Bake blind (unfilled) in a preheated moderately hot oven (190°C/375°F, Gas Mark 5) for 15 minutes. Cool, then spread with jam.

Beat the egg white until stiff, then gradually beat in the sugar. Fold in the cake crumbs, cocoa, vanilla and peanuts and spread over the jam. Return to the oven and bake for a further 25 minutes. Cut into slices to serve.

Variation:

Spicy Apple Slices: Use sweet shortcrust (pie) pastry (see page 106). Roll out and use to line the pan as above. Peel, core and slice 4 large apples and stew them gently with 100 g/4 oz (½ cup) sugar, 2 tablespoons water and a little grated lemon rind until tender. Cool, then spread the apple mixture over the dough. Sift 75 g/3 oz plain flour (¾ cup all-purpose flour) and 1 tablespoon ground cinnamon into a bowl and stir in 2½ tablespoons sugar. Rub in 50 g/ 2 oz (4 tablespoons) butter to make a dough. Chill until firm, then press the dough through a colander or grate it onto the apple mixture. Bake as above, allowing 35 to 40 minutes. Cool, then cut into slices.

Oslo Apple Cake

Metric/Imperial	American
3 large cooking apples, peeled, cored and sliced	3 large tart apples, peeled, cored and sliced
50 g/2 oz sugar	¼ cup sugar
1 teaspoon grated lemon rind	1 teaspoon grated lemon rind
1 tablespoon lemon juice	1 tablespoon lemon juice
Dough:	**Dough:**
225 g/8 oz self-raising flour	2 cups self-rising flour
100 g/4 oz butter	8 tablespoons (1 stick) butter
100 g/4 oz caster sugar	½ cup sugar
1 small egg, beaten	1 egg, beaten

Put the apples, sugar, lemon rind and juice in a saucepan and poach gently until the apples are tender but not soft. Drain the apples and cool.

Sift the flour into a mixing bowl and rub in the butter. Stir in half the sugar and the egg and mix well together, then knead in the remaining sugar. Roll out two-thirds of the dough to a 20 cm/8 inch round and place it in a greased 20 cm/8 inch cake pan. Top with the apples.

Roll out the remaining dough and cut it into strips. Lay these in a lattice over the apples. Bake in a preheated moderate oven (180°C/350°F, Gas Mark 4) for about 40 minutes. Serve hot or cold, with cream.

Variations:

Empress Cake: Replace the apples with a mixture of 75 g/3 oz caster sugar (6 tablespoons sugar), 75 g/3 oz (¾ cup) finely chopped blanched almonds, ½ egg white and a little water. Bake as above.

Apple Shortcake: Make the dough as above, divide it in half and roll out into two 20 cm/8 inch rounds. Place one round in a greased 20 cm/8 inch sandwich tin (layer cake pan). Spread with 1 to 2 tablespoons marmalade. Peel, core and grate 3 apples and scatter them over the marmalade. Sprinkle with the grated rind and juice of ½ lemon and 1 tablespoon sugar. Place the second dough round on top and press to seal the edges. Brush with water and sprinkle with more sugar. Bake as above.

Walnut Pie

Metric/Imperial
1 quantity spiced wholemeal pastry
(see page 106)
2 eggs, separated
100 g/4 oz soft brown sugar
100 g/4 oz walnuts, chopped
grated rind and juice of 1 lemon
walnut halves to decorate

American
1 quantity spiced wholewheat pastry
(see page 106)
2 eggs, separated
⅔ cup light brown sugar
1 cup chopped walnuts
grated rind and juice of 1 lemon
walnut halves to decorate

Roll out the dough and use to line a 20 cm/8 inch flan ring on a baking sheet or a tart pan. Bake blind (unfilled) in a preheated moderately hot oven (200°C/400°F, Gas Mark 6) for 15 minutes.

Meanwhile, beat the egg yolks and sugar together until pale and thick. Stir in the chopped walnuts and lemon rind and juice. Beat the egg whites until stiff and fold into the walnut mixture. Pour into the pastry case.

Return to the oven, reduce the temperature to moderate (180°C/350°F, Gas Mark 4) and bake for a further 30 minutes or until lightly browned and risen. Decorate with walnut halves and serve warm or cold.

Eccles Cakes

Metric/Imperial
25 g/1 oz butter, softened
25 g/1 oz soft brown sugar
25 g/1 oz chopped mixed peel
50 g/2 oz currants
¼ teaspoon ground mixed spice
½ quantity puff pastry (see page 103)
beaten egg white
caster sugar for dredging

American
2 tablespoons butter, softened
2½ tablespoons brown sugar
2½ tablespoons chopped mixed
candied peel
⅓ cup currants
¼ teaspoon apple pie spice
½ quantity puff pastry (see page 103)
beaten egg white
sugar for dredging

Mix together the butter, sugar, peel, currants and spice. Roll out the dough thinly and cut out 10 cm/4 inch plain rounds. Place a spoonful of the fruit mixture in the centre of each round, then moisten the edges with water and draw them up to meet in the centre, enclosing the filling. Press well together to seal, then turn over so the join is underneath. Roll lightly with a rolling pin until the currants just show through the dough and the cake is about 7 mm/⅓ inch thick. Place on baking sheets and leave for 10 minutes.

Make three slits in the top of each cake. Brush with egg white and dredge with sugar. Bake in a preheated very hot oven (230°C/450°F, Gas Mark 8) for about 15 minutes or until golden brown and crisp. Cool on a wire rack.
Makes 8–10

Banbury Cakes: Add 2 to 3 tablespoons fine cake crumbs to the fruit mixture and moisten with a little orange juice, brandy or rum. Cut the dough into ovals instead of rounds, and proceed as above.

Deluxe Apple Pie

Metric/Imperial	American
275 g/10 oz plain flour	2½ cups all-purpose flour
pinch of salt	pinch of salt
50 g/2 oz icing sugar	½ cup confectioners' sugar
225 g/8 oz butter, cut into pieces	½ lb (2 sticks) butter, cut into pieces
2 egg yolks	2 egg yolks
grated rind of 1 lemon	grated rind of 1 lemon
1 tablespoon lemon juice	1 tablespoon lemon juice
Filling:	**Filling:**
5 cooking apples, peeled, cored and thinly sliced	5 tart apples, peeled, cored and thinly sliced
3–4 tablespoons apricot jam	3–4 tablespoons apricot jam
milk to glaze	milk to glaze
sugar to dredge	sugar to dredge

Sift the flour, salt and sugar into a bowl. Add the butter, egg yolks and lemon rind and juice and work to a soft dough. Chill for 30 minutes.

Roll out two-thirds of the dough and use to line a 28 × 18 cm/11 × 7 inch cake pan. Arrange the apple slices in the pastry case and dot with the jam.

Roll out the remaining dough and lay over the apples. Press the edges together to seal. Slit the top in several places, then brush all over with milk and dredge with sugar.

Bake in a preheated hot oven (220°C/425°F, Gas Mark 7) for 15 minutes, then reduce the temperature to moderate (180°C/350°F, Gas Mark 4) and continue baking for 25 to 30 minutes. Serve warm, drizzled with glacé icing (see page 42), if liked.

Yorkshire Apple Tart

Metric/Imperial
1 quantity rich shortcrust pastry (see
   page 104)
350 g/12 oz cooking apples, peeled,
   cored and sliced
2 tablespoons sugar
1 tablespoon water
milk
sugar to dredge
100 g/4 oz Cheddar cheese, sliced

American
1 quantity rich pie pastry (see page
   104)
¾ lb tart apples, peeled, cored and
   sliced
2 tablespoons sugar
1 tablespoon water
milk
sugar to dredge
¼ lb Cheddar cheese, sliced

Roll out two-thirds of the dough and use to line a 20 cm/8 inch flan ring on a
baking sheet. Fill with the apples and sprinkle over the sugar and water.

Roll out the remaining dough and lay it over the apples. Press the edges
together to seal. Brush with milk and sprinkle with sugar.

Bake in a preheated moderately hot oven (190°C/375°F, Gas Mark 5) for
20 to 25 minutes or until the pastry is lightly browned.

Cool slightly, then carefully remove the top crust. Place the cheese slices
on top of the apples. Replace the crust. Return to the oven and continue
baking for 10 to 15 minutes. Serve hot.

French Orange Tarts

Metric/Imperial
2 thin-skinned oranges, thinly sliced
1 quantity spiced wholemeal pastry
   (see page 106)
1 egg, beaten
50 g/2 oz ground almonds
1 tablespoon sugar
2 tablespoons clear honey

American
2 thin-skinned oranges, thinly sliced
1 quantity spiced wholewheat pastry
   (see page 106)
1 egg, beaten
½ cup ground almonds
1 tablespoon sugar
2 tablespoons clear honey

Put the orange slices in a saucepan, cover with water and simmer gently for
about 30 minutes or until the peel is tender. Drain.

Roll out the dough and use to line four 10 cm/4 inch flan rings on a baking
sheet, or tartlet pans. Bake blind (unfilled) in a preheated moderately hot
oven (200°C/400°F, Gas Mark 6) for 15 minutes.

Meanwhile, beat the egg, almonds and sugar together. Spoon into the
pastry cases and arrange the orange slices on top, overlapping slightly.
Spoon over the honey.

Return to the oven, reduce the temperature to moderate (180°C/350°F,
Gas Mark 4) and bake for a further 20 minutes. Serve warm or cold.
Makes 4

Stuffed Monkey

Metric/Imperial
175 g/6 oz plain flour
¼ teaspoon ground cinnamon
100 g/4 oz butter
100 g/4 oz soft brown sugar
1 egg, beaten
flaked almonds to sprinkle
Filling:
40 g/1½ oz butter, melted
50 g/2 oz chopped mixed peel
50 g/2 oz blanched almonds,
   chopped
50 g/2 oz sultanas
25 g/1 oz sugar
1 egg yolk
few drops of almond essence
½ teaspoon ground cinnamon
½ teaspoon ground mixed spice

American
1½ cups all-purpose flour
¼ teaspoon ground cinnamon
8 tablespoons (1 stick) butter
⅔ cup light brown sugar
1 egg, beaten
slivered almonds to sprinkle
Filling:
3 tablespoons butter, melted
⅓ cup chopped mixed candied peel
½ cup chopped blanched almonds
⅓ cup seedless white raisins
2 tablespoons sugar
1 egg yolk
few drops of almond extract
½ teaspoon ground cinnamon
½ teaspoon ground allspice

Sift the flour and cinnamon into a bowl and rub in the butter. Stir in the sugar, then bind to a soft dough with the egg (reserving a little of the egg white to glaze the dough). Divide the dough in half and roll out each half to an 18 cm/ 7 inch square. Place one square on the bottom of a greased 18 cm/7 inch square cake pan.

Mix together all the ingredients for the filling and spread over the dough in the pan. Place the second dough square on top and seal the edges. Brush with the reserved egg white and sprinkle with almonds.

Bake in a preheated moderately hot oven (190°C/375°F, Gas Mark 5) for 30 minutes. Cut into squares to serve.

Jam Tarts

Metric/Imperial
½ quantity shortcrust pastry (see
   page 106)
raspberry or other jam

American
½ quantity pie pastry (see page 106)
raspberry or other jam

Roll out the dough and cut out 12 rounds with a fluted cutter. Use these to line 12 bun tins (tartlet or muffin tins).

Fill each pastry case with jam, then bake in a preheated hot oven (220°C/ 425°F, Gas Mark 7) for 10 to 15 minutes.
Makes 12

Apple and Apricot Tart

Metric/Imperial
1 quantity sweet shortcrust pastry (see page 106)
3 large cooking apples, peeled, cored and sliced
sugar to taste
50 g/2 oz nuts, chopped
6 tablespoons apricot jam
desiccated coconut (optional)

American
1 quantity sweet pie pastry (see page 106)
3 large tart apples, peeled, cored and sliced
sugar to taste
½ cup chopped nuts
6 tablespoons apricot jam
shredded coconut (optional)

Roll out about three-quarters of the dough and use to line a 20 cm/8 inch flan ring on a baking sheet or a tart pan. Bake blind (unfilled) in a preheated moderately hot oven (200°C/400°F, Gas Mark 6) for 10 minutes or until set.

Meanwhile, cook the apples gently with a very little water and sugar to taste until they form a thick purée. Remove from the heat and mix in the nuts and 2 tablespoons of the jam.

Spread another 2 tablespoons of the jam over the bottom of the pastry case. Top with the apple mixture, spreading it out evenly. Melt the remaining jam and brush it over the top of the filling.

Roll out the remaining dough and cut it into strips. Lay these in a lattice over the filling, and press onto the edge of the pastry case to seal.

Return to the oven, reduce the heat to moderate (180°C/350°F, Gas Mark 4) and continue baking for 15 to 20 minutes or until the pastry lattice is crisp and golden brown. Top with coconut, if you like, and serve warm or cold.

Pumpkin Pie

Metric/Imperial
1 quantity shortcrust pastry (see page 106)
1 × 750 g/1½ lb can puréed pumpkin
100 g/4 oz brown sugar
1 teaspoon ground allspice
½ teaspoon ground ginger
2 eggs, beaten
250 ml/8 fl oz single cream

American
1 quantity pie pastry (see page 106)
1 × 1½ lb can puréed pumpkin
⅔ cup brown sugar
1 teaspoon ground allspice
½ teaspoon ground ginger
2 eggs, beaten
1 cup light cream

Roll out the dough and use to line a 20 cm/8 inch flan ring on a baking sheet or a pie pan.

Mix together the pumpkin, sugar, spices, eggs and cream and pour into the pastry case. Bake in a preheated moderately hot oven (190°C/375°F, Gas Mark 5) for 40 to 45 minutes or until the filling has set and the pastry is golden brown.

French Apple Flan

Metric/Imperial	American
1 quantity sweet shortcrust pastry (see page 106)	1 quantity sweet pie pastry (see page 106)
1 kg/2 lb cooking apples, peeled, cored and quartered	2 lb tart apples, peeled, cored and quartered
150 ml/¼ pint white wine	⅔ cup white wine
pared rind of ½ lemon	pared rind of ½ lemon
50 g/2 oz butter	4 tablespoons butter
100 g/4 oz sugar	½ cup sugar
4 crisp eating apples	4 crisp eating apples
3 tablespoons apricot jam	3 tablespoons apricot jam
1 tablespoon lemon juice	1 tablespoon lemon juice

Roll out the dough and use to line a 20 cm/8 inch flan ring on a baking sheet or a tart pan.

Poach the apples in the wine with the lemon rind, butter and half the sugar. When the apples are tender, discard the lemon rind and purée the apple mixture with a sieve (strainer) or blender. Pour into the pastry case. Peel, core and slice the eating apples and arrange them on top of the purée, overlapping slightly. Sprinkle with the remaining sugar.

Bake in a preheated moderately hot oven (190°C/375°F, Gas Mark 5) for 25 to 30 minutes. Meanwhile melt the jam with the lemon juice, sieve (strain) and then use to glaze the hot cooked flan.

Spiced Cranberry and Apple Pie

Metric/Imperial	American
500 g/1 lb cooking apples, peeled, cored and sliced	1 lb tart apples, peeled, cored and sliced
grated rind and juice of 1 orange	grated rind and juice of 1 orange
225 g/8 oz cranberries	½ lb cranberries
75 g/3 oz sugar	6 tablespoons sugar
1 quantity spiced wholemeal pastry (see page 106), with 50 g/2 oz finely chopped nuts added	1 quantity spiced wholewheat pastry (see page 106), with ½ cup finely chopped nuts added
beaten egg to glaze	beaten egg to glaze

Put the apples, orange rind and juice, cranberries and sugar in a 900 ml/1½ pint (4 cup capacity) pie dish and mix well.

Roll out the dough and lay over the dish. Press the edges to the dish to seal, and make a slit in the centre. Brush with beaten egg.

Bake in a preheated moderately hot oven (200°C/400°F, Gas Mark 6) for 30 to 40 minutes or until crisp and brown. Serve hot.

Apple and Sultana (Raisin) Pie

Metric/Imperial
1 quantity rich sweet shortcrust
  pastry (see page 104)
2 tablespoons apricot jam
1 kg/2 lb cooking apples, peeled,
  cored and sliced
75 g/3 oz sugar
25 g/1 oz sultanas
grated rind and juice of 1 lemon
1 teaspoon ground cinnamon
25 g/1 oz plain flour, sifted
1 tablespoon butter, melted
1 egg white, lightly beaten
sugar to dredge

American
1 quantity rich sweet pie pastry (see
  page 104)
2 tablespoons apricot jam
2 lb tart apples, peeled, cored and
  sliced
6 tablespoons sugar
2½ tablespoons seedless white
  raisins
grated rind and juice of 1 lemon
1 teaspoon ground cinnamon
¼ cup all-purpose flour, sifted
1 tablespoon butter, melted
1 egg white, lightly beaten
sugar to dredge

Roll out about two-thirds of the dough and use to line a greased 23 × 30 cm/
9 × 12 inch cake pan. Spread the jam over the bottom of the pastry case.
  Mix together the apples, sugar, sultanas (raisins), lemon rind and juice,
cinnamon, flour and butter and spoon into the pastry case. Roll out the rest of
the dough and lay it over the apple filling. Crimp the edges together to seal.
Brush the dough with the egg white and sprinkle with sugar.
  Bake in a preheated hot oven (220°C/425°F, Gas Mark 7) for 20 minutes,
then reduce the temperature to moderately hot (200°C/400°F, Gas Mark 6)
and continue baking for 20 minutes or until browned. Cut into squares.

Yogurt Greengage Flan

Metric/Imperial
1 quantity shortcrust pastry (see
  page 106)
450 ml/¾ pint plain yogurt
3 egg yolks
2 tablespoons sugar
500 g/1 lb greengages

American
1 quantity pie pastry (see page 106)
2 cups unflavored yogurt
3 egg yolks
2 tablespoons sugar
1 lb greengages

Roll out the dough and use to line a 20 cm/8 inch flan ring on a baking sheet.
  Mix together the yogurt, egg yolks and sugar and pour half the mixture into
the pastry case. Bake in a preheated moderately hot oven (200°C/400°F,
Gas Mark 6) for 20 minutes.
  Arrange the greengages on top of the filling and spoon the remaining
yogurt mixture around the fruit. Return to the oven and bake for a further 20
minutes. Serve hot or cold.

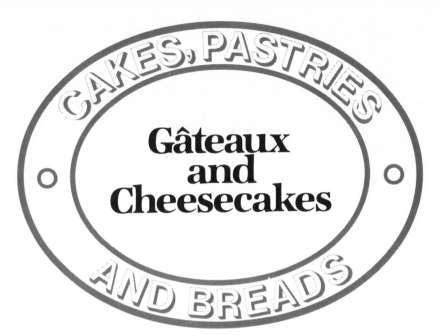

CAKES, PASTRIES AND BREADS

Gâteaux and Cheesecakes

Neapolitan Cheese Tart

Metric/Imperial
350 g/12 oz ricotta or curd cheese
75 g/3 oz caster sugar
3 eggs, beaten
50 g/2 oz blanched almonds, finely
   chopped
75 g/3 oz chopped mixed peel
grated rind of ½ lemon
grated rind of ½ orange
½ teaspoon vanilla essence
1 quantity pasta frolla (see page 107)
icing sugar to dredge

American
1½ cups ricotta or small-curd cottage
   cheese
6 tablespoons sugar
3 eggs, beaten
½ cup finely chopped blanched
   almonds
½ cup chopped mixed candied peel
grated rind of ½ lemon
grated rind of ½ orange
½ teaspoon vanilla extract
1 quantity pasta frolla (see page 107)
confectioners' sugar to dredge

Sieve (strain) the cheese, then beat in the sugar and eggs, followed by the nuts, peel, fruit rinds and vanilla.

Roll out the dough and use to line an 18 cm/7 inch flan ring on a baking sheet or a tart pan. Reserve the dough trimmings.

Fill the pastry case with the cheese mixture and smooth the surface. Roll out the dough trimmings and cut them into 1 cm/½ inch wide strips with a fluted cutter. Use to make a lattice over the filling.

Bake in a preheated moderate oven (180°C/350°F, Gas Mark 4) for about 45 minutes. Cool on a wire rack, then dredge with icing (confectioners') sugar.

Strawberry Meringue Gâteau

Metric/Imperial	American
6 egg whites	6 egg whites
350 g/12 oz caster sugar	1½ cups sugar
450 ml/¾ pint double cream	2 cups heavy cream
500 g/1 lb strawberries	1 lb strawberries

Line three baking sheets with non-stick silicone paper and draw a 20 cm/ 8 inch circle on each.

Beat the egg whites until stiff. Add 4 tablespoons of the sugar and continue beating for 1 minute, then fold in all but 3 tablespoons of the remaining sugar. Divide the meringue into three portions and spread in the circles on the paper.

Dry out in a preheated cool oven (140°C/275°F, Gas Mark 1) for 3 hours or until set. Cool, then remove from the paper.

Whip the cream until thick. Slice half the strawberries and fold into the cream with the reserved sugar.

Sandwich together the three meringue rounds with the cream mixture. Decorate the top and sides with the whole strawberries. Serve soon after assembling.

Serves 6

Variations:

Chestnut Vacherin: Make the three meringue rounds as above. Whip 300 ml/½ pint double cream (1¼ cups heavy cream) until thick. Set aside about 6 tablespoons of the cream, and fold a 250 g/9 oz can sweetened chestnut purée and 1 tablespoon dry sherry into the remainder. Use this mixture to sandwich together the meringue rounds. Decorate the top with the remaining whipped cream, 3 marrons glacés and piped melted plain (dark) chocolate.

Serves 8–10

Strawberry Hazelnut Gâteau: Make the meringue mixture using 4 egg whites and 275 g/10 oz (1¼ cups) caster sugar, and fold in 100 g/4 oz (1 cup) ground hazelnuts, 1 teaspoon vinegar, ½ teaspoon vanilla essence (extract) and 4 tablespoons black coffee with the last of the sugar. Spread the mixture evenly in two greased and floured 20 cm/8 inch loose-bottomed cake pans. Bake in a preheated moderate oven (180°C/350°F, Gas Mark 4) for about 35 minutes, then cool on the pan bases. Melt 175 g/6 oz plain (dark sweet) chocolate. Whip 600 ml/1 pint double cream (2½ cups heavy cream) until thick. Spread half the chocolate over one of the meringue rounds and cover with a 2 cm/¾ inch layer of cream. Top with a layer of sliced strawberries, then place the second meringue round on top. Spread with the remaining chocolate and cream and decorate with whole strawberries.

Celebration Cake

Metric/Imperial
750 g/1½ lb butter
750 g/1½ lb caster sugar
finely grated rind of 3 oranges
finely grated rind of 2 lemons
12 eggs, beaten
550 g/1¼ lb self-raising flour, sifted
4 tablespoons orange juice
Buttercream:
750 g/1½ lb butter
1 kg/2 lb icing sugar, sifted
1 tablespoon grated orange rind
1 teaspoon grated lemon rind
about 2 tablespoons orange or
   lemon juice
yellow food colouring
Glacé Icing:
750 g/1½ lb icing sugar, sifted
3 tablespoons lemon juice

American
1½ lb (6 sticks) butter
3 cups sugar
finely grated rind of 3 oranges
finely grated rind of 2 lemons
12 eggs, beaten
5 cups self-rising flour, sifted
¼ cup orange juice
Buttercream:
1½ lb (6 sticks) butter
8 cups confectioners' sugar, sifted
1 tablespoon grated orange rind
1 teaspoon grated lemon rind
about 2 tablespoons orange or
   lemon juice
yellow food coloring
Glacé Icing:
6 cups confectioners' sugar, sifted
3 tablespoons lemon juice

Cream the butter with the sugar and orange and lemon rinds until light and fluffy. Gradually beat in the eggs. If the mixture curdles, add a little of the flour. Fold in the remaining flour, then stir in the orange juice. Divide the batter between three greased and floured deep round cake pans in the following diameters: one 28 cm/11 inches, one 23 cm/9 inches and one 18 cm/7 inches.

Bake in a preheated moderate oven (160°C/325°F, Gas Mark 3) for 30 minutes for the smallest pan, 35 to 40 minutes for the medium pan and 40 to 45 minutes for the large pan. Cool on a wire rack.

For the buttercream, cream the butter until softened, then gradually beat in the sugar followed by the fruit rinds and juice. Tint the buttercream golden with food colouring.

Cut each cake into two layers and sandwich them back together with about one-third to half of the buttercream. Place the largest cake on a serving plate. Spread a little buttercream over the base of the medium cake and place it in the centre of the large cake. Spread a little buttercream over the base of the smallest cake and place it in the centre of the medium cake.

For the icing, mix the sugar with the lemon juice and enough water to make a flowing consistency. Pour the icing over the three-tiered cake to coat it all over and leave to set.

Decorate with the remaining buttercream, piped around the base of each tier and on top of the smallest cake.

Chocolate Liqueur Gâteau

Metric/Imperial
150 g/5 oz plain flour
25 g/1 oz cornflour
25 g/1 oz cocoa powder
6 large eggs
225 g/8 oz caster sugar
75 g/3 oz butter, melted and cooled
4 tablespoons orange or coffee
 liqueur
600 ml/1 pint double cream
175 g/6 oz plain chocolate

American
1¼ cups all-purpose flour
¼ cup cornstarch
¼ cup unsweetened cocoa
6 eggs
1 cup sugar
6 tablespoons butter, melted and
 cooled
¼ cup orange or coffee liqueur
2½ cups heavy cream
6 oz dark sweet chocolate

Sift together the flour, cornflour (cornstarch) and cocoa. Beat the eggs and sugar together until the mixture is pale and very thick and the beater leaves a trail when lifted. Fold in the flour mixture alternately with the butter. Divide between two greased and floured or lined 25 cm/10 inch sandwich tins (layer cake pans).

Bake in a preheated moderately hot oven (190°C/375°F, Gas Mark 5) for about 30 minutes or until firm. Cool on a wire rack.

Cut each cake into two layers. Sprinkle three of the layers (not the top one) with the liqueur. Whip the cream until thick and use three-quarters to sandwich the cake layers together.

Melt the chocolate gently and pour it over the cake, allowing it to run down the sides. As it sets, use a palette knife to make a pattern on the top. Chill until set.

Pipe the remaining cream on top of the cake, then leave it for at least 1 hour before serving.
Serves 10–12

Butterscotch Caramel Gâteau

Metric/Imperial
175 g/6 oz butter
175 g/6 oz soft brown sugar
3 eggs, beaten
175 g/6 oz self-raising flour, sifted
1 teaspoon vanilla essence
1 tablespoon black treacle
1 quantity crème pâtissière (see
  page 42)
1 quantity butterscotch buttercream
  (see page 41)
Caramel:
100 g/4 oz caster sugar
4 tablespoons water

American
12 tablespoons (1½ sticks) butter
1 cup light brown sugar
3 eggs, beaten
1½ cups self-rising flour, sifted
1 teaspoon vanilla extract
1 tablespoon molasses
1 quantity crème pâtissière (see
  page 42)
1 quantity butterscotch buttercream
  (see page 41)
Caramel:
½ cup sugar
¼ cup water

Cream the butter with the brown sugar until pale and fluffy. Beat in the eggs
one at a time, adding a tablespoon of flour with each one. Fold in the
remaining flour with the vanilla and treacle (molasses). Pour into a greased
and floured or lined 20 cm/8 inch round deep cake pan.

Bake in a preheated moderately hot oven (190°C/375°F, Gas Mark 5) for
40 to 50 minutes or until well risen and firm to the touch. Cool on a wire rack.

When the cake is cold, cut it into three layers and sandwich back together
with the crème pâtissière. Spread most of the buttercream over the top and
sides of the cake, swirling it decoratively. Pipe a border of the remaining
buttercream around the top edge and base of the cake.

For the caramel, dissolve the sugar in the water, then bring to the boil and
boil until the syrup turns a dark caramel colour. Pour onto a greased baking
sheet and leave until set. Break into pieces and use to decorate the top of the
gâteau.

Serves 8

Pear and Chocolate Gâteau

Metric/Imperial	American
225 g/8 oz butter	½ lb (2 sticks) butter
225 g/8 oz caster sugar	1 cup sugar
4 large eggs	4 eggs
175 g/6 oz self-raising flour	1½ cups self-rising flour
25 g/1 oz cocoa powder	¼ cup unsweetened cocoa
50 g/2 oz ground almonds	½ cup ground almonds
1–2 tablespoons warm water	1–2 tablespoons warm water
450 ml/¾ pint double cream	2 cups heavy cream
1–2 tablespoons brandy	1–2 tablespoons brandy
1 × 425 g/15 oz can pears, drained	1 × 15 oz can pear slices, drained
toasted flaked almonds	toasted slivered almonds

Cream the butter with the sugar until light and fluffy. Beat in the eggs one at a time, adding a tablespoon of flour with each egg. Sift in the remaining flour with the cocoa and fold into the creamed mixture with the almonds. Add just enough water to give a soft consistency.

Divide the batter between two greased and floured or lined 23 cm/9 inch sandwich tins (layer cake pans). Bake in a preheated moderate oven (180°C/350°F, Gas Mark 4) for 25 to 30 minutes or until firm to the touch. Cool on a wire rack.

Whip the cream with the brandy until thick. Use about one-third of the cream and half the pear slices to sandwich together the cake layers. Spread most of the remaining cream over the top and sides of the cake. Decorate the top with the rest of the pear slices, the almonds and piped rosettes of cream.

Coffee Ice Cream Cake

Metric/Imperial	American
2 eggs, separated	2 eggs, separated
2 tablespoons coffee essence	2 tablespoons coffee flavoring
50 g/2 oz icing sugar, sifted	½ cup confectioners' sugar, sifted
150 ml/¼ pint double cream	⅔ cup heavy cream
1 × 18 cm/7 inch whisked sponge cake (see page 7)	1 × 7 inch whisked sponge cake (see page 7)

Beat the egg yolks and coffee essence (flavoring) together. Beat the egg whites until stiff, then gradually beat in the sugar. Fold in the egg yolk mixture. Whip the cream until thick and fold in. Pour the mixture into a freezer tray and freeze until set.

Split the cake into three layers. Sandwich together with the coffee ice cream and sprinkle the top with a little extra icing (confectioners') sugar.
Serves 4–6

Pear and Almond Gâteau

Metric/Imperial	American
100 g/4 oz butter	8 tablespoons (1 stick) butter
100 g/4 oz sugar	½ cup sugar
2 eggs	2 eggs
175 g/6 oz self-raising flour, sifted	1½ cups self-rising flour, sifted
few drops of vanilla essence	few drops of vanilla extract
3 tablespoons milk	3 tablespoons milk
300 ml/½ pint double cream	1¼ cups heavy cream
4 ripe pears, peeled, halved and cored	4 ripe pears, peeled, halved and cored
6 tablespoons apricot jam	6 tablespoons apricot jam
100 g/4 oz flaked almonds, toasted	1 cup slivered almonds, toasted
grapes to decorate	grapes to decorate

Cream the butter with the sugar until pale and fluffy. Beat in the eggs one at a time, adding a tablespoon of flour with each egg. Fold in the remaining flour alternately with the vanilla and milk.

Divide the batter between two greased 18 cm/7 inch sandwich tins (layer cake pans). Bake in a preheated moderate oven (180°C/350°F, Gas Mark 4) for 15 to 18 minutes or until well risen and firm to the touch. Cool on a wire rack.

Whip the cream until thick. Slice one of the pears. Sandwich the cake layers together with a little of the jam and cream, the sliced pear and about one-quarter of the nuts. Spread the top and sides of the cake with half the remaining jam and all the remaining cream. Press the remaining nuts against the sides of the cake. Place the remaining pear halves on top and decorate with grapes. Warm the rest of the jam and brush all over the fruit.

Strawberry Cream Gâteau

Metric/Imperial
4 large eggs
100 g/4 oz caster sugar
finely grated rind of ½ lemon
100 g/4 oz plain flour, sifted
2 teaspoons lemon juice
Filling:
300 ml/½ pint double cream
25 g/1 oz icing sugar, sifted
500 g/1 lb strawberries, hulled and
halved

American
4 eggs
½ cup sugar
finely grated rind of ½ lemon
1 cup all-purpose flour, sifted
2 teaspoons lemon juice
Filling:
1¼ cups heavy cream
¼ cup confectioners' sugar, sifted
1 lb strawberries, hulled and halved

Beat the eggs, sugar and lemon rind together until the mixture is pale and very thick and will make a ribbon trail on itself when the beater is lifted. Fold in the flour and lemon juice. Pour the batter into a greased and floured 20 cm/8 inch round deep cake pan.

Bake in a preheated moderate oven (160°C/325°F, Gas Mark 3) for 35 to 40 minutes or until just firm to the touch. Cool on a wire rack.

Cut the cake into three layers. Whip the cream with the sugar until thick. Use about two-thirds of the cream and strawberries to sandwich together the cake layers. Top with the remaining fruit and pipe the rest of the cream decoratively around the top edge.

Variations:
Use any fruit in season instead of the strawberries.

Apple Cream Sponge Cake: Make the cake as above, baking it in a 23 cm/9 inch round deep cake pan or 25 cm/10 inch ring mould for about 30 minutes. Cool. Core and slice 2 dessert apples and poach in a very little water, with sugar and lemon juice to taste, until tender but still firm. Drain the apple slices. Whip 150 ml/¼ pint double cream (⅔ cup heavy cream) with sugar to taste until thick. Pipe or spread the cream on top of the 23 cm/9 inch cake and top with the apple slices and halved rings of canned or fresh pineapple. Fill the centre of the ring cake with the fruit and cream.

Cream Sponge Flan: Make the batter as above, using 2 eggs, 75 g/3 oz caster sugar (6 tablespoons sugar) and 65 g/2½ oz plain flour (½ cup plus 2 tablespoons all-purpose flour), and omitting the lemon rind and juice. Bake in a 20 to 23 cm/8 to 9 inch sponge flan tin in a preheated moderately hot oven (190°C/375°F, Gas Mark 5) for about 12 minutes or until firm to the touch. Cool on a wire rack. Whip 300 ml/½ pint double cream (1¼ cups heavy cream) until thick. Mash most of 350 g/12 oz of raspberries or strawberries and fold into the cream with sugar to taste. Fill the sponge flan case with the fruit and cream mixture and decorate with the remaining whole fruit.

Gâteau St. Honoré

Metric/Imperial

rich shortcrust pastry (see page 104), made with 150 g/5 oz flour and 75 g/3 oz butter with 1½ teaspoons caster sugar added
½ quantity choux pastry (see page 104)
beaten egg to glaze
300 ml/½ pint double cream
Caramel:
225 g/8 oz sugar
150 ml/¼ pint water
Filling:
1 × 425 g/15 oz can apricot halves, drained
1 quantity crème pâtissière (see page 42)

American

rich pie pastry (see page 104), made with 1¼ cups flour and 6 tablespoons butter with 1½ teaspoons sugar added
½ quantity choux pastry (see page 104)
beaten egg to glaze
1¼ cups heavy cream
Caramel:
1 cup sugar
⅔ cup water
Filling:
1 × 15 oz can apricot halves, drained
1 quantity crème pâtissière (see page 42)

Roll out the shortcrust (pie) pastry dough to a 20 cm/8 inch round and place it on a greased baking sheet. Crimp the edges and prick it all over. Bake in a preheated moderate oven (180°C/350°F, Gas Mark 4) for 20 minutes or until lightly coloured. Cool on a wire rack.

Put the choux pastry in a pastry bag fitted with a 1 cm/½ inch plain tube (nozzle). Pipe a 20 cm/8 inch ring on another greased baking sheet, and pipe 16 to 20 walnut-sized balls on a third greased baking sheet. Glaze all the choux with beaten egg, then bake in a preheated hot oven (220°C/425°F, Gas Mark 7) for about 25 minutes or until golden brown and firm. Pierce each ball and the ring to allow steam to escape, then cool on a wire rack.

Whip the cream until thick. Use most of the cream to fill the choux balls.

For the caramel, dissolve the sugar in the water, then boil until straw-coloured. Spread a little caramel around the edge of the pastry round and position the choux ring on top. Dip the tops of the choux buns into the caramel. Put a dot of caramel on the bottom of each bun and stick them around the top of the choux ring. Pour any extra caramel over the buns.

Reserve six apricot halves for the decoration and chop the remainder. Spread half the crème pâtissière inside the choux ring and top with the chopped apricots. Cover with the rest of the crème pâtissière. Brush the top of the crème with a little of the apricot can syrup to prevent a skin forming, then decorate with the reserved apricot halves and cream.

Chocolate Meringue Gâteau

Metric/Imperial
4 egg whites
225 g/8 oz caster sugar
Filling:
150 ml/¼ pint milk
50 g/2 oz caster sugar
50 g/2 oz plain chocolate, broken up
3 egg yolks
175 g/6 oz unsalted butter
1 tablespoon rum (optional)
Topping:
150 ml/¼ pint double cream
2 tablespoons milk
6 marrons glacés, halved, or 12 raspberries
25 g/1 oz plain chocolate, grated

American
4 egg whites
1 cup sugar
Filling:
⅔ cup milk
¼ cup sugar
2 oz dark sweet chocolate, broken up
3 egg yolks
12 tablespoons (1½ sticks) sweet butter
1 tablespoon rum (optional)
Topping:
⅔ cup heavy cream
2 tablespoons milk
6 marrons glacés, halved, or 12 raspberries
1 oz dark sweet chocolate, grated

Beat the egg whites until very stiff, then gradually beat in the sugar. Divide the meringue into three portions. Draw a 20 cm/8 inch circle on three baking sheets lined with non-stick silicone paper and spread the meringue in the circles.

Bake in a preheated cool oven (150°C/300°F, Gas Mark 2) for about 1 hour. Turn off the oven and leave the meringue rounds inside until cool.

For the filling, put the milk, sugar and chocolate in a double boiler and heat until the chocolate melts. Stir a little of the chocolate mixture into the egg yolks, then stir this into the remaining chocolate mixture. Cook gently, stirring, until the mixture is thick enough to coat the back of the spoon. Cool.

Cream the butter until soft, then gradually beat in the chocolate custard. Stir in the rum, if using. Use the filling to sandwich together the three meringue rounds.

Whip the cream with the milk until stiff and spread half over the top of the meringue cake. Use the remainder to pipe 12 rosettes around the top edge. Place a half marron glacé or a raspberry on each cream rosette and sprinkle the chocolate over the centre. Leave the cake for 2 to 3 hours before serving.

Serves 8

Mocha Torte

Metric/Imperial
6 eggs, separated
100 g/4 oz caster sugar
100 g/4 oz plain chocolate, melted
1 teaspoon instant coffee powder
4 tablespoons warm water
2 tablespoons plain flour
toasted flaked almonds to decorate
Filling:
600 ml/1 pint double cream
2 tablespoons instant coffee powder
50–100 g/2–4 oz caster sugar

American
6 eggs, separated
½ cup sugar
⅔ cup semi-sweet chocolate chips, melted
1 teaspoon instant coffee powder
¼ cup warm water
2 tablespoons all-purpose flour
toasted slivered almonds to decorate
Filling:
2½ cups heavy cream
2 tablespoons instant coffee powder
¼–½ cup sugar

Beat the egg yolks and sugar together until the mixture is pale and very thick and will make a ribbon trail on itself when the whisk is lifted. Stir in the chocolate. Dissolve the coffee powder in the water and fold into the chocolate mixture with the flour. Beat the egg whites until stiff and fold in carefully. Divide the batter between three greased and floured or lined 20 cm/8 inch sandwich tins (layer cake pans).

Bake in a preheated moderate oven (160°C/325°F, Gas Mark 3) for 30 to 35 minutes. Cool on a wire rack.

For the filling, mix the ingredients together and chill for 1 hour, then whip until thick. Use about half the cream mixture to sandwich the cakes then spread the remainder over the top and sides. Decorate with almonds.

Pavlova

Metric/Imperial
4 egg whites
225 g/8 oz caster sugar
300 ml/½ pint double cream
fresh or canned fruit

American
4 egg whites
1 cup sugar
1¼ cups heavy cream
fresh or canned fruit

Beat the egg whites until stiff. Gradually beat in 2 tablespoons of the sugar, then fold in the remainder. Line a baking sheet with non-stick silicone paper and draw a 20 cm/8 inch circle on it. Spread about half the meringue in the circle, then pipe or spoon the remaining meringue around the edge of the round to make a basket.

Dry out in a preheated very cool oven (120°C/250°F, Gas Mark ½) for about 2½ hours or until crisp. Cool.

Transfer the meringue shell to a serving plate. Whip the cream until thick and pile in the meringue basket with the fruit.

Black Forest Gâteau

Metric/Imperial
3 large eggs
115 g/4½ oz caster sugar
75 g/3 oz plain flour
15 g/½ oz cocoa powder
1 × 425 g/15 oz can black cherries
2 teaspoons arrowroot
450 ml/¾ pint double cream
2–3 tablespoons kirsch or brandy
3 flaked chocolate bars

American
3 eggs
½ cup plus 1 tablespoon sugar
¾ cup all-purpose flour
2 tablespoons unsweetened cocoa
1 × 15 oz can black cherries
2 teaspoons arrowroot
2 cups heavy cream
2–3 tablespoons kirsch or brandy
3 flaked chocolate bars

Beat the eggs and sugar together until pale and very thick and the beater leaves a trail when lifted. Sift the flour and cocoa together twice and fold into the egg mixture. Pour into a greased and lined 23 cm/9 inch round deep cake pan.

Bake in a preheated moderately hot oven (190°C/375°F, Gas Mark 5) for about 30 minutes or until firm to the touch. Cool on a wire rack.

When the cake is cold, cut it into three layers. Drain the cherries, reserving the can syrup. Mix 150 ml/¼ pint (⅔ cup) of the syrup (adding water if necessary) with the arrowroot in a saucepan and bring to the boil, stirring. Simmer until thickened and clear.

Halve the cherries, remove the stones (pits) and add them to the pan, reserving a few for decoration. Cool. Whip the cream until thick.

Place the bottom cake layer on a serving plate and spread with half the cherry mixture and a layer of cream. Cover with the second cake layer. Sprinkle with the kirsch or brandy, then spread over the remaining cherry mixture and another layer of cream. Put the top layer of cake carefully on the cream.

Reserving a little cream for decoration, spread the remainder over the top and sides of the cake. Make a decorative pattern on the top. Flake or grate the chocolate and press most of it onto the sides of the cake. Pipe the reserved cream in whirls on top of the cake and decorate with the remaining chocolate and reserved cherries.

Leave the cake for 2 to 3 hours before serving.

Serves 8–10

Chestnut Gâteau

Metric/Imperial
65 g/2½ oz plain flour
15 g/½ oz cornflour
3 large eggs
75 g/3 oz caster sugar
40 g/1½ oz butter, melted and cooled
3–4 tablespoons sherry
300 ml/½ pint whipping cream
1 × 226 g/8 oz can sweetened
  chestnut purée
50 g/2 oz flaked almonds, toasted

American
½ cup plus 2 tablespoons all-purpose
  flour
2 tablespoons cornstarch
3 eggs
6 tablespoons sugar
3 tablespoons butter, melted and
  cooled
3–4 tablespoons sherry
1¼ cups whipping cream
1 × ½ lb can sweetened chestnut
  purée
½ cup toasted slivered almonds

Sift together the flour and cornflour (cornstarch). Beat the eggs and sugar
together until pale and very thick and the beater leaves a trail when lifted.
Fold in the flour mixture alternately with the butter. Pour into a greased and
floured or lined 20 cm/8 inch square deep cake pan.

Bake in a preheated moderately hot oven (190°C/375°F, Gas Mark 5) for
25 to 30 minutes or until well risen and firm to the touch. Cool on a wire rack.

Cut the cake in half and sprinkle each half with sherry. Whip the cream
until thick. Mix one-quarter of the cream with just under half of the chestnut
purée and use to sandwich the two pieces of cake together.

Spread the remaining cream over the top and sides of the cake. Pipe the
remaining chestnut purée in a trellis design over the top of the cake and add
a row of stars all around the top edge. Press the almonds onto the sides of
the cake.

Serves 6–8

Baked Cheesecake

Metric/Imperial	American
melted butter	melted butter
about 8 tablespoons crushed digestive biscuits	about ½ cup crushed graham crackers
750 g/1½ lb curd cheese	3 cups small-curd cottage cheese
finely grated rind and juice of 1 lemon	finely grated rind and juice of 1 lemon
1 teaspoon vanilla essence	1 teaspoon vanilla extract
175 g/6 oz caster sugar	¾ cup sugar
2 tablespoons cornflour	2 tablespoons cornstarch
3 eggs, separated	3 eggs, separated
150 ml/¼ pint double cream	⅔ cup heavy cream

Brush a 20 cm/8 inch springform pan with melted butter and sprinkle liberally with the crushed biscuits (crackers).

Beat the cheese with the lemon rind and juice, vanilla, sugar, cornflour (cornstarch) and egg yolks until smooth. Beat the egg whites until stiff. Whip the cream until thick. Fold the egg whites and cream into the cheese mixture. Spoon into the pan.

Bake in a preheated moderate oven (160°C/325°F, Gas Mark 3) for 45 minutes. Turn off the oven, open the door and leave the cheesecake inside to cool for 30 minutes.

Allow to cool completely before removing from the pan.

Variations:

When the 45 minutes baking time is completed, cover the top of the cheesecake with 150 ml/¼ pint (⅔ cup) soured cream. Leave to cool in the turned-off oven as above.

Baked Orange Cheesecake: Cream 50 g/2 oz (4 tablespoons) butter with 1 tablespoon honey, the grated rind of 2 oranges and 50 g/2 oz (¼ cup) sugar. Mix in 175 g/6 oz crushed digestive biscuits (1½ cups crushed graham crackers). Use to line the bottom and sides of an 18 cm/7 inch springform pan. For the filling, cream 50 g/2 oz (4 tablespoons) butter with the grated rind of 1 orange and 75 g/3 oz (6 tablespoons) sugar. Beat in 2 egg yolks, 25 g/ 1 oz cornflour (¼ cup cornstarch), 350 g/12 oz (1½ cups) cottage cheese and 2 tablespoons orange juice. Beat 2 egg whites until stiff and fold into the orange cheese mixture. Spoon into the crumb crust and bake as above, allowing 1¼ hours. Allow to cool in the oven, then remove from the pan. Dust the top of the cheesecake with sifted icing (confectioners') sugar and decorate with well drained canned mandarin orange segments.

Fresh Fruit Cheesecake

Metric/Imperial
100 g/4 oz self-raising flour, sifted
75 g/3 oz butter
50 g/2 oz icing sugar, sifted
1 egg
100–175 g/4–6 oz fresh soft fruit
Filling:
2 tablespoons cornflour
2 tablespoons natural yogurt
50 g/2 oz butter, softened
2 eggs, separated
1 × 225 g/8 oz packet cream cheese
225 g/8 oz cottage cheese
50 g/2 oz caster sugar
½ teaspoon vanilla essence

American
1 cup self-rising flour, sifted
6 tablespoons butter
½ cup confectioners' sugar, sifted
1 egg
¼–½ lb fresh soft fruit
Filling:
2 tablespoons cornstarch
2 tablespoons unflavored yogurt
4 tablespoons butter, softened
2 eggs, separated
1 × ½ lb package cream cheese
1 cup cottage cheese
¼ cup sugar
½ teaspoon vanilla extract

Put the flour, butter, icing (confectioners') sugar and egg in a bowl and beat together until smooth. Press over the bottom of a greased 23 cm/9 inch springform pan. Bake in a preheated moderately hot oven (190°C/375°F, Gas Mark 5) for 15 minutes. Cool.

For the filling, mix the cornflour (cornstarch) with the yogurt, then beat in the butter, egg yolks, cream and cottage cheeses, sugar and vanilla. Beat the egg whites until stiff and fold into the filling. Spread over the pastry base, then bake for a further 25 minutes or until just firm. Cool.

Remove the cheesecake from the pan and decorate the top with fresh fruit (raspberries, sliced strawberries, grapes, etc.).

Variation:
Omit the vanilla and use the finely grated rind of 1 lemon or 1 small orange instead.

Refrigerator Orange Cheesecake

Metric/Imperial
1 tablespoon gelatine
75 g/3 oz caster sugar
2 eggs, separated
200 ml/7 fl oz milk
grated rind and juice of 1 orange
2 teaspoons lemon juice
350 g/12 oz curd or cottage cheese
50 g/2 oz butter
100 g/4 oz digestive biscuits or
  gingernuts, crushed
whipped cream to decorate

American
1½ envelopes unflavored gelatin
6 tablespoons sugar
2 eggs, separated
¾ cup plus 2 tablespoons milk
grated rind and juice of 1 orange
2 teaspoons lemon juice
1½ cups cottage cheese
4 tablespoons butter
1 cup crushed graham crackers or
  ginger snaps
whipped cream to decorate

Put the gelatine, sugar, egg yolks and milk in a saucepan and bring to the boil, stirring to be sure the gelatine dissolves. Stir in the orange rind and juice and lemon juice and cool.

Sieve (strain) the cottage cheese and stir into the orange mixture. Leave until on the point of setting.

Beat the egg whites until stiff and fold into the cheese mixture. Pour into a greased 18 cm/7 inch springform pan.

Melt the butter and stir in the biscuit (cracker) crumbs. Spoon in an even layer over the cheesecake filling, then chill until firm.

Remove the cheesecake from the pan and invert it onto a serving plate. Decorate with whirls of whipped cream.

Variation:

Apricot Cheesecake: Drain a 425 g/15 oz can of apricot halves and make up the can syrup to 300 ml/½ pint (1¼ cups) with water. Add the grated rind and juice of 1 lemon to the syrup mixture. Dissolve 15 g/½ oz (2 envelopes unflavored) gelatine in a little of the warmed syrup mixture, then add to the remainder. Beat in a 225 g/8 oz package of cream cheese and set aside to stiffen slightly. Chop all but 6 of the apricot halves. Mix the chopped apricots into the cream cheese mixture. Whip 150 ml/¼ pint double cream (⅔ cup heavy cream) with 50 g/2 oz sugar until thick and fold into the cheese mixture. Pour into a dampened 18 cm/7 inch round deep cake pan. Chill until lightly set. Cream 50 g/2 oz (4 tablespoons) butter with 25 g/1 oz sifted icing sugar (¼ cup sifted confectioners' sugar) and mix in 100 g/4 oz crushed digestive biscuits (1 cup crushed graham crackers). Press this on top of the cheesecake and chill for several hours. Invert onto a serving plate to serve, decorated with the reserved apricot halves and whipped cream.

Blackberry Cheesecake

Metric/Imperial
500 g/1 lb blackberries
6 tablespoons water
175 g/6 oz caster sugar
2 eggs, separated
1 tablespoon gelatine
350 g/12 oz cottage cheese
300 ml/½ pint double cream
100 g/4 oz digestive biscuits,
  crushed
1 tablespoon brown sugar
50 g/2 oz butter, melted

American
1 lb blackberries
6 tablespoons water
¾ cup sugar
2 eggs, separated
1½ envelopes unflavored gelatin
1½ cups cottage cheese
1¼ cups heavy cream
1 cup crushed graham crackers
1 tablespoon brown sugar
4 tablespoons butter, melted

Reserve a few blackberries for the decoration and put the remainder in a saucepan with 4 tablespoons of the water and 50 g/2 oz (¼ cup) of the sugar. Cook until pulped, then sieve or blend to a purée. Cool.

Beat the egg yolks and remaining sugar together until pale and thick. Dissolve the gelatine in the remaining water and add to the egg yolk mixture with the fruit purée. Sieve (strain) the cottage cheese and mix into the fruit mixture. Leave until on the point of setting.

Whip the cream until thick. Fold most of it into the fruit mixture. Beat the egg whites until stiff and fold into the fruit mixture. Spoon into a 20 cm/8 inch springform pan lined with dampened greaseproof (wax) paper. Mix the biscuit (cracker) crumbs with the brown sugar and butter and sprinkle over the fruit filling. Chill until set.

Invert the cheesecake onto a serving plate and decorate with the remaining cream and reserved blackberries.

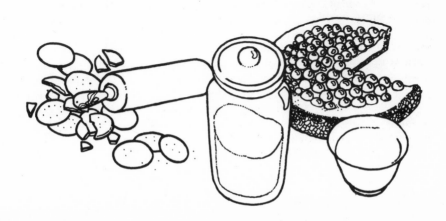

Chilled Redcurrant Cheesecake

Metric/Imperial
50 g/2 oz butter, melted
100 g/4 oz digestive biscuits,
  crushed
Filling:
2 teaspoons gelatine
2 tablespoons water
225 g/8 oz cottage cheese
1 egg, separated
50 g/2 oz caster sugar
finely grated rind and juice of ½
  lemon
5 tablespoons double cream
stewed redcurrants
2 tablespoons redcurrant jelly,
  melted
whipped cream to decorate

American
4 tablespoons butter melted
1 cup crushed graham crackers
Filling:
1½ envelopes unflavored gelatin
2 tablespoons water
1 cup cottage cheese
1 egg, separated
¼ cup sugar
finely grated rind and juice of ½
  lemon
5 tablespoons heavy cream
stewed redcurrants
2 tablespoons redcurrant jelly,
  melted
whipped cream to decorate

Mix the melted butter with the biscuit (cracker) crumbs and press over the bottom and sides of a 20 cm/8 inch flan ring on a baking sheet or a tart pan. Chill until set.

Meanwhile, for the filling, dissolve the gelatine in the warmed water. Sieve (strain) the cottage cheese, then beat in the egg yolk, sugar, lemon rind and juice and gelatine. Whip the cream until thick and fold in. Chill until the mixture has thickened and is on the point of setting.

Beat the egg white until stiff and fold into the cheese mixture. Turn into the crumb crust and chill until set.

Remove the cheesecake from the flan ring or pan and place on a plate. Top with stewed redcurrants and brush with the jelly. Pipe a border of whipped cream around the edge.

Variation:

Minted Cheesecake: Make the crumb crust using 150 g/5 oz (1¼ cups) crushed shortbread. Press over the bottom of a greased 18 cm/7 inch springform pan and chill until set. For the filling, dissolve 1 tablespoon (2 envelopes) unflavoured gelatine in 4 tablespoons water. Cream 1 × 225 g/ 8 oz package cream cheese with 100 g/4 oz (½ cup) sugar, then beat in ½ teaspoon vanilla essence (extract), 1 teaspoon peppermint essence (mint flavoring) and 2 tablespoons lemon juice. Mix in the gelatine with 1 small can chilled evaporated milk. Pour into the crumb crust and chill until set.

Soured Cream Cheesecake

Metric/Imperial
225 g/8 oz digestive biscuits,
  crushed
100 g/4 oz butter, melted
1 × 225 g/8 oz packet cream cheese
225 g/8 oz cottage cheese
3 eggs
25 g/1 oz cornflour
225 g/8 oz sugar
150 ml/¼ pint milk
300 ml/½ pint soured cream
grated rind of 2 lemons
1 teaspoon lemon juice

American
2 cups crushed graham crackers
8 tablespoons (1 stick) butter,
  melted
1 × ½ lb package cream cheese
1 cup cottage cheese
3 eggs
¼ cup cornstarch
1 cup sugar
⅔ cup milk
1¼ cups sour cream
grated rind of 2 lemons
1 teaspoon lemon juice

Mix together the biscuit (cracker) crumbs and butter and press onto the
bottom and sides of a greased 20 cm/8 inch springform pan.

Beat the cheeses together until smooth. Beat in the eggs one at a time,
then add the cornflour (cornstarch) and sugar and mix well. Stir in the milk,
soured cream and lemon rind and juice. Pour into the crumb crust.

Bake in a preheated moderate oven (160°C/325°F, Gas Mark 3) for 50 to
60 minutes. Turn off the oven and leave the cheesecake inside to cool. Chill
for several hours before serving.

Variation:

Chocolate Cream Cheesecake: Make the crumb crust as above. Beat
1 × 225 g/8 oz package cream cheese with 150 ml/¼ pint (⅔ cup) whipping
cream until thick. Stir in 75 g/3 oz melted plain (dark sweet) chocolate. Beat
3 eggs with 175 g/6 oz (¾ cup) sugar until pale and very thick and fold into
the chocolate mixture with 2 tablespoons rum and 1 teaspoon vanilla
essence (extract). Sift together 40 g/1½ oz plain flour (6 tablespoons all-
purpose flour), a pinch of salt and a pinch of bicarbonate of soda (baking
soda) and fold into the chocolate mixture. Pour into the crumb crust. Bake in
a preheated cool oven (150°C/300°F, Gas Mark 2) for 55 to 60 minutes. Cool,
then chill. Top with sweetened whipped cream and drizzle over melted
chocolate.

Chocolate Nut Cheesecake

Metric/Imperial
100 g/4 oz plain chocolate biscuits,
  crushed
40 g/1½ oz butter, melted
1 × 225 g/8 oz packet cream cheese
100 g/4 oz sugar
1 teaspoon vanilla essence
2 eggs, separated
100 g/4 oz plain chocolate, melted
pinch of salt
300 ml/½ pint whipping cream
3 tablespoons finely chopped
  walnuts

American
1 cup crushed plain chocolate
  cookies
3 tablespoons butter, melted
1 × ½ lb package cream cheese
½ cup sugar
1 teaspoon vanilla extract
2 eggs, separated
¼ lb dark sweet chocolate, melted
pinch of salt
1¼ cups whipping cream
3 tablespoons finely chopped
  walnuts

Mix together the biscuit (cookie) crumbs and butter and press onto the bottom of a 20 cm/8 inch springform pan. Bake in a preheated moderate oven (160°C/325°F, Gas Mark 3) for 8 minutes. Cool.

Cream the cheese with half the sugar and the vanilla. Beat in the egg yolks and chocolate. Beat the egg whites with the salt until stiff, then gradually beat in the remaining sugar. Fold into the chocolate mixture. Whip the cream until thick and fold into the chocolate mixture with the nuts.

Pour into the crumb crust and chill until the filling is set.

Quick Lemon Cheesecake

Metric/Imperial
50 g/2 oz butter
2 tablespoons golden syrup
150 g/5 oz digestive biscuits,
  crushed
1 × 225 g/8 oz packet cream cheese
1 × 500 g/16 oz can condensed milk
120 ml/4 fl oz lemon juice
whipped cream to decorate

American
4 tablespoons butter
2 tablespoons light corn syrup
1¼ cups crushed graham crackers
1 × ½ lb package cream cheese
1 × 16 oz can condensed milk
½ cup lemon juice
whipped cream to decorate

Melt the butter and syrup in a saucepan. Stir in the biscuit (cracker) crumbs. Press the mixture onto the bottom and sides of a foil-lined 20 cm/8 inch springform pan. Chill until set.

Soften the cream cheese, then beat in the condensed milk and lemon juice. Pour into the crumb crust and chill for at least 1 hour or until set.

Just before serving remove the cheesecake from the tin (pan) and decorate with whipped cream.
Serves 6

Variation:

Lemon Jelly Cheesecake: Mix 225 g/8 oz crushed digestive biscuits (2 cups crushed graham crackers) with 100 g/4 oz (8 tablespoons) melted butter. Press onto the bottom and sides of a 20 cm/8 inch springform pan and chill until set. For the filling, dissolve 1 packet lemon jelly (lemon-flavored gelatin) in 150 ml/¼ pint (⅔ cup) boiling water. Stir in 150 ml/¼ pint (⅔ cup) lemon juice and 1 teaspoon grated lemon rind. Cool. Whip a 500 g/16 oz can condensed milk until thick. Beat in a 225 g/8 oz package cream cheese and 1 teaspoon vanilla essence (extract). Combine thoroughly with the lemon mixture. Pour into the crumb crust and chill until set.

Pineapple Cheesecake

Metric/Imperial
175 g/6 oz digestive biscuits,
  crushed
50 g/2 oz butter, melted
Filling:
225 g/8 oz cream cheese
2 eggs, beaten
100 g/4 oz sugar
2–3 drops of vanilla essence
1 × 225 g/8 oz can pineapple
  chunks, drained and chopped
Topping:
150 ml/¼ pint soured cream
canned or crystallized pineapple
glacé cherries

American
1½ cups crushed graham crackers
4 tablespoons butter, melted
Filling:
1 × ½ lb package cream cheese
2 eggs, beaten
½ cup sugar
2–3 drops of vanilla extract
1 × ½ lb can pineapple chunks,
  drained and chopped
Topping:
⅔ cup sour cream
canned or candied pineapple
candied cherries

Mix the biscuit (cracker) crumbs with the butter and press over the bottom of a greased loose-bottomed 18 cm/7 inch square cake pan. Chill.

Beat together the cream cheese, eggs, sugar and vanilla, then fold in the pineapple. Pour over the crumb base.

Bake in a preheated moderately hot oven (190°C/375°F, Gas Mark 5) for 1 hour. Cool.

Spread the soured cream over the top of the cheesecake and decorate with the pineapple and cherries.

Coffee Cream Cheesecake

Metric/Imperial	American
225 g/8 oz digestive biscuits, crushed	2 cups crushed graham crackers
100 g/4 oz butter, melted	8 tablespoons (1 stick) butter, melted
350 g/12 oz cream cheese	1½ cups cream cheese
100 g/4 oz cottage cheese, sieved	½ cup cottage cheese, strained
2 tablespoons gelatine	2 envelopes unflavored gelatin
120 ml/4 fl oz water	½ cup water
2 tablespoons grated lemon rind	2 tablespoons grated lemon rind
2 tablespoons lemon juice	2 tablespoons lemon juice
300 ml/½ pint double cream	1¼ cups heavy cream
4 tablespoons coffee essence	¼ cup strong black coffee
1 egg white	1 egg white
175 g/6 oz caster sugar	¾ cup sugar

Mix together the biscuit (cracker) crumbs and butter and press onto the bottom and sides of a greased 20 cm/8 inch springform pan. Chill until set.

Beat together the cheeses. Dissolve the gelatine in the water and add to the cheeses with the lemon rind and juice. Whip the cream with the coffee essence (coffee) until thick and fold into the cheese mixture. Beat the egg white until stiff, then gradually beat in the sugar. Fold into the cheese mixture. Pour into the crumb crust.

Chill until the filling is set.

Variation:

Peach and Raspberry Cheesecake: Make the crumb crust as above. For the filling, sieve (strain) 350 g/12 oz (1½ cups) cottage cheese, then beat in 150 ml/¼ pint (⅔ cup) natural (unflavored) yogurt, 50 g/2 oz (¼ cup) caster sugar and the grated rind and juice of 1 lemon. Dissolve 15 g/½ oz (2 envelopes unflavored) gelatine in 2 tablespoons water, then stir into the cheese mixture. Beat 2 egg whites until stiff and fold into the cheese mixture. Pour into the crumb crust and chill until set. Peel, stone (pit) and slice 2 large peaches. Brush them with a little lemon juice to prevent discoloration, then arrange on top of the cheesecake with 225 g/8 oz raspberries.

Continental Cream Cheese Slices

Metric/Imperial	American
175 g/6 oz plain flour	1½ cups all-purpose flour
50 g/2 oz custard powder	½ cup custard powder
25 g/1 oz icing sugar	¼ cup confectioners' sugar
½ teaspoon baking powder	½ teaspoon baking powder
100 g/4 oz butter	8 tablespoons (1 stick) butter
4–6 tablespoons milk	4–6 tablespoons milk
Filling:	**Filling:**
50 g/2 oz butter	4 tablespoons butter
275 g/10 oz cream cheese	1¼ cups cream cheese
2 eggs	2 eggs
50 g/2 oz sugar	¼ cup sugar
50 g/2 oz sultanas	⅓ cup seedless white raisins
grated rind of 1 lemon	grated rind of 1 lemon
2 tablespoons lemon juice	2 tablespoons lemon juice

Sift the flour, custard powder, icing (confectioners') sugar and baking powder into a bowl. Rub in the butter, then bind to a stiff dough with the milk.

Roll out two-thirds of the dough and use to line a greased 28 × 18 cm/ 11 × 7 inch cake pan. Bake blind (unfilled) in a preheated moderate oven (180°C/350°F, Gas Mark 4) for 10 minutes. Cool.

For the filling, cream the butter with the cream cheese. Beat the eggs and sugar together until pale and very thick and beat into the cream cheese mixture. Fold in the sultanas (raisins) and lemon rind and juice. Pour into the pastry case.

Roll out the remaining dough and cut into strips. Arrange these in a diagonal lattice over the filling. Brush the strips with milk.

Return to the oven and bake for a further 35 to 45 minutes. Cut into slices while warm, then leave to cool in the pan.

Variation:

Cheesecake Squares: Make the dough as above using 100 g/4 oz (1 cup) each plain (all-purpose) flour and self-raising flour, 50 g/2 oz cornflour (½ cup cornstarch), 50 g/2 oz (½ cup) custard powder, 40 g/1½ oz icing sugar (6 tablespoons confectioners' sugar), 175 g/6 oz (12 tablespoons) butter, 2 to 3 tablespoons water and 1 teaspoon lemon juice. Roll out half the dough and use to line a pan as above. Spread with 100 g/4 oz (⅓ cup) apricot jam. For the filling, cream 75 g/3 oz (6 tablespoons) butter with 2 egg yolks, 50 g/2 oz (¼ cup) sugar, 50 g/2 oz (⅓ cup) raisins, ½ teaspoon grated lemon rind, 275 g/ 10 oz (1¼ cups) cottage cheese and 150 ml/¼ pint (⅔ cup) soured cream. Beat 2 egg whites until stiff and fold into the cheese mixture. Spread over the jam. Roll out the remaining dough and lay over the filling. Brush with beaten egg, then bake as above, allowing 30 to 40 minutes. Cool, cut into squares and sprinkle with icing (confectioners') sugar.

English Muffins

Metric/Imperial
½ teaspoon sugar
6 tablespoons lukewarm water
4 teaspoons dried yeast
500 g/1 lb plain flour
1 teaspoon salt
150 ml/¼ pint lukewarm milk
1 egg, beaten
25 g/1 oz butter, melted

American
½ teaspoon sugar
6 tablespoons lukewarm water
2 packages active dry yeast
4 cups all-purpose flour
1 teaspoon salt
⅔ cup lukewarm milk
1 egg, beaten
2 tablespoons butter, melted

Dissolve the sugar in the water. Sprinkle the yeast on top and leave in a warm place for about 20 minutes or until frothy.

Sift the flour and salt into a bowl. Add the yeast liquid, milk, egg and butter and mix to a softish dough. Knead until the dough is smooth and elastic, then leave to rise in a warm place until doubled in size.

Knead the dough lightly to knock out any air bubbles. Roll out to about 1 cm/½ inch thick and cut out 12 rounds with an 8.5 cm/3½ inch plain cutter. Put the rounds on greased and floured baking sheets and leave in a warm place to rise until doubled in size.

Bake in a preheated very hot oven (240°C/450°F, Gas Mark 8) for 5 minutes. Turn the muffins over and bake for a further 5 to 6 minutes.

To serve, toast on both sides, pull apart, butter and put together again.
Makes 12

White Bread

Metric/Imperial
1 teaspoon sugar
about 900 ml/1½ pints lukewarm
   water
15 g/½ oz dried yeast
1.35 kg/3 lb strong plain flour
1 tablespoon salt

American
1 teaspoon sugar
about 3¾ cups lukewarm water
2 packages active dry yeast
3 lb (12 cups) all-purpose flour
1 tablespoon salt

Dissolve the sugar in about one-third of the water. Sprinkle the yeast on top and leave in a warm place for about 20 minutes or until frothy.

Sift the flour and salt into a bowl. Make a well in the centre and put in the yeast liquid and the remaining water. Gradually draw the flour into the liquid and mix to a dough. Knead until the dough is smooth and elastic, then leave to rise in a warm place until doubled in size.

Knead the dough lightly to knock out any air bubbles, then divide into three portions. Form each portion into the shape you want: to bake in a greased 500 g/1 lb (4½ × 2½ × 1½ inch) loaf pan, form a portion of dough into an oblong, then fold it into three to fit the pan. The dough should just over half-fill the pan. Leave in a warm place to rise for 20 minutes.

Bake in a preheated hot oven (220°C/425°F, Gas Mark 7) for 20 to 25 minutes, then reduce the temperature to cool (150°C/300°F, Gas Mark 2) and continue baking for 15 to 20 minutes for the loaf pan described. To test if the bread is cooked, turn it out of the pan and knock firmly on the base: the bread should sound hollow.

Makes 3 loaves

Variations:

Rich White Bread: Use half milk and half water, and rub 25 to 50 g/1 to 2 oz (2 to 4 tablespoons) butter into the flour.

Milk Bread: Use all milk, plus an egg if wished, and rub 50 g/2 oz (4 tablespoons) butter into the flour.

Wholemeal (Wholewheat) Bread: Use half or all wholemeal (wholewheat) flour and adjust the quantity of liquid accordingly – wholemeal (wholewheat) flour absorbs more liquid.

Soft-Topped Baps: Make up one-third of the bread dough, being sure it is a soft consistency. Form it into small rounds instead of a loaf and arrange on greased baking sheets. Press the rounds lightly to flatten them, then brush with milk and sprinkle with flour. Let rise, then bake as above, allowing about 12 minutes.

Farmhouse Wholemeal (Wholewheat) Bread: Use 25 g/1 oz (2 tablespoons) Barbados sugar instead of the 1 teaspoon sugar, substitute wholemeal (wholewheat) flour for plain (all-purpose) flour and add 25 g/1 oz sea salt (1 tablespoon coarse dairy salt) with the flour. Add 1 tablespoon oil with the remaining water. Brush the tops of the loaves with beaten egg before baking.

Rye Bread

Metric/Imperial	American
1 tablespoon sugar	1 tablespoon sugar
300 ml/½ pint lukewarm water	1¼ cups lukewarm water
4 teaspoons dried yeast	2 packages active dry yeast
225 g/8 oz rye flour	2 cups rye flour
100 g/4 oz wholemeal flour	1 cup wholewheat flour
100 g/4 oz plain flour	1 cup all-purpose flour
1 teaspoon salt	1 teaspoon salt
1 teaspoon ground aniseed	1 teaspoon ground aniseed
150 ml/¼ pint milk	⅔ cup milk
1 tablespoon oil	1 tablespoon oil

Dissolve 1 teaspoon of the sugar in a little of the water. Sprinkle the yeast on top and leave in a warm place for about 20 minutes or until frothy.

Sift the flours, salt and aniseed into a bowl and stir in the remaining sugar. Make a well in the centre and put in the yeast liquid, the remaining water, the milk and oil. Gradually draw the flour into the liquid and mix to a dough. Knead until the dough is smooth and elastic, then leave to rise in a warm place until doubled in size.

Knead the dough lightly to knock out any air bubbles, then shape into a loaf and place in a greased 1 kg/2 lb (9 × 5 × 3 inch) loaf pan. Leave in a warm place to rise until the dough reaches the top of the pan.

Brush with a little sugar dissolved in warm water, then bake in a preheated hot oven (220°C/425°F, Gas Mark 7) for 40 to 45 minutes. Cool on a wire rack.

Variations:

Dark Rye Bread: Use 2 tablespoons black treacle (molasses) in place of the sugar and increase the other ingredients as follows: 900 ml/1½ pints (4 cups) water, 25 g/1 oz dried yeast (4 packages active dry yeast), 500 g/1 lb (4 cups) rye flour, 1 kg/2 lb wholemeal flour (8 cups wholewheat flour) and 1 tablespoon salt. Omit the aniseed, milk and oil, and rub 25 g/1 oz (2 tablespoons) butter into the flour before adding the liquids. Shape into two long, oval loaves and brush with 1 egg beaten with a pinch of salt. Sprinkle with cracked wheat or bran and cut several diagonal slashes in the tops of the loaves. Bake in a preheated very hot oven (230°C/450°F, Gas Mark 8) for 20 minutes, then reduce the temperature to moderately hot (200°C/400°F, Gas Mark 6) and bake for a further 20 minutes.

Light Rye Bread: Make up the dough using 1 tablespoon sugar, 120 ml/4 fl oz (½ cup) lukewarm water, 1 tablespoon dried yeast (2 packages active dry yeast), 50 g/2 oz (½ cup) rye flour, 275 g/10 oz plain flour (2½ cups all-purpose flour), ½ tablespoon salt, 1 teaspoon aniseed, 1 teaspoon caraway seeds, 1 teaspoon grated orange rind and 120 ml/4 fl oz (½ cup) milk. Shape, rise and bake as above.

Bran Bread

Metric/Imperial	American
25 g/1 oz Barbados sugar	2 tablespoons Barbados sugar
450 ml/¾ pint lukewarm water	2 cups lukewarm water
4 teaspoons dried yeast	2 packages active dry yeast
550 g/1¼ lb wholemeal flour	5 cups wholewheat flour
100 g/4 oz bran	2 cups bran
15 g/½ oz sea salt	1½ teaspoons coarse dairy salt
1 tablespoon corn oil	1 tablespoon corn oil
To finish:	**To finish:**
2 tablespoons cold water	2 tablespoons cold water
pinch of salt	pinch of salt
2 tablespoons rolled oats	2 tablespoons rolled oats

Dissolve a little of the sugar in a little of the water. Sprinkle over the yeast and leave in a warm place for about 20 minutes or until frothy.

Put the flour, bran, salt and remaining sugar in a bowl. Make a well in the centre and put in the yeast liquid, remaining water and the oil. Gradually draw the dry ingredients into the liquid and mix to a dough. Knead until the dough is smooth and elastic, then leave to rise in a warm place until doubled in size.

Knead the dough lightly to knock out any air bubbles, then divide it in half. Shape into two loaves and place in greased 500 g/1 lb (4½ × 2½ × 1½ inch) loaf pans. Leave in a warm place to rise until the dough reaches the tops of the pans.

Mix together the cold water and salt and brush over the tops of the loaves. Sprinkle with the oats. Bake in a preheated very hot oven (230°C/450°F, Gas Mark 8) for 35 minutes.

Makes 2 loaves

Bath Buns

Metric/Imperial	American
2 tablespoons plus ½ teaspoon sugar	2 tablespoons plus ½ teaspoon sugar
5 tablespoons lukewarm water	5 tablespoons lukewarm water
5 teaspoons dried yeast	2 packages active dry yeast
500 g/1 lb plain flour	4 cups all-purpose flour
1 teaspoon salt	1 teaspoon salt
50 g/2 oz butter	4 tablespoons butter
100 g/4 oz sultanas	⅔ cup seedless white raisins
50 g/2 oz chopped mixed peel	⅓ cup chopped mixed candied peel
150 ml/¼ pint lukewarm milk	⅔ cup lukewarm milk
1 egg	1 egg
beaten egg to glaze	beaten egg to glaze
8 sugar cubes, coarsely crushed	8 sugar cubes, coarsely crushed

Dissolve the ½ teaspoon sugar in the water. Sprinkle the yeast on top and leave in a warm place for about 20 minutes or until frothy.

Sift the flour and salt into a bowl. Rub in the butter, then stir in the remaining sugar, the sultanas (raisins) and peel. Mix to a soft dough with the yeast liquid, milk and egg. Knead until the dough is smooth and elastic, then leave to rise in a warm place until doubled in size.

Knead the dough lightly to knock out any air bubbles. Divide the dough into 12 to 14 portions and place them (leaving the shapes irregular) on a greased baking sheet. Leave in a warm place to rise until almost doubled in size.

Brush with beaten egg and sprinkle with the crushed sugar. Bake in a preheated hot oven (220°C/425°F, Gas Mark 7) for 20 to 25 minutes. Cool on a wire rack.

Makes 12–14

Variation:

Hot Cross Buns: Sift the flour with 1 teaspoon ground mixed spice (allspice), ½ teaspoon ground cinnamon and ½ teaspoon grated nutmeg. Substitute mixed dried fruit for the sultanas (seedless white raisins). Divide the dough into 12 portions, shape into balls and let rise. Before baking, cut a cross in the top of each bun. Omit the egg and sugar glaze. After baking, glaze with honey or melted apricot jam.

Saffron Bread

Metric/Imperial
1 teaspoon sugar
4 tablespoons lukewarm water
1 tablespoon dried yeast
500 g/1 lb plain flour
1½ teaspoons salt
150 ml/¼ pint lukewarm milk
½ teaspoon saffron powder
2 eggs, beaten

American
1 teaspoon sugar
¼ cup lukewarm water
2 packages active dry yeast
4 cups all-purpose flour
1½ teaspoons salt
⅔ cup lukewarm milk
½ teaspoon saffron powder
2 eggs, beaten

Dissolve the sugar in the water. Sprinkle the yeast on top and leave in a warm place for about 20 minutes or until frothy.

Sift the flour and salt into a bowl and make a well in the centre. Mix the milk with the saffron, stirring to dissolve the spice, then add to the bowl with the yeast liquid and eggs. Gradually draw the flour into the liquids and mix to a dough. Knead until the dough is smooth and elastic, then leave to rise in a warm place until doubled in size.

Knead the dough lightly to knock out any air bubbles, then shape into a loaf. Put into a greased 1 kg/2 lb (9 × 5 × 3 inch) loaf pan. Leave in a warm place to rise until the dough reaches the top of the pan.

Bake in a preheated moderately hot oven (190°C/375°F, Gas Mark 5) for 30 minutes.

Sugared Bun Cluster

Metric/Imperial
⅓ quantity risen rich white bread
    dough (see page 157)
demerara sugar
milk
4 tablespoons honey, melted
25 g/1 oz nuts, chopped

American
⅓ quantity risen rich white bread
    dough (see page 157)
raw brown sugar
milk
¼ cup honey, melted
¼ cup chopped nuts

Divide the dough into 8 portions. Work a little sugar into each portion, then shape into smooth balls. Arrange the balls in a greased 20 cm/8 inch round deep cake pan so that they just touch. Leave to rise in a warm place for about 20 minutes.

Brush the top of the bun cluster with milk, then spoon over the honey. Sprinkle with more sugar and the nuts.

Bake in a preheated very hot oven (230°C/450°F, Gas Mark 8) for 15 minutes, then reduce the temperature to moderately hot (200°C/400°F, Gas Mark 6) and continue baking for 10 minutes. Cool on a wire rack.
Makes 8

Brioche

Metric/Imperial	American
1 teaspoon sugar	1 teaspoon sugar
1 tablespoon lukewarm water	1 tablespoon lukewarm water
2 teaspoons dried yeast	1 package active dry yeast
225 g/8 oz plain flour	2 cups all-purpose flour
½ teaspoon salt	½ teaspoon salt
2 eggs, beaten	2 eggs, beaten
50 g/2 oz butter, melted and cooled	4 tablespoons butter, melted and cooled
Glaze:	
1 egg	**Glaze:**
1 tablespoon water	1 egg
pinch of sugar	1 tablespoon water
	pinch of sugar

Dissolve the sugar in the water. Sprinkle the yeast on top and leave in a warm place for about 20 minutes or until frothy.

Sift the flour and salt into a bowl. Make a well in the centre and put in the yeast liquid, eggs and butter. Gradually draw the flour into the liquids and mix to a soft dough. Knead until the dough is smooth and elastic, then leave in a warm place to rise until doubled in size.

Knead the dough lightly to knock out any air bubbles, then divide it into 12 portions. Shape three-quarters of each portion into a ball and place in a greased 7.5 cm/3 inch brioche or deep bun (muffin) tin. Press a hole firmly in the centre of each ball with your finger. Roll the remaining one-quarter of each dough portion into a small ball, slightly taper one side and place it on top of the larger ball. Leave to rise in a warm place until doubled in size.

Beat the egg for the glaze lightly with the water and sugar. Brush this over the brioches, then bake in a preheated very hot oven (230°C/450°F, Gas Mark 8) for 10 minutes. Serve warm.
Makes 12

Cheese and Poppy Seed Pinwheels

Metric/Imperial
⅓ quantity risen rich white bread
   dough (see page 157)
1 egg
pinch of salt
25 g/1 oz Parmesan cheese, grated
poppy seeds

American
⅓ quantity risen rich white bread
   dough (see page 157)
1 egg
pinch of salt
¼ cup grated Parmesan cheese
poppy seeds

Divide the dough into 12 portions and roll each into a long thin sausage
shape. Flatten the sausages lightly with the palm of the hand. Beat the egg
with the salt and brush over the dough strips. Sprinkle with the cheese, then
roll up the strips tightly and press the ends to seal.

Arrange the pinwheels on greased baking sheets, well apart, and brush
again with the egg mixture. Sprinkle with poppy seeds. Leave to rise in a
warm place for about 20 minutes.

Bake in a preheated hot oven (220°C/425°F, Gas Mark 7) for 15 minutes.

Sally Lunn Cake

Metric/Imperial
50 g/2 oz butter
200 ml/⅓ pint milk
1 teaspoon sugar
2 eggs, beaten
2 teaspoons dried yeast
500 g/1 lb plain flour
1 teaspoon salt
Glaze:
1 tablespoon sugar
1 tablespoon water

American
4 tablespoons butter
¾ cup plus 2 tablespoons milk
1 teaspoon sugar
2 eggs, beaten
1 package active dry yeast
4 cups all-purpose flour
1 teaspoon salt
Glaze:
1 tablespoon sugar
1 tablespoon water

Melt the butter in a saucepan. Remove from the heat and stir in the milk,
sugar, eggs and yeast. Sift the flour and salt into a bowl. Add the yeast liquid
and mix to a smooth dough. Knead lightly.

Divide the dough in half and roll out each into a round. Place in two greased
12.5 cm/5 inch round deep cake pans. Leave to rise in a warm place until the
dough almost reaches the tops of the pans.

Bake in a preheated very hot oven (230°C/450°F, Gas Mark 8) for 15 to 20
minutes.

For the glaze, boil the sugar with the water for 2 minutes. Brush over the
hot loaves, then cool on a wire rack.
Makes 2

All-Bran Tea Bread

Metric/Imperial
25 g/1 oz plus 1 teaspoon sugar
150 ml/¼ pint lukewarm water
1 tablespoon dried yeast
75 g/3 oz All-Bran
150 ml/¼ pint milk
500 g/1 lb plain flour
1 teaspoon salt
grated rind of ½ orange
1 egg, beaten
100 g/4 oz icing sugar, sifted
glacé cherries, chopped
glacé pineapple, chopped
candied angelica, chopped

American
2 tablespoons plus 1 teaspoon sugar
⅔ cup lukewarm water
2 packages active dry yeast
1½ cups All-Bran
⅔ cup milk
4 cups all-purpose flour
1 teaspoon salt
grated rind of ½ orange
1 egg, beaten
1 cup confectioners' sugar, sifted
candied cherries, chopped
candied pineapple, chopped
candied angelica, chopped

Dissolve the 1 teaspoon sugar in the water. Sprinkle the yeast on top and leave in a warm place for about 20 minutes or until frothy.

Put the All-Bran and milk into a bowl and leave to soak for 10 minutes.

Sift the flour and salt into the bowl containing the All-Bran. Add the remaining sugar, the orange rind, egg and yeast mixture and mix to a soft dough. Knead until the dough is smooth and elastic, then leave in a warm place until doubled in size.

Knead the dough lightly to knock out any air bubbles. Divide it into three and roll into ropes about 37 cm/15 inches long. Plait (braid) these together and press the ends together to make a ring. Place on a greased baking sheet. Leave in a warm place to rise until doubled in size.

Bake in a preheated hot oven (220°C/425°F, Gas Mark 7) for 15 to 20 minutes. Cool on a wire rack.

Mix the icing (confectioners') sugar with enough hot water to make a coating consistency. Trickle this icing over the tea bread, then leave until almost set. Decorate with the fruits.

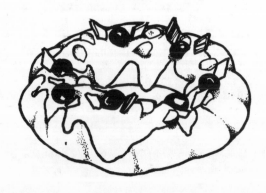

Spiced Almond Ring

Metric/Imperial
½ teaspoon sugar
7 tablespoons lukewarm milk
2 teaspoons dried yeast
225 g/8 oz plain flour
½ teaspoon salt
15 g/½ oz butter, melted
1 egg, beaten
Filling and decoration:
15 g/½ oz butter, melted
50 g/2 oz soft brown sugar
1 teaspoon ground allspice
25 g/1 oz blanched almonds,
  chopped
50 g/2 oz icing sugar, sifted
1½ teaspoons warm water
4 glacé cherries, halved
1 tablespoon flaked almonds

American
½ teaspoon sugar
7 tablespoons lukewarm milk
1 package active dry yeast
2 cups all-purpose flour
½ teaspoon salt
1 tablespoon butter, melted
1 egg, beaten
Filling and decoration:
1 tablespoon butter, melted
⅓ cup light brown sugar
1 teaspoon ground allspice
¼ cup chopped blanched almonds
½ cup confectioners' sugar, sifted
1½ teaspoons warm water
4 candied cherries, halved
1 tablespoon slivered almonds

Dissolve the sugar in the milk. Sprinkle the yeast on top and leave in a warm place for about 20 minutes or until frothy.

Sift the flour and salt into a bowl. Add the yeast liquid, butter and egg and mix to a dough. Knead until the dough is smooth and elastic, then leave in a warm place to rise until doubled in size.

Knead the dough lightly to knock out any air bubbles. Roll it out to a 30 × 23 cm/12 × 9 inch oblong. Brush with the melted butter for the filling and sprinkle over the sugar, spice and chopped almonds. Roll up from one of the long sides like a Swiss (jelly) roll and press the edges together to seal. Shape the roll into a ring and place it on a greased baking sheet. With scissors, snip at 2.5 cm/1 inch intervals to within 1 cm/½ inch of the centre of the ring and separate by turning each piece gently sideways. Leave in a warm place to rise until doubled in size.

Bake in a preheated moderately hot oven (190°C/375°F, Gas Mark 5) for 30 to 35 minutes. Cool on a wire rack.

Mix the icing (confectioners') sugar with the water to make a smooth icing and pour it over the ring. Decorate with the cherries and flaked (slivered) almonds.

Danish Pastries

Metric/Imperial	American
25 g/1 oz plus 1 teaspoon caster sugar	2 tablespoons plus 1 teaspoon sugar
150 ml/¼ pint lukewarm water	⅔ cup lukewarm water
1 tablespoon dried yeast	2 packages active dry yeast
500 g/1 lb plain flour	4 cups all-purpose flour
1 teaspoon salt	1 teaspoon salt
50 g/2 oz lard	¼ cup lard
2 eggs, beaten	2 eggs, beaten
275 g/10 oz butter	1¼ cups (2½ sticks) butter
beaten egg to glaze	beaten egg to glaze

Dissolve the 1 teaspoon sugar in the water and sprinkle over the yeast. Leave in a warm place for about 20 minutes or until frothy.

Sift the flour and salt into a bowl and rub in the lard. Stir in the remaining sugar. Add the yeast liquid and eggs and mix to a soft dough. Knead the dough until smooth and elastic, then chill for 10 minutes.

Shape the butter into a oblong about 25 × 10 cm/10 × 4 inches.

Roll out the dough to a 28 cm/11 inch square. Place the butter in the centre and fold over the dough to enclose it. Seal with a rolling pin, then roll out to a strip three times as long as it is wide. Fold the bottom third up and the top third down. Seal the edges and chill for 10 minutes.

Repeat the rolling, folding and chilling twice, leaving the dough to chill for 30 minutes after the second folding. Shape as suggested below.

Crescents: Roll out one-third of the dough to a 23 cm/9 inch round and cut into 8 even wedges. Put 1 teaspoon almond paste (see page 42) or crème pâtissière (see page 42) or stewed apple at the base of each wedge and roll up towards the point. Curve into a crescent and place on a baking sheet. Leave to rise in a warm place until puffy. Brush with beaten egg, then bake in a preheated hot oven (220°C/425°F, Gas Mark 7) for 10 to 15 minutes or until light golden brown. Transfer to a wire rack and brush with glacé icing (see page 42) while still warm. Sprinkle with chopped nuts and cool.
Makes 8

Cocks' Combs: Roll out one-third of the dough thinly and cut into 11 × 12 inch/4½ × 5 inch strips. Spread half the width of each strip with almond paste (see page 42) or crème pâtissière (see page 42) or stewed apple sprinkled with ground cinnamon and currants. Fold over the other half to enclose the filling and seal with beaten egg. Make four or five cuts into the folded edge and put onto greased baking sheets, curving each strip slightly to open out the cuts. Rise, glaze and bake as for crescents, above, allowing about 20 minutes baking. Brush with glacé icing (see page 42) and sprinkle with chopped nuts while still warm, then cool.
Makes 6–8

Fruit Pinwheels: Roll out one-third of the dough thinly and cut into an oblong 30 × 20 cm/12 × 8 inches. Spread all over with a mixture of 25 g/1 oz (2 tablespoons) butter, 25 g/1 oz (2½ tablespoons) soft brown sugar and 1 teaspoon ground cinnamon. Sprinkle with a few currants and a little chopped mixed candied peel. Roll up like a Swiss (jelly) roll, starting at the narrow end, and seal with beaten egg. Cut into 2.5 cm/1 inch slices and place on a baking sheet. Flatten slightly. Rise, glaze and bake as for crescents, above. Brush with glacé icing (see page 42) and sprinkle with chopped nuts and glacé (candied) cherries while still warm, then cool.
Makes 8

Chelsea Buns

Metric/Imperial	American
225 g/8 oz plain flour	2 cups all-purpose flour
½ teaspoon sugar	½ teaspoon sugar
2 teaspoons dried yeast	1 package active dry yeast
120 ml/4 fl oz lukewarm milk	½ cup lukewarm milk
½ teaspoon salt	½ teaspoon salt
50 g/2 oz butter	4 tablespoons butter
1 egg, beaten	1 egg, beaten
75 g/3 oz mixed dried fruit	½ cup mixed dried fruit
25 g/1 oz chopped mixed peel	2½ tablespoons chopped mixed
50 g/2 oz soft brown sugar	candied peel
clear honey	⅓ cup light brown sugar
	clear honey

Sift 50 g/2 oz (½ cup) of the flour into a bowl and stir in the sugar, yeast and milk. Leave in a warm place for about 20 minutes or until frothy.

Sift the remaining flour and the salt into another bowl. Rub in 40 g/1½ oz (3 tablespoons) of the butter, then mix in the egg and yeast mixture to make a fairly soft dough that leaves the sides of the bowl clean.

Knead the dough until smooth and no longer sticky, then leave to rise in a warm place until doubled in size.

Knead the dough lightly to knock out any air bubbles, then roll out to a 30 × 23 cm/12 × 9 inch oblong. Melt the remaining butter and brush all over the dough. Sprinkle with the fruit, peel and brown sugar. Roll up from the longest side like a Swiss (jelly) roll and press the edges together to seal. Cut into nine equal slices and place these, cut sides down, in a greased 18 cm/7 inch square cake pan. Leave to rise in a warm place until the dough feels springy.

Bake in a preheated moderately hot oven (190°C/375°F, Gas Mark 5) for 30 to 35 minutes. Lift the buns out of the pan, place them on a wire rack and brush them with honey. Cool.
Makes 9

Iced Fruit Plait (Braid)

Metric/Imperial
225 g/8 oz strong plain flour
large pinch of salt
25 g/1 oz butter
50 g/2 oz plus 1 teaspoon caster
  sugar
75 g/3 oz mixed dried fruit
5 tablespoons lukewarm milk
1½ teaspoons dried yeast
2 eggs
double quantity glacé icing (see
  page 42)
To decorate:
25 g/1 oz flaked almonds, toasted
25 g/1 oz glacé cherries, chopped

American
2 cups all-purpose flour
large pinch of salt
2 tablespoons butter
¼ cup plus 1 teaspoon sugar
½ cup mixed dried candied fruit
5 tablespoons lukewarm milk
1 package active dry yeast
2 eggs
double quantity glacé icing (see
  page 42)
To decorate:
¼ cup toasted slivered almonds
2½ tablespoons chopped candied
  cherries

Sift the flour and salt into a bowl and rub in the butter. Stir in 50 g/2 oz (¼ cup) of the sugar and the fruit.

Dissolve the remaining sugar in the milk and sprinkle the yeast on top. Leave in a warm place for about 20 minutes or until frothy.

Add the yeast liquid and one of the eggs to the flour mixture and mix to a soft dough. Knead the dough until elastic and smooth, then leave in a warm place to rise until doubled in size.

Knead the dough lightly to knock out any air bubbles. Divide the dough into three portions and roll into long thin sausages. Starting in the middle of the sausages, plait (braid) them together and press the ends together to seal. Place on a greased baking sheet and leave in a warm place to rise until doubled in size.

Beat the second egg and brush over the plait (braid). Bake in a preheated hot oven (220°C/425°F, Gas Mark 7) for about 20 minutes or until golden brown. Cool on a wire rack.

Pour the icing over the plait (braid). Scatter over the almonds and cherries and leave to set.

Variation:

The risen dough can be shaped into 8 to 10 buns and baked for 10 to 15 minutes, or shaped into a large flattish round loaf, marked into wedges and baked for about 20 minutes.

Devonshire Splits

Metric/Imperial
25 g/1 oz plus 1 teaspoon caster
  sugar
300 ml/½ pint lukewarm milk
1½ teaspoons dried yeast
500 g/1 lb strong plain flour
1 teaspoon salt
50 g/2 oz butter
sifted icing sugar to dredge
Filling:
raspberry jam
Devonshire, clotted or whipped
  cream

American
2 tablespoons plus 1 teaspoon sugar
1¼ cups lukewarm milk
1 package active dry yeast
4 cups all-purpose flour
1 teaspoon salt
4 tablespoons butter
sifted confectioners' sugar to dredge
Filling:
raspberry jam
whipped cream

Dissolve the 1 teaspoon sugar in half the milk and sprinkle over the yeast.
Leave in a warm place for about 20 minutes or until frothy.

Sift the flour and salt into a bowl. Melt the butter and remaining sugar in the
remaining milk and allow to cool to lukewarm. Add the milk to the flour with
the yeast liquid and mix to a soft dough. Knead the dough until smooth and
elastic, then leave to rise in a warm place until doubled in size.

Knead the dough lightly to knock out any air bubbles. Divide the dough
into 15 pieces and shape into balls. Place on a greased baking sheet and
flatten slightly. Leave to rise in a warm place until doubled in size.

Bake in a preheated hot oven (220°C/425°F, Gas Mark 7) for 15 to 20
minutes or until golden brown. Cool on a wire rack.

To serve, split the buns open, spread with jam and cream, reassemble and
dredge the tops with icing (confectioners') sugar.
Makes 15

Variation:
Swiss Buns: Divide the risen dough into 12 pieces and roll each into a
sausage shape. Place on greased baking sheets and let rise. Bake as
above. Cool, then coat with glacé icing (double the quantity – see page 42).

Fresh Cherry Tart

Metric/Imperial
250 g/9 oz plain flour
pinch of salt
75 g/3 oz sugar
15 g/½ oz fresh yeast
2 eggs
100 g/4 oz butter, softened
Filling:
25 g/1 oz cornflour
550 ml/18 fl oz warm milk
4 eggs
150 g/5 oz sugar
750 g/1½ lb cherries, stoned

American
2¼ cups all-purpose flour
pinch of salt
6 tablespoons sugar
½ cake compressed yeast
2 eggs
8 tablespoons (1 stick) butter,
  softened
Filling:
¼ cup cornstarch
2¼ cups warm milk
4 eggs
⅔ cup sugar
1½ lb cherries, pitted

Sift the flour and salt onto a working surface and stir in the sugar. Crumble the yeast and work it thoroughly into the mixture. Make a well in the centre and put in the eggs and butter. Mix the ingredients together to make a smooth, supple dough. Cover and leave to rise at room temperature for 2 hours.

For the filling, dissolve the cornflour (cornstarch) in a little of the milk. Beat in the eggs and sugar, then gradually stir in the remaining milk. Pour the mixture into a saucepan and heat gently, stirring constantly, until the custard thickens. Remove from the heat.

Roll out the dough and use to line a 25 cm/10 inch flan ring placed on a baking sheet or a tart pan. Arrange the cherries in the pastry case and carefully pour in the custard. Bake in a preheated moderately hot oven (190°C/375°F, Gas Mark 5) for 20 to 30 minutes or until the custard is set and the pastry is golden. Serve warm or cold.
Serves 10–12

Raisin Apricot Bread

Metric/Imperial	American
100 g/4 oz sugar	½ cup sugar
350 ml/12 fl oz lukewarm milk	1½ cups lukewarm milk
4 teaspoons dried yeast	2 packages active dry yeast
500 g/1 lb plain flour	4 cups all-purpose flour
1½ teaspoons ground cardamom	1½ teaspoons ground cardamom
100 g/4 oz butter	8 tablespoons (1 stick) butter
100 g/4 oz raisins	⅔ cup raisins
150 g/5 oz dried apricots, chopped	¾ cup chopped dried apricots

Dissolve 1 teaspoon of the sugar in a little of the milk. Sprinkle the yeast on top and leave in a warm place for about 20 minutes or until frothy.

Sift the flour and cardamom into a bowl and stir in the remaining sugar. Make a well in the centre and put in the yeast liquid. Melt the butter in the remaining milk and add to the bowl. Gradually draw the flour into the liquid and mix to a dough. Knead until the dough is smooth and elastic, then leave to rise in a warm place until doubled in size.

Knead the dough lightly to knock out any air bubbles, then work in the raisins and apricots. Shape into a loaf and place in a greased 1 kg/2 lb (9 × 5 × 3 inch) loaf pan. Leave in a warm place to rise until the dough reaches the top of the pan.

Brush with a little sugar dissolved in warm water, then bake in a preheated moderately hot oven (190°C/375°F, Gas Mark 5) for 45 to 55 minutes. Cool on a wire rack.

Variation:

Cream Buns: Make the dough as above, using only 300 ml/½ pint (1¼ cups) milk, omitting the cardamom, using only 50 g/2 oz (4 tablespoons) butter and adding 1 beaten egg with the butter and milk mixture. Omit the raisins and apricots and use 40 g/1½ oz sultanas (¼ cup seedless white raisins) instead. Let rise, then divide into 16 portions and shape into balls. Place on a greased baking sheet and rise again. Bake in a preheated moderate oven (180°C/350°F, Gas Mark 4) for 15 to 20 minutes or until golden brown. Dissolve 1 tablespoon (unflavored) gelatine and 1 tablespoon sugar in 150 ml/¼ pint (⅔ cup) water. Brush this glaze over the buns while still warm, then cool. Cut out a small section, about 5 mm/¼ inch wide, from the top of each bun and pipe in whipped cream. Sprinkle with icing (confectioners') sugar or drop a little raspberry jam into the centre of the row of cream.
Makes 16

Coffee Walnut Buns

Metric/Imperial	American
50 g/2 oz sugar	¼ cup sugar
600 ml/1 pint lukewarm milk	2½ cups lukewarm milk
4 teaspoons dried yeast	2 packages active dry yeast
1 kg/2 lb plain flour	8 cups all-purpose flour
pinch of salt	pinch of salt
50 g/2 oz butter	4 tablespoons butter
2 eggs, beaten	2 eggs, beaten
75 g/3 oz sultanas	½ cup seedless white raisins
Glaze:	**Glaze:**
1 tablespoon gelatine	2 envelopes unflavored gelatin
1 tablespoon sugar	1 tablespoon sugar
150 ml/¼ pint water	⅔ cup water
Icing:	**Frosting:**
225 g/8 oz icing sugar	2 cups confectioners' sugar
1 teaspoon instant coffee powder	1 teaspoon instant coffee powder
1 tablespoon butter	1 tablespoon butter
milk	milk
chopped walnuts	chopped walnuts

Dissolve 1 teaspoon of the sugar in a little of the milk. Sprinkle the yeast on top and leave in a warm place for about 20 minutes or until frothy.

Sift the flour and salt into a bowl and stir in the remaining sugar. Make a well in the centre and put in the yeast liquid. Melt the butter in the remaining milk and add to the bowl with the eggs. Gradually draw the flour into the liquid and mix to a dough. Work in the sultanas (raisins), kneading the dough until it is smooth and elastic. Leave to rise in a warm place until doubled in size.

Knead the dough lightly to knock out any air bubbles, then divide into lemon-sized portions. Roll each portion between the palms of the hands to a long roll and tie into a knot. Place the knots, about 2.5 cm/1 inch apart, on greased baking sheets. Leave in a warm place to rise until almost doubled in size.

Bake in a preheated moderate oven (180°C/350°F, Gas Mark 4) for 20 to 25 minutes or until golden brown.

Meanwhile, make the glaze (see cream buns recipe on page 171). Brush the glaze over the hot buns and cool slightly.

For the icing, sift the sugar and coffee into a double boiler and add the butter and enough milk to make a fairly thin consistency. Heat, stirring, until the icing is shiny, then drizzle over the buns and sprinkle with walnuts.
Makes about 20

Cinnamon Snails

Metric/Imperial	American
2 tablespoons sugar	2 tablespoons sugar
120 ml/4 fl oz lukewarm milk	½ cup lukewarm milk
4 teaspoons dried yeast	2 packages active dry yeast
350 g/12 oz plain flour	3 cups all-purpose flour
pinch of salt	pinch of salt
225 g/8 oz butter	½ lb (2 sticks) butter
3 egg yolks	3 egg yolks
Filling:	**Filling:**
75 g/3 oz walnuts, finely chopped	¾ cup finely chopped walnuts
225 g/8 oz sugar	1 cup sugar
1 tablespoon ground cinnamon	1 tablespoon ground cinnamon
1 egg, beaten	1 egg, beaten
2 egg whites	2 egg whites
Glaze:	**Glaze:**
1 tablespoon gelatine	2 envelopes unflavored gelatin
1 tablespoon sugar	1 tablespoon sugar
150 ml/¼ pint water	⅔ cup water

Dissolve 1 teaspoon of the sugar in a little of the milk. Sprinkle the yeast on top and leave in a warm place for about 20 minutes or until frothy.

Sift the flour and salt into a bowl and stir in the remaining sugar. Rub in the butter. Add the yeast liquid, the remaining milk and the egg yolks and mix to a soft dough. Chill overnight.

The next day, remove the dough from the refrigerator 30 minutes before using. Roll out the dough to an oblong about 5 mm/¼ inch thick.

For the filling, mix together the walnuts, sugar, cinnamon and beaten egg. Beat the egg whites until stiff. Spread the egg whites over the dough, then cover with the walnut mixture. Roll up like a Swiss (jelly) roll. Cut into 4 cm/ 1½ inch thick slices and arrange them close together, cut sides up, in a greased shallow cake pan. Leave in a warm place to rise for 30 to 45 minutes.

Bake in a preheated hot oven (220°C/425°F, Gas Mark 7) for 20 minutes or until browned.

Meanwhile, make the glaze (see cream buns recipe on page 171). Brush the glaze over the hot buns and cool.

Makes about 12

Variation:

Instead of the filling given above, brush the rolled-out dough with 100 g/4 oz (8 tablespoons) melted butter and sprinkle over a mixture of 75 g/3 oz sultanas (½ cup seedless white raisins), 150 g/5 oz (¾ cup) dark brown sugar, 75 g/3 oz (¾ cup) chopped blanched almonds and 1 tablespoon ground cinnamon. Roll up the dough and continue as above.

Fruit Malt Loaf

Metric/Imperial	American
1 teaspoon sugar	*1 teaspoon sugar*
5 tablespoons lukewarm water	*5 tablespoons lukewarm water*
4 teaspoons dried yeast	*2 packages active dry yeast*
225 g/8 oz wholemeal flour	*2 cups wholewheat flour*
¼ teaspoon salt	*¼ teaspoon salt*
100 g/4 oz sultanas	*⅔ cup seedless white raisins*
25 g/1 oz butter	*2 tablespoons butter*
50 g/2 oz malt extract	*3 tablespoons malt extract*
25 g/1 oz black treacle	*1½ tablespoons molasses*
1 tablespoon clear honey to glaze	*1 tablespoon clear honey to glaze*

Dissolve the sugar in the water. Sprinkle the yeast on top and leave in a warm place for about 20 minutes or until frothy.

Put the flour, salt and sultanas (raisins) in a bowl. Put the butter, malt extract and treacle (molasses) in a saucepan and heat gently until the butter has melted. Cool.

Add the melted mixture and the yeast liquid to the dry ingredients and mix to a soft dough. Knead until the dough is smooth and elastic, then leave to rise in a warm place until doubled in size.

Knead the dough lightly to knock out any air bubbles, then shape it into a loaf. Put into a greased 500 g/1 lb (4½ × 2½ × 1½ inch) loaf pan. Leave in a warm place to rise until the dough reaches the top of the pan.

Bake in a preheated moderately hot oven (200°C/400°F, Gas Mark 6) for 45 minutes. Turn out onto a wire rack, brush with the honey and cool.

Croissants

Metric/Imperial	American
1 teaspoon caster sugar	1 teaspoon sugar
200 ml/7 fl oz lukewarm water	¾ cup plus 2 tablespoons lukewarm water
1 tablespoon dried yeast	2 packages active dry yeast
500 g/1 lb strong plain flour	4 cups all-purpose flour
2 teaspoons salt	2 teaspoons salt
25 g/1 oz lard	2 tablespoons lard
1 egg, beaten	1 egg, beaten
175 g/6 oz butter	12 tablespoons (1½ sticks) butter
beaten egg to glaze	beaten egg to glaze

Dissolve the sugar in the water and sprinkle over the yeast. Leave in a warm place for about 20 minutes or until frothy.

Sift the flour and salt into a bowl and rub in the lard. Add the yeast liquid and egg and mix to a pliable dough. Knead the dough until smooth and elastic.

Roll out the dough to a rectangle about 50 × 20 cm/20 × 8 inches. Divide the butter into three portions and soften each with the back of a knife. Dot one portion over the top two-thirds of the dough rectangle, leaving a margin clear all around. Fold the bottom third up and the top third down on top of it. Turn the dough so the folds are to the sides.

Repeat this process twice, using the rest of the butter. Chill the dough for 30 minutes.

Repeat the rolling and folding three more times, then chill for at least 1 hour.

Roll out the dough to a rectangle about 58 × 35 cm/23 × 14 inches. Leave to rest for 10 minutes. Trim the rectangle to 52 × 30 cm/21 × 12 inches, then cut it in half lengthways. Cut each strip into six triangles 15 cm/6 inches high. Brush all over with beaten egg and roll up each triangle loosely beginning at the base. Form into a crescent shape and place on baking sheets, putting the tip of the crescent underneath. Brush again with egg, then leave in a warm place to rise until puffy.

Glaze again with egg. Bake in a preheated hot oven (220°C/425°F, Gas Mark 7) for about 20 minutes or until well risen and golden brown.
Makes 12

Aniseed Bread

Metric/Imperial	American
1 tablespoon sugar	1 tablespoon sugar
300 ml/½ pint lukewarm milk	1¼ cups lukewarm milk
1 tablespoon dried yeast	2 packages active dry yeast
500 g/1 lb plain flour	4 cups all-purpose flour
pinch of salt	pinch of salt
1 egg, beaten	1 egg, beaten
2 teaspoons aniseed	2 teaspoons aniseed

Dissolve the sugar in 2 tablespoons of the milk. Sprinkle the yeast on top and leave in a warm place for about 20 minutes or until frothy.

Sift the flour and salt into a bowl and make a well in the centre. Put in the yeast liquid, the remaining milk, the egg and aniseed. Gradually draw the flour into the liquids and mix to a dough. Knead until the dough is smooth and elastic, then leave to rise in a warm place until doubled in size.

Knead the dough lightly to knock out any air bubbles, then shape into a loaf. Put into a 1 kg/2 lb (9 × 5 × 3 inch) loaf pan. Leave to rise in a warm place until the dough reaches the top of the pan. Bake in a preheated moderately hot oven (200°C/400°F, Gas Mark 6) for 40 minutes.

Cheese Loaf

Metric/Imperial	American
1 teaspoon sugar	1 teaspoon sugar
150 ml/¼ pint lukewarm water	⅔ cup lukewarm water
2 teaspoons dried yeast	1 package active dry yeast ·
225 g/8 oz wholemeal flour	2 cups wholewheat flour
1 teaspoon salt	1 teaspoon salt
1 teaspoon dry mustard	1 teaspoon dry mustard
100 g/4 oz Cheddar cheese, grated	1 cup grated Cheddar cheese

Dissolve the sugar in a little of the water. Sprinkle the yeast on top and leave in a warm place for about 20 minutes or until frothy.

Put the flour, salt, mustard and cheese in a bowl and mix well. Add the yeast liquid and remaining water and mix to a soft dough. Knead until the dough is smooth and elastic, then leave to rise in a warm place until doubled in size.

Knead the dough lightly to knock out any air bubbles, then shape it into a loaf. Put it into a greased 500 g/1 lb (4½ × 2½ × 1½ inch) loaf pan. Leave to rise in a warm place until the dough rises to the top of the pan.

Bake in a preheated hot oven (220°C/425°F, Gas Mark 7) for 10 minutes, then reduce the temperature to moderately hot (190°C/375°F, Gas Mark 5) and continue baking for 35 minutes.

Lardy Cake

Metric/Imperial	American
50 g/2 oz plus ½ teaspoon sugar	*¼ cup plus ½ teaspoon sugar*
300 ml/½ pint lukewarm water	*1¼ cups lukewarm water*
2 teaspoons dried yeast	*1 package active dry yeast*
500 g/1 lb plain flour	*4 cups all-purpose flour*
2 teaspoons salt	*2 teaspoons salt*
100 g/4 oz lard	*½ cup lard*
1 teaspoon ground mixed spice	*1 teaspoon apple pie spice*

Dissolve the ½ teaspoon sugar in 120 ml/4 fl oz (½ cup) of the water. Sprinkle the yeast on top and leave in a warm place for about 20 minutes or until frothy.

Sift the flour and salt into a bowl. Add the yeast liquid and the remaining water and mix to a dough. Knead until the dough is smooth and elastic, then leave to rise in a warm place until doubled in size.

Knead the dough lightly to knock out any air bubbles, then roll it out to a large oblong. Cut the lard into flakes and dot half of these over the top two-thirds of the dough oblong. Sprinkle with 2 tablespoons of the remaining sugar and ½ teaspoon of the spice. Dredge lightly with flour. Fold up the bottom third over the centre and the top third down over that. Seal the edges with a rolling pin, then turn the dough so that the folds are to the right and left.

Roll out again into an oblong and proceed as before, using up the remaining lard, sugar and spice. Fold and turn, then roll out to an oval about 1 cm/½ inch thick. Transfer to a greased baking sheet and leave in a warm place to rise until light and puffy.

Bake in a preheated hot oven (220°C/425°F, Gas Mark 7) for about 30 minutes. Serve warm.

Cheese Buns

Metric/Imperial
25 g/1 oz sugar
5 tablespoons lukewarm water
2 teaspoons dried yeast
225 g/8 oz plain flour
¼ teaspoon salt
175 g/6 oz butter
1 egg, beaten
double quantity glacé icing (see
    page 42) made with lemon juice
    instead of water
Filling:
500 g/1 lb curd cheese
1 egg, beaten
50 g/2 oz sugar
50 g/2 oz sultanas (optional)

American
2 tablespoons sugar
5 tablespoons lukewarm water
1 package active dry yeast
2 cups all-purpose flour
¼ teaspoon salt
12 tablespoons (1½ sticks) butter
1 egg, beaten
double quantity glacé icing (see
    page 42) made with lemon juice
    instead of water
Filling:
2 cups small-curd cottage cheese
1 egg, beaten
¼ cup sugar
⅓ cup seedless white raisins
    (optional)

Dissolve 1 teaspoon of the sugar in the water. Sprinkle the yeast on top and leave in a warm place for about 20 minutes or until frothy.

Sift the flour and salt into a bowl and stir in the remaining sugar. Rub in 25 g/1 oz (2 tablespoons) of the butter. Make a well in the centre and put in the yeast liquid and egg. Mix to a soft dough, adding more water if necessary. Knead until the dough is smooth and elastic, then roll it out to an oblong.

Cut the remaining butter into small pieces and divide into three portions. Dot one portion over the top two-thirds of the dough oblong, leaving a margin clear all around. Fold the bottom third up and the top third down on top of it. Turn the dough so the folds are to the sides. Repeat this process twice, using the rest of the butter, then chill for 30 minutes.

Beat together the ingredients for the filling until smooth.

Roll out the dough thinly and cut it into 5 cm/2 inch squares. Place a teaspoon of the filling in the centre of each square. Dampen the edges, then fold each corner to the centre. Place on greased baking sheets and leave to rise in a warm place until puffy.

Bake in a preheated very hot oven (230°C/450°F, Gas Mark 8) for 15 minutes. Spread the buns with the glacé icing while they are still warm.

Variations:

Jam Buns: Use jam instead of the cheese filling.

Fruity Buns: Roll out the dough into a square and brush it with melted butter. Mix together sultanas (seedless white raisins) or other dried fruit, sugar and ground cinnamon and sprinkle over the dough. Dampen the edges and roll up tightly like a Swiss (jelly) roll. Cut into slices and place, cut sides down, on greased baking sheets. Rise and bake as above. Coat with glacé icing, then sprinkle with chopped blanched almonds.

Kuchen

Metric/Imperial
100 g/4 oz plus 1 teaspoon sugar
2 tablespoons lukewarm water
4 tablespoons dried yeast
500 g/1 lb plain flour
½ teaspoon salt
100 g/4 oz butter
2 eggs, beaten
50–100 g/2–4 oz sultanas (optional)
Topping:
75 g/3 oz plain flour
50 g/2 oz butter
50 g/2 oz sugar
½ teaspoon ground cinnamon

American
½ cup plus 1 teaspoon sugar
2 tablespoons lukewarm water
2 packages active dry yeast
4 cups all-purpose flour
½ teaspoon salt
8 tablespoons (1 stick) butter
2 eggs, beaten
⅓–⅔ cup seedless white raisins
  (optional)
Topping:
¾ cup all-purpose flour
4 tablespoons butter
¼ cup sugar
½ teaspoon ground cinnamon

Dissolve the 1 teaspoon sugar in the water. Sprinkle the yeast on top and leave in a warm place for about 20 minutes or until frothy.

Sift the flour and salt into a bowl and rub in the butter. Stir in the remaining sugar, then make a well in the centre. Put in the yeast liquid and eggs and beat well to make a stiff dough, adding more water if necessary. Work in the sultanas (raisins), if using. Knead until the dough is smooth and elastic.

Roll out the dough lightly and place in a greased 30 × 23 cm/12 × 9 inch cake pan. Leave to rise in a warm place until doubled in size.

For the topping, sift the flour into a bowl and rub in the butter. Stir in the sugar and cinnamon.

Sprinkle the topping over the dough. Bake in a preheated moderately hot oven (200°C/400°F, Gas Mark 6) for 1 hour.

Traditional Jam Doughnuts

Metric/Imperial
50 g/2 oz plus ½ teaspoon sugar
6 tablespoons lukewarm milk
2 teaspoons dried yeast
225 g/8 oz plain flour
½ teaspoon salt
15 g/½ oz butter
1 egg, beaten
jam
oil for deep frying
½ teaspoon ground cinnamon

American
¼ cup plus ½ teaspoon sugar
6 tablespoons lukewarm milk
1 package active dry yeast
2 cups all-purpose flour
½ teaspoon salt
1 tablespoon butter
1 egg, beaten
jam
oil for deep frying
½ teaspoon ground cinnamon

Dissolve the ½ teaspoon sugar in the milk. Sprinkle the yeast on top and leave in a warm place for about 20 minutes or until frothy.

Sift the flour and salt into a bowl. Rub in the butter, then add the yeast liquid and egg and mix to a soft dough. Knead until the dough is smooth and elastic. Leave to rise in a warm place until doubled in size.

Knead the dough lightly to knock out any air bubbles. Divide the dough into 12 portions and roll into balls. Make a deep depression in each ball with the handle of a wooden spoon, fill with a little jam and pinch the edges around the jam to enclose it completely. Leave in a warm place to rise until the balls are doubled in size.

Deep fry in hot oil for about 4 minutes or until puffed up and golden brown. Drain on paper towels. Mix the remaining sugar with the cinnamon and use to coat the doughnuts.

Makes 12

Rum Babas

Metric/Imperial	American
1 tablespoon plus 1 teaspoon caster sugar	1 tablespoon plus 1 teaspoon sugar
3 tablespoons lukewarm milk	3 tablespoons lukewarm milk
1½ teaspoons dried yeast	1 package active dry yeast
100 g/4 oz strong plain flour	1 cup all-purpose flour
pinch of salt	pinch of salt
2 eggs, beaten	2 eggs, beaten
50 g/2 oz butter, softened	4 tablespoons butter, softened
50 g/2 oz currants	⅓ cup currants
Rum Syrup:	**Rum Syrup:**
2 tablespoons water	2 tablespoons water
2 tablespoons clear honey	2 tablespoons clear honey
1–2 tablespoons rum	1–2 tablespoons rum
Filling:	**Filling:**
150–300 ml/¼–½ pint double cream	⅔–1¼ cups heavy cream
8 glacé cherries	8 candied cherries

Dissolve the 1 teaspoon sugar in the milk and sprinkle over the yeast. Stir in 25 g/1 oz (¼ cup) of the flour. Leave in a warm place for about 20 minutes or until frothy.

Sift the remaining flour and salt together. Stir into the yeast batter with the remaining sugar, the eggs, butter and currants. Beat until smooth.

Divide the batter between 8 greased small ring tins (moulds) or two 600 ml/ 1 pint (2½ cup capacity) ring moulds. The batter should only half fill the tins (moulds). Leave to rise in a warm place until the tins (moulds) are two-thirds full.

Bake in a preheated moderately hot oven (200°C/400°F, Gas Mark 6) for 15 to 20 minutes for small babas, or 25 to 30 minutes for the larger ones, or until well risen and firm to the touch. Turn out onto a wire rack.

Put the water, honey and rum into a saucepan and bring to the boil. Spoon the syrup over the babas while they are still warm, then cool.

Whip the cream until stiff. Pipe a large whirl into the centre of each small baba and top with a cherry. Fill the large babas in a similar way.

Makes 8 small or 2 large babas

Variation:

Orange Savarin: Make up double the quantity of batter as above, omitting the currants. Pour into a greased 20 cm/8 inch ring mould (the dough should half-fill the mould), then rise and bake as above, allowing 20 minutes. Cool, then place the savarin on a serving plate and prick it all over with a skewer. Mix the juice of 2 oranges and 2 tablespoons rum and spoon over the savarin. Whip 150 ml/¼ pint (⅔ cup) whipping cream until thick and fold in 3 peeled and segmented oranges and 100 g/4 oz halved and pipped (seeded) grapes. Pile into the centre of the savarin.

CAKES, PASTRIES AND BREADS

Bread without Yeast

Scones

Metric/Imperial
225 g/8 oz self-raising flour
1 teaspoon baking powder
pinch of salt
50 g/2 oz butter
1 tablespoon caster sugar
150 ml/¼ pint milk

American
2 cups self-rising flour
1 teaspoon baking powder
pinch of salt
4 tablespoons butter
1 tablespoon sugar
⅔ cup milk

Sift the flour, baking powder and salt into a bowl. Rub in the butter, then stir in the sugar. Bind to a soft but not sticky dough with the milk.

Roll out the dough on a floured surface to about 4 cm/1½ inches thick and cut into 5 cm/2 inch rounds. Place the rounds on a greased baking sheet.

Bake in a preheated very hot oven (230°C/450°F, Gas Mark 8) for 8 to 10 minutes or until well risen and golden. Cool on a wire rack and serve warm.
Makes 16–18

Variations:

Strawberry Shortcake: Roll out the dough to 2.5 cm/1 inch thick and cut into six 10 cm/4 inch rounds. Bake in a preheated hot oven (220°C/425°F, Gas Mark 7) for 15 to 20 minutes. Cool to lukewarm, then split open the scones and butter them. Sandwich with sliced strawberries and whipped cream.
Serves 6

Wholemeal (Wholewheat) Scones: Use 100 g/4 oz (1 cup) each self-raising flour and wholemeal (wholewheat) flour and increase the baking powder to 2 teaspoons.

Sultana (Raisin) Scones: Use 350 g/12 oz self-raising flour (3 cups self-rising flour), a pinch of salt (omit the baking powder), 75 g/3 oz (6 tablespoons) butter and 40 g/1½ oz (3 tablespoons) sugar. Stir in 50 g/2 oz sultanas (⅓ cup seedless white raisins), then bind to a soft dough with 1 beaten egg and about 150 ml/¼ pint (⅔ cup) milk. Roll out to a 2 cm/¾ inch square and cut into 14 to 16 triangles. Place on a floured baking sheet and bake in a very hot oven (230°C/450°F, Gas Mark 8) for 12 to 15 minutes or until lightly browned.

Cheese and Onion Scones: Follow the recipe for sultana (raisin) scones above, omitting the sugar and sultanas (raisins) and adding 50 g/2 oz (½ cup) grated Cheddar cheese and 1 to 2 tablespoons finely grated onion to the dry ingredients.

Spiced Treacle (Molasses) Scones: Follow the recipe for basic scones, sifting ¾ teaspoon ground mixed spice (apple pie spice) with the flour and increasing the sugar to 2 tablespoons. Add 1 tablespoon black treacle (molasses) with the milk.

Honey and Walnut Scones: Follow the recipe for basic scones, but omit the baking powder and stir in 25 g/1 oz (¼ cup) chopped walnuts with the sugar. Reduce the milk to 2 to 3 tablespoons and add to the dry ingredients with 1 beaten egg and 1 tablespoon thin honey.

Cream Scones: Sift 225 g/8 oz self-raising flour (2 cups self-rising flour) into a bowl. Mix together 1 egg, 2 tablespoons sugar, 4 tablespoons single (light) cream and 4 tablespoons milk. Add to the flour and mix to a soft dough. Pat out the dough to 2 cm/¾ inch thick and cut into 5 cm/2 inch rounds. Bake as above, allowing 10 to 12 minutes.
Makes 12

Cheese-Topped Scones: Make the scone dough using 350 g/12 oz self-raising flour (3 cups self-rising flour), ½ teaspoon salt, 40 g/1½ oz (3 tablespoons) butter and about 300 ml/½ pint (1¼ cups) milk. Cut into rounds as above and place on a baking sheet. For the topping, melt 75 g/3 oz (6 tablespoons) butter in a saucepan. Cool slightly, then stir in 75 g/3 oz (¾ cup) grated cheese, a pinch each of salt and pepper and ½ teaspoon dry mustard. Place a teaspoon of the topping on each scone, then bake as above, allowing 10 to 15 minutes.
Makes about 15

Date Scones: Follow the recipe for basic scones, but omit the baking powder, increase the sugar to 50 g/2 oz (¼ cup) and add 1 beaten egg with the milk. Work in 175 g/6 oz (1 cup) finely chopped stoned (pitted) dates. Glaze the tops of the scones with milk before baking.

Wholemeal (Wholewheat) Yogurt Scones: Follow the recipe for basic scones, using wholemeal (wholewheat) flour instead of self-raising, increasing the baking powder to 1½ teaspoons and using only 25 g/1 oz (2 tablespoons) butter. Substitute natural (unflavored) yogurt for the milk.

Herb Scones

Metric/Imperial
250 ml/8 fl oz water
65 g/2½ oz butter
175 g/6 oz plain flour, sifted
3 eggs
275 g/10 oz freshly mashed potatoes
salt and black pepper
4 tablespoons chopped mixed fresh
   herbs (chervil, dill, chives and
   parsley)
lard or oil for cooking

American
1 cup water
5 tablespoons butter
1½ cups all-purpose flour, sifted
3 eggs
1¼ cups freshly mashed potatoes
salt and black pepper
¼ cup chopped mixed fresh herbs
   (chervil, dill, chives and parsley)
lard or oil for cooking

Put the water and butter in a saucepan and bring to the boil, stirring to melt the butter. Remove from the heat and stir in the flour to make a thick paste. Beat in the eggs one at a time, then beat in the hot mashed potatoes. Season to taste and stir in the herbs. Cool.

Lightly grease a griddle or heavy frying pan and heat it. Form the herb mixture into flat round cakes and cook them on the griddle or pan until golden brown on both sides. Serve hot.
Makes about 16

Fruited Girdle Scones

Metric/Imperial
225 g/8 oz plain flour
1 teaspoon bicarbonate of soda
2 teaspoons cream of tartar
1 teaspoon salt
25 g/1 oz butter
25 g/1 oz caster sugar
40 g/1½ oz currants
about 150 ml/¼ pint milk
lard or oil for cooking

American
2 cups all-purpose flour
1 teaspoon baking soda
2 teaspoons cream of tartar
1 teaspoon salt
2 tablespoons butter
2 tablespoons sugar
¼ cup currants
about ⅔ cup milk
lard or oil for cooking

Sift the flour, soda, cream of tartar and salt into a bowl. Rub in the butter, then stir in the sugar and currants. Mix to a soft dough with the milk and knead lightly until smooth.

Divide the dough in half and roll out each portion to a round about 5 mm/ ¼ inch thick. Cut each round into six wedges.

Grease a girdle, griddle, hot plate or heavy frying pan with lard or oil and heat. Cook one dough round at a time for about 5 minutes on each side or until well risen and an even golden brown. Serve warm.
Makes 12

Variation:

Welsh Cakes: Make the dough as before using 225 g/8 oz self-raising flour (2 cups self-rising flour), a pinch of salt, 100 g/4 oz (8 tablespoons) butter, 50 g/2 oz (¼ cup) sugar, 50 g/2 oz (⅓ cup) currants, 25 g/1 oz (¼ cup) chopped nuts, 1 beaten egg and 2 tablespoons milk. Roll out and cut into 5 cm/2 inch rounds. Cook as before. **Makes 8–10**

Potato and Onion Cakes: Make the dough as for Welsh cakes above, sifting 1 teaspoon dry mustard with the flour and omitting the sugar, currants and nuts. Add 1 small grated onion, 1 large grated potato, 2 tablespoons chopped parsley and 50 g/2 oz (½ cup) grated Cheddar cheese after rubbing in the butter. Roll out to a 23 cm/9 inch round and cut into 8 wedges. Cook as before. **Makes 8**

Drop Scones (Scotch Pancakes)

Metric/Imperial	American
100 g/4 oz self-raising flour	*1 cup self-rising flour*
pinch of salt	*pinch of salt*
1 tablespoon caster sugar	*1 tablespoon sugar*
1 egg	*1 egg*
150 ml/¼ pint milk	*⅔ cup milk*
lard or oil for cooking	*lard or oil for cooking*

Sift the flour and salt into a bowl and stir in the sugar. Make a well in the centre and put in the egg and half the milk. Gradually draw in the flour to make a smooth mixture, then beat in the remaining milk.

Grease a griddle or large heavy frying pan with a little lard or oil and heat the griddle or pan. Pour on spoonsful of the batter, keeping them well spaced apart, and cook until bubbles rise to the surface. Turn over and cook the other sides until golden brown. Serve warm.

Makes about 16

Variations:

Oat and Treacle (Molasses) Drop Scones: Sift 1 tablespoon baking powder with the flour and salt, then stir in 25 g/1 oz demerara sugar (2½ tablespoons raw brown sugar) and 100 g/4 oz (⅔ cup) fine oatmeal. Melt 50 g/2 oz (4 tablespoons) butter with 2 tablespoons black treacle (molasses) and add to the dry ingredients with the egg and milk. Beat until smooth. Cook as above.

Makes 25–30

Buttermilk Drop Scones: Use plain (all-purpose) flour with ¼ teaspoon bicarbonate of soda (baking soda) instead of the self-raising flour. Substitute buttermilk or soured milk for the milk.

Savoury Drop Scones: Omit the sugar and add 1 small grated onion, 1 teaspoon dry mustard and 50 g/2 oz (½ cup) grated Parmesan cheese to the batter. Cook as above.

Honeyed Banana Scones

Metric/Imperial
100 g/4 oz self-raising flour
100 g/4 oz plain flour
½ teaspoon salt
25 g/1 oz butter
2 bananas, mashed
7–8 tablespoons milk
2 tablespoons honey

American
1 cup self-rising flour
1 cup all-purpose flour
½ teaspoon salt
2 tablespoons butter
2 bananas, mashed
7–8 tablespoons milk
2 tablespoons honey

Sift the flours and salt into a bowl and rub in the butter. Mix together the bananas, milk and honey and add to the dry ingredients. Mix to a soft dough. Pat the dough out to 2 cm/¾ inch thick and cut out 5 cm/2 inch rounds. Place them on a greased baking sheet. Brush with a little milk.
　　Bake in a preheated very hot oven (230°C/450°F, Gas Mark 8) for 12 to 15 minutes.
Makes 12

Ring Doughnuts

Metric/Imperial
350 g/12 oz self-raising flour
1 teaspoon salt
1 teaspoon ground cinnamon
100 g/4 oz butter
50 g/2 oz caster sugar
1 egg, beaten
175 ml/6 fl oz milk
oil for deep frying
sugar for sprinkling

American
3 cups self-rising flour
1 teaspoon salt
1 teaspoon ground cinnamon
8 tablespoons (1 stick) butter
¼ cup sugar
1 egg, beaten
¾ cup milk
oil for deep frying
sugar for sprinkling

Sift the flour, salt and cinnamon into a bowl. Rub in the butter, then stir in the sugar. Bind to a soft but not sticky dough with the egg and milk. Knead until smooth.
　　Roll out the dough to 1 cm/½ inch thick and cut into 5 cm/2 inch rounds. Cut out the centres with a 2.5 cm/1 inch cutter.
　　Deep fry the doughnuts, in batches, for 3 to 4 minutes, turning once. Drain on paper towels and toss in sugar.
Makes about 20

Bran Nut Muffins

Metric/Imperial
75 g/3 oz bran
1 large egg
250 ml/8 fl oz milk
100 g/4 oz self-raising flour, sifted
pinch of salt
50 g/2 oz sugar
25 g/1 oz butter, melted
2–3 tablespoons chopped walnuts or
   pecans

American
1 cup bran
1 egg
1 cup milk
1 cup self-rising flour, sifted
pinch of salt
¼ cup sugar
2 tablespoons butter, melted
2–3 tablespoons chopped walnuts or
   pecans

Mix together the bran, egg and milk and allow to stand for 15 minutes.
   Beat in the flour, salt and sugar, then fold in the butter and nuts. Divide between 12 to 16 greased deep patty or muffin tins.
   Bake in a preheated moderately hot oven (190°C/375°F, Gas Mark 5) for about 20 minutes or until firm. Serve warm or cold.
Makes 12–16

Apple Muffins

Metric/Imperial
225 g/8 oz self-raising flour
pinch of salt
50 g/2 oz brown sugar
½ teaspoon ground cinnamon
2 eggs, beaten
50 g/2 oz butter, melted and cooled
150 ml/¼ pint milk
2 apples, peeled, cored and grated

American
2 cups self-rising flour
pinch of salt
⅓ cup brown sugar
½ teaspoon ground cinnamon
2 eggs, beaten
4 tablespoons butter, melted and
   cooled
⅔ cup milk
2 apples, peeled, cored and grated

Sift the flour, salt, sugar and cinnamon into a bowl. Add the eggs, butter and milk and mix to a smooth batter. Fold in the apples. Pour into 12 greased patty (muffin) tins.
   Bake in a preheated moderately hot oven (190°C/375°F, Gas Mark 5) for 20 to 25 minutes. Serve warm.
Makes 12

Syrup Ginger Buns

Metric/Imperial	American
100 g/4 oz butter	8 tablespoons (1 stick) butter
100 g/4 oz caster sugar	½ cup sugar
175 g/6 oz golden syrup	½ cup light corn syrup
1 egg	1 egg
225 g/8 oz plain flour	2 cups all-purpose flour
½ teaspoon ground mixed spice	½ teaspoon apple pie spice
1 teaspoon ground ginger	1 teaspoon ground ginger
½ teaspoon bicarbonate of soda	½ teaspoon baking soda
150 ml/¼ pint hot water	⅔ cup hot water
1–2 tablespoons finely chopped preserved ginger	1–2 tablespoons finely chopped candied ginger

Cream the butter with the sugar and syrup until pale and fluffy. Gradually beat in the egg. Sift the flour with the spices. Dissolve the soda in the water. Fold the flour mixture into the creamed mixture alternately with the liquid. Fold in the ginger.

Divide the batter between 20 patty tins lined with paper cake cases. Bake in a preheated moderately hot oven (200°C/400°F, Gas Mark 6) for 15 to 20 minutes.

Makes 20

Rock Buns

Metric/Imperial	American
225 g/8 oz self-raising flour	2 cups self-rising flour
pinch of salt	pinch of salt
½ teaspoon mixed spice	½ teaspoon apple pie spice
½ teaspoon grated nutmeg	½ teaspoon grated nutmeg
100 g/4 oz butter	8 tablespoons (1 stick) butter
100 g/4 oz currants	⅔ cup currants
90 g/3½ oz caster sugar	7 tablespoons sugar
1 tablespoon chopped mixed peel	1 tablespoon chopped mixed candied peel
1 egg, beaten	1 egg, beaten
1–2 tablespoons milk	1–2 tablespoons milk

Sift the flour, salt and spices into a bowl. Rub in the butter, then mix in the currants, sugar and peel. Mix to a stiff dough with the egg and milk.

Drop the dough in 10 to 12 mounds on a greased baking sheet, leaving space between them. Bake in a preheated moderately hot oven (200°C/400°F, Gas Mark 6) for 15 to 20 minutes. Cool on a wire rack.

Makes 10–12

Variations:

Mixed Fruit Buns: Use mixed dried fruit instead of just currants.

Vanilla Buns: Omit the spices, currants and mixed candied peel. Add ¼ teaspoon vanilla essence (extract) with the egg and milk. Crush a few sugar lumps and sprinkle them over the buns before baking, as above.

Jam Buns: Make the vanilla buns dough as above and drop in mounds on a baking sheet. Make an indentation in each mound with a floured finger and put in a little jam. Bring the dough around the jam to enclose it. Sprinkle with a little sugar and bake as above.

Orange Buns: Omit the spices, currants and mixed candied peel. Add the grated rind of 2 oranges and a little chopped candied orange peel with the sugar. Bake as above and cool, then dust with icing (confectioners') sugar.

Caramel Fruit Buns

Metric/Imperial	American
140 g/5½ oz butter	11 tablespoons butter
100 g/4 oz soft brown sugar	⅔ cup light brown sugar
50 g/2 oz walnuts, chopped	½ cup chopped walnuts
350 g/12 oz self-raising flour	3 cups self-rising flour
pinch of salt	pinch of salt
50 g/2 oz caster sugar	¼ cup sugar
1 egg	1 egg
150–300 ml/¼–½ pint milk	⅔–1¼ cups milk
100 g/4 oz raisins	⅔ cup raisins

Cream together 100 g/4 oz (8 tablespoons) of the butter and the brown sugar until light and fluffy. Spread half this mixture over the bottom of a greased and lined 23 cm/9 inch square cake pan. Sprinkle over the walnuts.

Sift the flour, salt and sugar into a bowl. Rub in the remaining butter, then add the egg and enough milk to mix to a soft dough. Roll out the dough to a 35 × 23 cm/14 × 9 inch oblong. Spread with the remaining butter and brown sugar mixture and sprinkle with the raisins. Roll up like a Swiss (jelly) roll and cut into 16 slices. Arrange these in the pan, cut sides up.

Bake in a preheated moderately hot oven (190°C/375°F, Gas Mark 5) for 30 to 35 minutes.

Makes 16

ɔda Bread

ric/Imperial	American
ɔɔɔ g/1 lb plain flour	4 cups all-purpose flour
2 teaspoons bicarbonate of soda	2 teaspoons baking soda
2 teaspoons cream of tartar	2 teaspoons cream of tartar
1 teaspoon salt	1 teaspoon salt
50 g/2 oz lard	¼ cup lard
300 ml/½ pint sour milk or fresh milk soured with 1 tablespoon lemon juice	1¼ cups sour milk or fresh milk soured with 1 tablespoon lemon juice

Sift the flour, soda, cream of tartar and salt into a bowl. Rub in the lard, then mix to a soft manageable dough with the milk.

Turn the dough onto a floured surface and shape it into a round about 18 cm/7 inches in diameter. Transfer to a floured baking sheet. Dredge with flour and mark into quarters.

Bake in a hot oven (220°C/ 425°F, Gas Mark 7) for about 30 minutes or until well risen and golden. Cool on a wire rack.

Cheese and Date Bread

Metric/Imperial	American
225 g/8 oz self-raising flour	2 cups self-rising flour
1 teaspoon dry mustard	1 teaspoon dry mustard
salt	salt
pepper	pepper
50 g/2 oz butter	4 tablespoons butter
100 g/4 oz Cheddar or Gruyère cheese, grated	1 cup grated Cheddar or Gruyère cheese
50–75 g/2–3 oz stoned dates, chopped	½ cup chopped pitted dates
2 eggs, beaten	2 eggs, beaten
150 ml/¼ pint milk or buttermilk	⅔ cup milk or buttermilk

Sift the flour, mustard and seasoning to taste into a bowl. Rub in the butter, then mix in the cheese and dates. Bind to a dough with most of the eggs (reserve a little to brush on top of the loaf) and milk or buttermilk. Put into a greased and floured 1 kg/2 lb (9 × 5 × 3 inch) loaf pan, and brush with the reserved egg.

Bake in a preheated moderate oven (180°C/350°F, Gas Mark 4) for 45 to 50 minutes or until quite firm to the touch. Serve warm or cold, sliced with butter.

Variation:
Edam Tea Ring: Make the dough as above, using 225 /8 oz plain flour (2

cups all-purpose flour), 4½ teaspoons baking powder, 1 teaspoon salt, 1 teaspoon paprika, 225 g/8 oz (2 cups) grated Edam cheese, 4 tablespoons chopped sweet pickle (relish), 1 egg and 150 ml/¼ pint (⅔ cup) milk. Divide the dough into 6 portions and shape into rolls. Place on a baking sheet in a ring, leaving a little space between each roll. Brush with milk and sprinkle with a little more grated cheese. Bake in a preheated hot oven (220°C/425°F, Gas Mark 7) for 25 minutes. Cool on a wire rack.
Makes 6

Cottage Cheese Griddlecakes

Metric/Imperial	American
25 g/1 oz butter, melted	2 tablespoons butter, melted
100 g/4 oz cottage cheese	½ cup cottage cheese
2 eggs, beaten	2 eggs, beaten
50 g/2 oz self-raising flour, sifted	½ cup self-rising flour, sifted
1 tablespoon milk	1 tablespoon milk
lard or oil for cooking	lard or oil for cooking

Beat together the butter and cottage cheese, then beat in the eggs. Fold in the flour and milk to make a smooth thick batter.

Grease a girdle, griddle, hot plate or heavy frying pan with lard or oil and heat. Drop tablespoons of the batter onto the girdle and cook for 1 minute or until just set. Turn over and cook the other side for 1 minute. Turn over again and cook until golden. Serve hot.
Makes 10–12

Popovers

Metric/Imperial	American
100 g/4 oz self-raising flour	1 cup self-rising flour
pinch of salt	pinch of salt
2 eggs	2 eggs
250 ml/8 fl oz milk	1 cup milk
2 teaspoons oil or melted butter	2 teaspoons oil or melted butter

Sift the flour and salt into a bowl. Beat in the eggs, then gradually beat in the milk. Add the oil or butter. Divide the batter between 8 to 12 warmed, greased deep patty tins, custard cups or popover pans (they should be only half full).

Bake in a preheated hot oven (220°C/425°F, Gas Mark 7) for about 20 minutes, then reduce the oven temperature to cool (150°C/300°F, Gas Mark 2) and bake for a further 15 to 20 minutes or until crisp and brown. Serve hot.
Makes 8–12

Corn Bread

Metric/Imperial	American
175 g/6 oz cornmeal	1 cup plus 3 tablespoons cornmeal
100 g/4 oz plain flour	1 cup all-purpose flour
2 teaspoons baking powder	2 teaspoons baking powder
1 teaspoon salt	1 teaspoon salt
50 g/2 oz butter, melted and cooled	4 tablespoons butter, melted and
175 ml/6 fl oz milk	cooled
2 eggs, beaten	¾ cup milk
	2 eggs, beaten

Sift the cornmeal, baking powder and salt into a bowl. Mix together the butter, milk and eggs and add to the dry ingredients. Combine thoroughly, then pour into a greased 20 cm/8 inch square cake pan.

Bake in a preheated moderately hot oven (200°C/400°F, Gas Mark 6) for 20 to 25 minutes or until a skewer inserted into the centre of the bread comes out clean. Serve warm, cut into squares.

Quick Brown Bread

Metric/Imperial	American
225 g/8 oz wholemeal flour	2 cups wholewheat flour
225 g/8 oz plain flour	2 cups all-purpose flour
1 teaspoon salt	1 teaspoon salt
1 teaspoon bicarbonate of soda	1 teaspoon baking soda
1 teaspoon cream of tartar	1 teaspoon cream of tartar
150 ml/¼ pint lukewarm milk	⅔ cup lukewarm milk
300 ml/½ pint lukewarm water	1¼ cups lukewarm water
1 tablespoon golden syrup	1 tablespoon light corn syrup
1 teaspoon vinegar	1 teaspoon vinegar

Sift the flours, salt, soda and cream of tartar into a bowl. Mix together the milk, water, syrup and vinegar and gradually stir into the dry ingredients. Pour into a greased 1 kg/2 lb (9 × 5 × 3 inch) loaf pan.

Bake in a preheated moderately hot oven (200°C/400°F, Gas Mark 6) for 20 minutes, then reduce the temperature to moderate (180°C/350°F, Gas Mark 4) and continue baking for 30 minutes.

Quickly Cooked Treats

Coffee Cream Roll

Metric/Imperial
225 g/8 oz plain sweet biscuits,
   crushed
100 g/4 oz icing sugar, sifted
75 g/3 oz ground almonds
150 ml/¼ pint hot black coffee
½ teaspoon vanilla essence
Filling:
300 ml/½ pint whipping cream
40 g/1½ oz icing sugar, sifted
1–2 teaspoons rum

American
2 cups crushed plain sweet cookies
1 cup confectioners' sugar, sifted
¾ cup ground almonds
⅔ cup hot black coffee
½ teaspoon vanilla extract
Filling:
1¼ cups whipping cream
6 tablespoons confectioners' sugar,
   sifted
1–2 teaspoons rum

Mix together the biscuits (cookies), sugar, almonds, coffee and vanilla to make a soft dough. Roll out the dough on a sheet of greaseproof (wax) paper sprinkled with icing (confectioners') sugar to a rectangle about 23 × 30 cm/ 9 × 12 inches.

Whip the cream with the sugar and rum until thick. Spread over the dough rectangle, then roll it up carefully like a Swiss (jelly) roll, using the paper to lift it. Chill until firm.

Biscuit (Cookie) Cake

Metric/Imperial	American
50 g/2 oz butter	4 tablespoons butter
25 g/1 oz sugar	2 tablespoons sugar
1 tablespoon golden syrup	1 tablespoon light corn syrup
1 teaspoon vanilla essence	1 teaspoon vanilla extract
3 tablespoons cocoa powder, sifted	3 tablespoons unsweetened cocoa, sifted
225 g/8 oz digestive biscuits, broken into small pieces	2 cups coarsely crushed graham crackers

Put the butter, sugar and syrup into a saucepan and heat until the butter has melted and the sugar dissolved. Remove from the heat and stir in the vanilla and cocoa, then fold in the biscuits (crackers).

Pour into a greased and lined 15 cm/6 inch round cake pan and smooth the surface level. Chill overnight.

Almond and Strawberry Malakoff

Metric/Imperial	American
18 sponge fingers	18 ladyfingers
grated rind and juice of 2 oranges	grated rind and juice of 2 oranges
2 tablespoons sherry	2 tablespoons sherry
100 g/4 oz butter	8 tablespoons (1 stick) butter
100 g/4 oz soft brown sugar	2/3 cup light brown sugar
225 g/8 oz curd cheese	1 cup small-curd cottage cheese
175 g/6 oz ground almonds	1½ cups ground almonds
350 g/12 oz strawberries, sliced	¾ lb strawberries, sliced

Trim one end off each sponge (lady) finger so they are the same height as a greased and lined 15 × 7 cm/6 × 3 inch round deep cake pan. Reserve the trimmings.

Mix the orange juice with the sherry. Dip the sponge (lady) fingers in the liquid to soften them slightly, then arrange them, rounded ends down, to line the sides of the pan.

Cream the butter with the sugar until light and fluffy. Beat in the cheese, almonds, orange rind and any remaining orange juice mixture. Spread one-third of the almond mixture on the bottom of the pan and cover with a layer of strawberries and sponge (lady) finger trimmings. Continue making layers in this way, ending with the almond mixture, and reserving some of the strawberries for the decoration.

Put a small plate on top of the pan and weight it down. Chill for at least 4 hours or until firm.

Turn out of the pan and decorate with the reserved strawberries.

Cheese Chocolate Triangle

Metric/Imperial
100 g/4 oz butter
100 g/4 oz sugar
500 g/1 lb curd cheese
grated rind of ¼ lemon
1 egg, beaten
few drops of vanilla essence
36 plain sweet oblong biscuits
milk

Icing:
100 g/4 oz sugar
3 tablespoons cocoa powder
2 tablespoons water
1 teaspoon strong black coffee
75 g/3 oz butter, cut into pieces

American
8 tablespoons (1 stick) butter
½ cup sugar
2 cups small-curd cottage cheese
grated rind of ¼ lemon
1 egg, beaten
few drops of vanilla extract
36 plain sweet oblong cookies
milk

Frosting:
½ cup sugar
3 tablespoons unsweetened cocoa
2 tablespoons water
1 teaspoon strong black coffee
6 tablespoons butter, cut into pieces

Cream the butter with the sugar until light and fluffy. Beat in the cheese, lemon rind, egg and vanilla. Dip the biscuits (cookies) in milk, then arrange four rows of three biscuits (cookies) each on a sheet of foil. Spread with a layer of the cheese mixture. Repeat these layers twice more, then cover with the remaining cheese mixture, piling it up in the centre. Put your hands under the foil and bring the outer row of biscuits (cookies) to meet in the centre, forming a triangle. Chill.

For the icing, put the sugar, cocoa, water and coffee in a saucepan and bring to the boil, stirring to dissolve the sugar. Boil until thick. Remove from the heat and stir in the butter a piece at a time. Beat well. Cool, then pour over the cake and leave to set overnight in the refrigerator.

Nutty Fruit Chews

Metric/Imperial
500 g/1 lb mixed dried fruit (raisins,
    figs, dates, prunes and apricots)
100 g/4 oz mixed nuts, chopped
100 g/4 oz clear honey

American
3 cups mixed dried fruit (raisins, figs,
    dates, prunes and apricots)
1 cup chopped mixed nuts
⅓ cup clear honey

Put the fruit in a bowl and pour over boiling water to cover. Leave for 5 minutes, then drain. Mince (grind) the fruit, then stir in the nuts and honey.

Press into a foil-lined 20 cm/8 inch square cake pan. Cover with more foil and weight down. Chill for 12 hours.

Cut into squares to serve.
Makes 16

Chocolate Oat Chews

Metric/Imperial	American
50 g/2 oz caster sugar	¼ cup sugar
2 tablespoons golden syrup	2 tablespoons light corn syrup
75 g/3 oz butter	6 tablespoons butter
225 g/8 oz quick-cook oats	1⅓ cups quick-cook oatmeal flakes
3 tablespoons cocoa powder	3 tablespoons unsweetened cocoa
1 teaspoon vanilla or rum essence	1 teaspoon vanilla or rum extract
25 g/1 oz walnuts, chopped	¼ cup chopped walnuts
50 g/2 oz raisins, chopped	⅓ cup chopped raisins

Put the sugar, syrup and butter in a saucepan and heat until the sugar has dissolved and the butter melted. Bring to the boil. Remove from the heat and stir in the remaining ingredients.

Spread out in a greased 20 cm/8 inch square cake pan. Chill until set, then cut into 5 cm/2 inch squares.
Makes 16

Biscotten Torte

Metric/Imperial	American
100 g/4 oz butter	8 tablespoons (1 stick) butter
100 g/4 oz caster sugar	½ cup sugar
2 eggs, separated	2 eggs, separated
100 g/4 oz ground almonds	1 cup ground almonds
few drops of almond essence	few drops of almond extract
300 ml/½ pint milk	1¼ cups milk
1½ tablespoons rum	1½ tablespoons rum
350 g/12 oz (about 24) plain sweet oblong biscuits	¾ lb (about 24) plain sweet oblong cookies
300 ml/½ pint whipping cream	1¼ cups whipping cream
toasted flaked almonds	toasted slivered almonds

Cream the butter with the sugar until light and fluffy. Beat in the egg yolks, then fold in the ground almonds, almond essence (extract) and half the milk. Beat the egg whites until stiff and fold into the creamed mixture.

Mix together the remaining milk and the rum. Arrange six of the biscuits (cookies) lengthways in two rows (three to a row) beside each other on a sheet of greaseproof (wax) paper. Brush liberally with the rum and milk mixture, then spread over one-third of the creamed mixture. Continue making layers in this way, ending with biscuits (cookies). Wrap in foil and chill overnight.

The next day, place on a serving plate. Whip the cream until thick and spread all over the cake to cover it completely. Decorate with almonds.

Chocolate Cherry Slice

Metric/Imperial

100 g/4 oz unsalted butter
3 tablespoons golden syrup
350 g/12 oz digestive biscuits,
  crushed
50 g/2 oz sultanas
50 g/2 oz glacé cherries, quartered
100 g/4 oz plain chocolate, chopped
50–100 g/2–4 oz blanched almonds,
  chopped (optional)

Icing:

50 g/2 oz plain chocolate, chopped
1½ tablespoons water
25 g/1 oz butter
175 g/6 oz icing sugar, sifted

To decorate:

5–6 glacé cherries, halved
candied angelica leaves
50 g/2 oz blanched almonds,
  chopped

American

8 tablespoons sweet butter
3 tablespoons light corn syrup
3 cups crushed plain sweet cookies
⅓ cup seedless white raisins
⅓ cup quartered candied cherries
¼ lb dark sweet chocolate, chopped
½–1 cup chopped blanched almonds
  (optional)

Frosting:

2 oz dark sweet chocolate, chopped
1½ tablespoons water
2 tablespoons butter
1½ cups confectioners' sugar, sifted

To decorate:

5–6 candied cherries, halved
candied angelica leaves
½ cup chopped blanched almonds

Melt the butter with the syrup in a saucepan. Remove from the heat and stir in the biscuit (cookie) crumbs, sultanas (raisins), cherries, chocolate and nuts, if used. Return to the heat and cook gently, stirring, until the chocolate melts. Pour into a 28 × 18 cm/11 × 7 inch Swiss (jelly) roll tin lined with greased greaseproof (wax) paper. Spread out evenly, then chill for 3 hours or until set.

Cut the cake crossways into three equal slices.

For the icing, melt the chocolate gently with the water and butter. Gradually beat in the sugar. Use about two-thirds of the icing to sandwich together the cake slices, then spread the remainder over the top and mark it with a fork to make a decorative design. Decorate with the cherries, angelica and nuts.

Chocolate Rum Cream Pie

Metric/Imperial
225 g/8 oz plain sweet biscuits,
  crushed
½ teaspoon grated nutmeg
100 g/4 oz butter, melted
Filling:
1 tablespoon gelatine
4 tablespoons milk
100 g/4 oz sugar
3 tablespoons cornflour
550 ml/18 fl oz hot milk
4 eggs, separated
100 g/4 oz plain chocolate, chopped
3 tablespoons rum
150 ml/¼ pint whipping cream
grated chocolate to decorate

American
2 cups crushed plain sweet cookies
½ teaspoon grated nutmeg
8 tablespoons (1 stick) butter
Filling:
1½ envelopes unflavored gelatin
4 tablespoons milk
½ cup sugar
3 tablespoons cornstarch
2¼ cups hot milk
4 eggs, separated
4 squares dark sweet chocolate,
  chopped
3 tablespoons rum
⅔ cup whipping cream
grated chocolate to decorate

Mix together the biscuit (cookie) crumbs, nutmeg and butter and press onto the bottom and sides of a greased 18 cm/7 inch flan ring on a baking sheet or a pie pan.

For the filling, dissolve the gelatine in the 4 tablespoons of milk. Mix the sugar with the cornflour (cornstarch) and stir in the hot milk. Beat in the egg yolks. Pour the mixture into a saucepan and cook gently, stirring, until the custard thickens. Stir in the gelatine, chocolate and rum until the chocolate melts. Cool. Beat the egg whites until stiff and fold into the chocolate mixture.

Pour into the crumb crust and chill until set. Whip the cream until thick, sweeten to taste and then spread over the filling. Decorate with grated chocolate.

Continental Chocolate Squares

Metric/Imperial
100 g/4 oz butter
100 g/4 oz sugar
3 tablespoons cocoa powder
1 egg
1 teaspoon vanilla essence
225 g/8 oz wheatmeal biscuits,
   crushed
75 g/3 oz desiccated coconut
75 g/3 oz walnuts, chopped
Topping:
50 g/2 oz butter
275 g/10 oz icing sugar
2 tablespoons custard powder
4 tablespoons hot water
100 g/4 oz plain chocolate

American
8 tablespoons (1 stick) butter
½ cup sugar
3 tablespoons unsweetened cocoa
1 egg
1 teaspoon vanilla extract
2 cups crushed graham crackers
1 cup shredded coconut
¾ cup chopped walnuts
Topping:
4 tablespoons butter
2½ cups confectioners' sugar
2 tablespoons custard powder
¼ cup hot water
¼ lb dark sweet chocolate

Put the butter, sugar and cocoa in a saucepan and cook gently, stirring, until the butter melts and the sugar dissolves. Stir in the egg and vanilla and cook for 1 minute longer. Remove from the heat and mix in the biscuit (cookie) crumbs, coconut and walnuts. Press into a greased 28 × 18 cm/11 × 7 inch cake pan. For the topping, cream the butter. Sift over the sugar and custard powder and beat in well with the water. When the mixture is light and fluffy, spread it over the crumb base. Chill until set. Melt the chocolate gently and spread it over the topping. Chill until set. Cut into small squares to serve.
Makes about 24

Variations:

Chocolate Peppermint Squares: Make the biscuit (cracker) mixture as above and press into a greased 33 × 25 cm/13 × 10 inch cake pan. Chill until set. For the filling, mix 150 g/5 oz sifted icing sugar (1¼ cups sifted confectioners' sugar) with 25 g/1 oz (2 tablespoons) melted butter, 3 tablespoons milk and ½ teaspoon peppermint essence (mint flavoring). Spread over the biscuit (cracker) base and chill until firm. Melt 175 g/6 oz plain (dark sweet) chocolate with 25 g/1 oz (2 tablespoons) butter and spread over the filling. Chill until set, then cut into small squares. **Makes about 36**
Chocolate Fruit Squares: Mix together 100 g/4 oz drinking chocolate (1 cup hot chocolate powder), 100 g/4 oz desiccated coconut (1¼ cups shredded coconut), 50 g/2 oz sultanas (⅓ cup seedless white raisins), 50 g/2 oz (½ cup) crushed cornflakes, 40 g/1½ oz (⅓ cup) chopped walnuts, 1 teaspoon sherry or fruit juice, 2 tablespoons crushed sweet biscuits (cookies) and 4 tablespoons condensed milk. Press into a greased 18 cm/7 inch square cake pan. Melt 75 g/3 oz plain (dark sweet) chocolate and spread over the mixture in the pan. Mark with a fork, then chill until set. Cut into small squares to serve. **Makes about 18**

Chocolate Caramel Crisps

Metric/Imperial
225 g/8 oz plain chocolate
100 g/4 oz butter
100 g/4 oz sugar
100 g/4 oz stoned dates, chopped
225 g/8 oz Rice Krispies

American
½ lb dark sweet chocolate
8 tablespoons (1 stick) butter
½ cup sugar
⅔ cup chopped pitted dates
2 cups Rice Krispies

Melt the chocolate gently, then spread half of it over the bottom of a greased 28 × 18 cm/11 × 7 inch cake pan. Chill until set.

Put the butter, sugar and dates in another saucepan and cook gently, stirring, until the dates are soft. Stir in the cereal to make a firm but spreadable mixture. Spread over the chocolate base in the pan.

Warm the remaining chocolate, then spread it over the cereal mixture. Chill until set. Cut into small squares to serve.

Makes about 24

Chocolate Quickies

Metric/Imperial
100 g/4 oz butter
2 tablespoons cocoa powder
1 tablespoon demerara sugar
2 tablespoons golden syrup
225 g/8 oz semi-sweet biscuits, crushed
100 g/4 oz plain or milk chocolate, broken up

American
8 tablespoons (1 stick) butter
2 tablespoons unsweetened cocoa
1 tablespoon raw brown sugar
2 tablespoons light corn syrup
2 cups crushed plain semi-sweet cookies
¼ lb dark or milk chocolate, broken up

Melt the butter in a saucepan and stir in the cocoa, sugar and syrup. Bring to the boil and boil for 1 minute. Remove from the heat and stir in the biscuit (cookie) crumbs. Pour into a greased 18 cm/7 inch square cake pan and press out evenly.

Melt the chocolate gently and pour over the biscuit (cookie) mixture. As the chocolate sets, mark it into swirls with a knife. Chill until set, then cut into squares or bars.

Makes 12–16

Date and Nut Fingers

Metric/Imperial
225 g/8 oz sweet biscuits, crushed
grated rind of 1 lemon
1 tablespoon lemon juice
100 g/4 oz nuts, chopped
100 g/4 oz stoned dates, chopped
about 150 ml/¼ pint sweetened
    condensed milk
sifted icing sugar

American
2 cups crushed plain sweet cookies
grated rind of 1 lemon
1 tablespoon lemon juice
1 cup chopped nuts
⅔ cup chopped pitted dates
about ⅔ cup sweetened condensed
    milk
sifted confectioners' sugar

Mix together the biscuits (cookies), lemon rind and juice, nuts and dates, then bind with the condensed milk. Coat a 20 cm/8 inch sandwich tin (layer cake pan) with icing (confectioners') sugar and put in the date mixture. Spread it out evenly and sprinkle with more icing (confectioners') sugar. Chill until set, then cut into fingers.

Lemon Cream Pie

Metric/Imperial
225 g/8 oz plain sweet biscuits,
    crushed
½ teaspoon grated nutmeg
100 g/4 oz butter, melted
Filling:
1 teaspoon gelatine
4 tablespoons water
175 g/6 oz lemon curd
300 ml/¼ pint whipping cream

American
2 cups crushed plain sweet cookies
½ teaspoon grated nutmeg
8 tablespoons (1 stick) butter
Filling:
1 envelope unflavored gelatin
¼ cup water
½ cup lemon curd or cheese
1¼ cups whipping cream

Mix together the biscuit (cookie) crumbs, nutmeg and butter and press onto the bottom and sides of a greased 18 cm/7 inch flan ring on a baking sheet or a pie pan.
   Dissolve the gelatine in the water, then stir in the lemon curd (or cheese). Whip the cream until thick and fold into the lemon mixture. Pour into the crumb crust and chill until the filling is set.

Grape Meringue Flan

Metric/Imperial
50 g/2 oz butter
75 g/3 oz soft brown sugar
75 g/3 oz demerara sugar
8 tablespoons golden syrup
225 g/8 oz bran buds

Filling:
225 g/8 oz white grapes, halved and pipped
50–100 g/2–4 oz black grapes, halved and pipped
4 tablespoons apricot jam
3 tablespoons water
10–12 small meringues, bought or homemade (see page 34)

American
4 tablespoons butter
½ cup light brown sugar
½ cup raw brown sugar
½ cup light corn syrup
2 cups bran buds

Filling:
½ lb green grapes, halved and seeded
about ¼ lb purple grapes, halved and seeded
¼ cup apricot jam
3 tablespoons water
10–12 small meringues, bought or homemade (see page 34)

Melt the butter with the sugars and syrup in a saucepan. Remove from the heat and stir in the bran buds. Press into a 20 cm/8 inch flan ring on a serving plate or a tart pan. Chill until set.

Arrange the grapes in the flan case. Melt the jam with the water, then sieve (strain) it. Brush the grapes with the warm jam glaze and leave to cool. Arrange the meringues around the top edge and serve with cream.

Variations:

Use crushed digestive biscuits (graham crackers) instead of the bran buds, or use another cereal such as cornflakes.
Substitute other fresh fruit for the grapes.

Sponge (Lady) Finger Gâteau

Metric/Imperial
about 30 sponge fingers
600 ml/1 pint double cream
sugar to taste
750 g–1 kg/1½–2 lb fresh fruit, sliced or chopped, etc.

American
about 30 ladyfingers
2½ cups heavy cream
sugar to taste
1½–2 lb fresh fruit, sliced or chopped, etc.

Make a layer of about one-third of the sponge (lady) fingers on a serving plate. Whip the cream with sugar to taste and spread about one-third of it over the fingers. Add a layer of fruit. Make two more layers on top in the same way – sponge (lady) fingers, cream and fruit. Leave for 1 to 2 hours before serving.

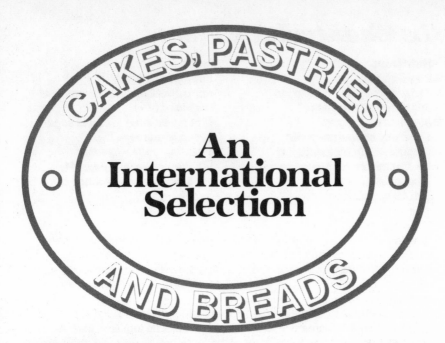

Nougatines

Metric/Imperial
1 × 20 cm/8 inch whisked sponge
 cake (see page 7)
½ quantity coffee-flavoured
 buttercream (see page 41)
toasted flaked almonds
Praline:
225 g/8 oz sugar
6 tablespoons water
225 g/8 oz unblanched almonds,
 chopped

American
1 × 8 inch whisked sponge cake
 (see page 7)
½ quantity coffee-flavored
 buttercream (see page 41)
toasted slivered almonds
Praline:
1 cup sugar
6 tablespoons water
2 cups chopped unblanched
 almonds

Cut the cake into wedges and trim the corners to give a smooth outer edge.
 For the praline, dissolve the sugar in the water, then bring to the boil and boil until the syrup turns golden brown. Stir in the almonds and cool slightly, then spread about two-thirds of the praline over the flat sides of the cake wedges. Pour the rest of the praline onto an oiled board and cool until set. Crush with a rolling pin to a fine powder.
 Beat the crushed praline into the buttercream and use to cover the exposed cake. Coat with the toasted almonds.
Makes about 8

Le Chantecler

Metric/Imperial
8 egg whites
115 g/4½ oz ground almonds
200 g/7 oz caster sugar
25 g/1 oz plain flour
1 quantity coffee-flavoured
  buttercream (see page 41)
1 × 23 cm/9 inch whisked sponge
  cake (see page 7)
rum for sprinkling

American
8 egg whites
1 cup plus 2 tablespoons ground
  almonds
¾ cup plus 2 tablespoons sugar
¼ cup all-purpose flour
1 quantity coffee-flavored
  buttercream (see page 41)
1 × 9 inch whisked sponge cake
  (see page 7)
rum for sprinkling

Beat the egg whites until stiff, then fold in the ground almonds, sugar and flour. Divide the mixture between two greased and floured 23 cm/9 inch sandwich tins (layer cake pans) and spread out evenly. Bake in a preheated cool oven (150°C/300°F, Gas Mark 2) for 30 minutes. Cool the macaroon layers on a wire rack.

Place one macaroon layer on a serving plate and spread with about one-quarter of the buttercream. Place the sponge cake on top, sprinkle it with rum and cover with another quarter of the buttercream. Top with the second macaroon layer and spread the rest of the buttercream over the top and sides. Chill before serving.

Tuiles aux Amandes

Metric/Imperial
100 g/4 oz butter, softened
225 g/8 oz caster sugar
100 g/4 oz plain flour, sifted
4 egg whites
75 g/3 oz flaked almonds

American
8 tablespoons (1 stick) butter,
  softened
1 cup sugar
1 cup all-purpose flour, sifted
4 egg whites
¾ cup slivered almonds

Beat together the butter, sugar, flour and egg whites until the mixture is smooth. Put large spoonsful of the mixture on greased baking sheets, shaping them into ovals about 18 cm/7 inches long. Sprinkle with the almonds.

Bake in a preheated moderately hot oven (190°C/375°F, Gas Mark 5) for 5 minutes or until golden brown.

Lift the tuiles, one at a time, off the baking sheet and drape over a rolling pin to cool.
Makes about 16

Beignets aux Cerises

Metric/Imperial
500 g/1 lb black or Morello cherries,
   stoned
150 ml/¼ pint water
50–100 g/2–4 oz sugar
1 teaspoon arrowroot
3–4 tablespoons cherry brandy
1 quantity choux pastry (see page
   104)
oil for deep frying

American
1 lb bing or Morello cherries, pitted
⅔ cup water
¼–½ cup sugar
1 teaspoon arrowroot
3–4 tablespoons cherry brandy
1 quantity choux pastry (see page
   104)
oil for deep frying

Put the cherries, water and sugar in a saucepan and simmer for about 5 minutes. Dissolve the arrowroot in the cherry brandy and add to the pan. Simmer, stirring, until thickened. Remove from the heat and keep hot.

Drop spoonsful of the choux pastry into oil heated to 185°C/365°F and deep fry until golden brown. Drain on paper towels and keep hot.

When all the beignets have been fried, pile them up on a serving plate and pour over the hot cherry sauce.

Serves 6–8

Variation:

Beignets à la Confiture: Serve the beignets with a sauce made by heating 225 g/8 oz (⅔ cup) jam.

Nicciollette

Metric/Imperial
100 g/4 oz butter
40 g/1½ oz icing sugar, sifted
1½ tablespoons honey
100 g/4 oz plain flour, sifted
75 g/3 oz toasted ground hazelnuts
sifted icing sugar to dredge

American
8 tablespoons (1 stick) butter
6 tablespoons confectioners' sugar,
   sifted
1½ tablespoons honey
1 cup all-purpose flour, sifted
¾ cup toasted ground hazelnuts
sifted confectioners' sugar to dredge

Cream the butter with the sugar and honey until light and fluffy. Fold in the flour and nuts to make a smooth dough. Divide the dough into walnut-sized pieces and shape them into ovals. Arrange on greased baking sheets, well spaced apart.

Bake in a preheated moderate oven (180°/350°F, Gas Mark 4) for about 15 minutes or until firm. Cool slightly, then coat with icing (confectioners') sugar.

Makes about 24

Galette Perougienne

Metric/Imperial	American
25 g/1 oz fresh yeast	1 cake compressed yeast
4–6 tablespoons lukewarm water	4–6 tablespoons lukewarm water
350 g/12 oz plain flour	3 cups all-purpose flour
1 teaspoon salt	1 teaspoon salt
grated rind of 1 lemon	grated rind of 1 lemon
25 g/1 oz caster sugar	2 tablespoons sugar
2 eggs, beaten	2 eggs, beaten
200 g/7 oz butter, softened	14 tablespoons butter, softened
Topping:	**Topping:**
40 g/1½ oz sugar	3 tablespoons sugar
75 g/3 oz butter, cut into pieces	6 tablespoons butter, cut into pieces

Mix the yeast with 3 tablespoons of the water. Sift the flour and salt into a bowl and stir in the lemon rind and sugar. Make a well in the centre and put in the yeast mixture, the eggs and the butter. Work the ingredients together to make a smooth, pliable dough, adding more of the remaining water if necessary. Cover and leave to rise in a warm place for 1 hour.

Knead the dough lightly, then roll it out to a large round about 60 cm/24 inches in diameter, or into two smaller rounds. Place on a greased baking sheet. Sprinkle with the sugar and dot with the butter.

Bake in a preheated very hot oven (230°C/450°F, Gas Mark 8) for 8 minutes or until risen and the top is golden brown. Serve hot.**Serves 6–8**
Note: dried yeast may be substituted for fresh – use 4 teaspoons dried yeast (2 packages active dry yeast) and follow the package instructions for dissolving it.

Eier Kichlach

Metric/Imperial	American
3 eggs	3 eggs
4 tablespoons oil	¼ cup oil
25 g/1 oz sugar	2 tablespoons sugar
¼ teaspoon salt	¼ teaspoon salt
100 g/4 oz plain flour, sifted	1 cup all-purpose flour, sifted

Beat the eggs with the oil, then beat in the sugar, salt and flour. Drop teaspoons of the mixture onto greased baking sheets, well spaced apart.

Bake in a preheated moderate oven (160°C/325°F, Gas Mark 3) for 15 to 20 minutes or until brown and puffy.

Kouign-Amann

Metric/Imperial
175 g/6 oz plain flour
½ teaspoon salt
15 g/½ oz fresh yeast
150 ml/¼ pint lukewarm water
100 g/4 oz butter, softened
100 g/4 oz sugar
milk to glaze

American
1½ cups all-purpose flour
½ teaspoon salt
½ cake compressed yeast
⅔ cup lukewarm water
8 tablespoons (1 stick) butter,
   softened
½ cup sugar
milk to glaze

Sift 100 g/4 oz (1 cup) of the flour and the salt onto a working surface. Mix the yeast with 2 tablespoons of the water. Make a well in the centre of the flour and put in the yeast mixture. Gradually add the remaining water, drawing in the flour to make a very sticky dough. Knead until the dough becomes elastic. Slowly incorporate the remaining flour to make a smooth, manageable dough.

Press out the dough to a rectangle about 2.5 cm/1 inch thick. Spread with the butter, then sprinkle over the sugar. Fold the dough into three, give it a quarter turn and press the edges together to seal. Roll out to a rectangle again. Repeat the folding and rolling three times more.

Press the dough into a greased shallow 18 cm/7 inch cake pan. Brush with milk and mark a criss-cross pattern over the top with a sharp knife. Leave to rise in a warm place for 20 minutes.

Bake in a preheated moderately hot oven (200°C/400°F, Gas Mark 6) for 30 minutes or until well risen and golden brown. Serve warm.

Pinoccate

Metric/Imperial
75 g/3 oz ground almonds
200 g/7 oz caster sugar
few drops of vanilla essence
2 egg whites
pinch of salt
100 g/4 oz pine nuts

American
¾ cup ground almonds
¾ cup plus 2 tablespoons sugar
few drops of vanilla extract
2 egg whites
pinch of salt
1 cup pine nuts

Pound the almonds with half the sugar to a fine powder using a pestle and mortar, or blend for about 1 minute. Stir in the vanilla.

Beat the egg whites with the salt until stiff, then gradually beat in the remaining sugar. Fold into the almond mixture.

Spread out the pine nuts on a sheet of greaseproof (wax) paper. Drop teaspoons of the almond mixture onto the nuts and roll them gently to coat with the nuts. Place on greased and floured baking sheets well spaced apart.

Bake in a preheated moderately hot oven (200°C/400°F, Gas Mark 6) for about 10 minutes or until golden.
Makes 20–24

Danish Cream Cheese and Strawberry Flan

Metric/Imperial
150 g/5 oz plain flour
pinch of salt
75 g/3 oz butter
50 g/2 oz caster sugar
1 egg yolk
Filling:
1 × 75 g/3 oz packet cream cheese
2 tablespoons single cream
350 g/12 oz strawberries, hulled
3 tablespoons redcurrant jelly,
  melted

American
1¼ cups all-purpose flour
pinch of salt
6 tablespoons butter
¼ cup sugar
1 egg yolk
Filling:
1 × 3 oz package cream cheese
2 tablespoons light cream
¾ lb strawberries, hulled
3 tablespoons redcurrant jelly,
  melted

Sift the flour and salt into a bowl. Rub in the butter, then mix in the sugar and egg yolk to form a paste. Press the paste into a 20 cm/8 inch flan ring on a baking sheet or a tart pan. Bake blind (unfilled) in a preheated moderately hot oven (200°C/400°F, Gas Mark 6) for about 20 minutes or until the pastry is golden brown. Cool. Beat the cream cheese with the cream until smooth. Spread this mixture over the bottom of the pastry shell. Arrange the strawberries on top. Brush the redcurrant jelly glaze over the fruit.

Cassata alla Siciliana

Metric/Imperial

4 eggs, separated
150 g/5 oz caster sugar
grated rind of ½ lemon
75 g/3 oz plain flour
25 g/1 oz cornflour
2 tablespoons warm water

Filling and Icing:

750 g/1½ lb ricotta or curd cheese
175 g/6 oz caster sugar
5–6 tablespoons orange liqueur
50 g/2 oz plain chocolate, finely
  chopped
75 g/3 oz chopped mixed peel

To decorate:

glacé fruits
strips of candied peel
coarsely grated chocolate

American

4 eggs, separated
⅔ cup sugar
grated rind of ½ lemon
¾ cup all-purpose flour
¼ cup cornstarch
2 tablespoons warm water

Filling and Frosting:

3 cups ricotta or small-curd cottage
  cheese
¾ cup sugar
5–6 tablespoons orange liqueur
¼ cup finely chopped dark sweet
  chocolate
½ cup chopped mixed candied peel

To decorate:

candied fruits
strips of candied peel
coarsely grated chocolate

Beat the egg yolks, sugar and lemon rind together until pale and fluffy. Sift the flour with the cornflour (cornstarch) and fold into the egg yolk mixture, followed by the water. Beat the egg whites until stiff and fold in. Pour into a greased and floured 1.75 l/3 pint (7½ cup capacity) springform pan.

Bake in a preheated moderate oven (180°C/350°F, Gas Mark 4) for 45 to 50 minutes or until firm to the touch. Cool on a wire rack.

For the filling, sieve (strain) the cheese, then beat in the sugar and 2 tablespoons of the liqueur. Chill half the mixture; add the chocolate and peel to the remainder.

Cut the cake into three layers. Sprinkle the bottom two layers with the remaining liqueur, then sandwich together the three layers with the chocolate cheese mixture. Press the cake together and chill.

About 1 hour before serving, spread the chilled plain cheese mixture over the top and sides of the cake. Decorate with the fruits, peel and chocolate.

Brazo de Gitano

Metric/Imperial
4 eggs
100 g/4 oz caster sugar
100 g/4 oz self-raising flour, sifted
pinch of salt
sifted icing sugar
Filling:
150 ml/¼ pint milk
1 vanilla pod
2 tablespoons rum or strong black
  coffee
2 egg yolks
50 g/2 oz caster sugar
2 tablespoons cornflour

American
4 eggs
½ cup sugar
1 cup self-rising flour, sifted
pinch of salt
sifted confectioners' sugar
Filling:
⅔ cup milk
1 vanilla bean
2 tablespoons rum or strong black
  coffee
2 egg yolks
¼ cup sugar
2 tablespoons cornstarch

Beat the eggs and sugar together until the mixture is pale and very thick and
will make a ribbon trail on itself when the beater is lifted. Sift over the flour
and salt and fold in gently. Pour into a greased and floured 36 × 25 cm/
14 × 10 inch Swiss (jelly) roll pan, tilting the pan to spread out the mixture.
Bake in a preheated moderately hot oven (200°C/400°F, Gas Mark 6) for 12
to 15 minutes or until golden and springy to the touch.

    Turn out the cake onto a sugared sheet of greaseproof (wax) paper and
cover with another sheet of paper. Roll up while still warm, with the paper
inside, and cool.

    For the filling, put the milk into a saucepan with the vanilla and rum or
coffee. Bring slowly to the boil, then remove from the heat and cool.

    Beat together the egg yolks, sugar and cornflour (cornstarch). Remove the
vanilla pod (bean) from the milk, then stir in the egg yolk mixture. Cook
gently, stirring, for 5 minutes or until thick and smooth. Cool.

    Unroll the cake, remove the paper and spread with the filling. Roll up again
very carefully. Wrap in foil and chill before serving, dusted with icing
(confectioners') sugar.

Torta à la Gallega

Metric/Imperial
100 g/4 oz plain flour
1 teaspoon baking powder
100 g/4 oz sugar
5 tablespoons olive oil
3 tablespoons milk
2 eggs, separated
grated rind and juice of 1 lemon

American
1 cup all-purpose flour
1 teaspoon baking powder
½ cup sugar
5 tablespoons olive oil
3 tablespoons milk
2 eggs, separated
grated rind and juice of 1 lemon

Sift the flour and baking powder into a bowl and stir in the sugar. Add the oil, milk, egg yolks and lemon rind and juice and mix well.

Beat the egg whites until stiff and fold into the lemon mixture. Spoon into a greased 500 g/1 lb (4½ × 2½ × 1½ inch) loaf pan. Bake in a preheated moderate oven (180°C/350°F, Gas Mark 4) for about 45 minutes. Cool on a wire rack.

Lebskuchen

Metric/Imperial
2 eggs
50 g/2 oz granulated sugar
100 g/4 oz brown sugar
2 tablespoons grated plain chocolate
1 tablespoon honey
grated rind of ½ lemon
grated rind of ½ orange
few drops of vanilla essence
25 g/1 oz nuts, chopped
100 g/4 oz plain flour
½ teaspoon baking powder
½ teaspoon ground mixed spice
1 quantity glacé icing (see page 42)

American
2 eggs
¼ cup granulated sugar
⅔ cup brown sugar
2 tablespoons grated dark sweet
 chocolate
1 tablespoon honey
grated rind of ½ lemon
grated rind of ½ orange
few drops of vanilla extract
¼ cup chopped nuts
1 cup all-purpose flour
½ teaspoon baking powder
½ teaspoon ground allspice
1 quantity glacé icing (see page 42)

Beat the eggs with the sugars until thick. Beat in the chocolate, honey, grated fruit rinds, vanilla and nuts. Sift the flour with the baking powder and spice and fold into the egg mixture. Spread out in a greased 30 × 23 cm/ 12 × 9 inch cake pan.

Bake in a preheated moderate oven (180°C/350°F, Gas Mark 4) for 30 minutes. Spread with glacé icing while still warm and cut into squares when cold.

Chinese Sesame Seed Biscuits (Crackers)

Metric/Imperial
225 g/8 oz self-raising flour, sifted
25 g/1 oz sugar
2 tablespoons sesame seeds
1 tablespoon lard
4 tablespoons water
oil for deep frying

American
2 cups self-rising flour, sifted
2 tablespoons sugar
2 tablespoons sesame seeds
1 tablespoon lard
¼ cup water
oil for deep frying

Mix together the flour, sugar and sesame seeds and rub in the lard. Mix to a soft dough with the water. Roll out the dough to 3 mm/⅛ inch thick and cut into 2 × 5 cm/¾ × 2 inch rectangles. Make a slit in the centre of each rectangle and bring one end of the rectangle through the slit to form a twist.

Heat the oil to 160°C/325°F. Deep fry the biscuits (crackers) until golden brown. Drain on paper towels and serve hot or cold.

Chinese Sponge Cake

Metric/Imperial
4 eggs
100 g/4 oz caster sugar
120 ml/4 fl oz milk
225 g/8 oz self-raising flour
½ teaspoon bicarbonate of soda
pinch of salt
25 g/1 oz lard, melted and cooled
3 tablespoons oil

American
4 eggs
½ cup sugar
½ cup milk
2 cups self-rising flour
½ teaspoon baking soda
pinch of salt
2 tablespoons lard or shortening, melted and cooled
3 tablespoons oil

Beat the eggs with the sugar until pale and thick. Stir in the milk. Sift the flour, soda and salt together and fold into the egg mixture, followed by the lard and oil. Pour into a greased 20 cm/8 inch round deep cake pan.

Steam the cake for 20 minutes. Remove the cake from the pan while it is still hot and serve warm or cold.

Gevickelte Kichlen

Metric/Imperial
100 g/4 oz self-raising flour
100 g/4 oz plain flour
pinch of salt
100 g/4 oz butter
100 g/4 oz sugar
1–2 eggs, beaten
icing sugar to dredge
Filling:
jam
chopped nuts
sultanas
chopped mixed peel
ground cinnamon

American
1 cup self-rising flour
1 cup all-purpose flour
pinch of salt
8 tablespoons (1 stick) butter
½ cup sugar
1–2 eggs, beaten
confectioners' sugar to dredge
Filling:
jam
chopped nuts
seedless white raisins
chopped mixed candied peel
ground cinnamon

Sift the flours and salt into a bowl and rub in the butter. Stir in the sugar, then bind to a stiff dough with the eggs. Divide the dough into four portions and roll out each into an oblong.

Spread jam over the dough oblongs to within 1 cm/½ inch of the edge. Sprinkle with nuts, sultanas (raisins), peel and cinnamon. Dampen the edges, then roll up like Swiss (jelly) rolls. Place on greased baking sheets.

Bake in a preheated hot oven (220°C/425°F, Gas Mark 7) for 20 minutes. Cool, then dredge with icing (confectioners') sugar and cut into slices.

Variation:

Poppy Seed Kichlen: Make the dough using all self-raising (self-rising) flour and increasing the butter and sugar to 150 g/5 oz (10 tablespoons). Work in 25 g/1 oz (¼ cup) poppy seeds. Roll out the dough thinly, cut into shapes and place on greased baking sheets. Brush with beaten egg, then bake in a preheated moderately hot oven (190°C/375°F, Gas Mark 5) for 15 to 20 minutes.

Makes about 36

Sachertorte

Metric/Imperial
275 g/10 oz plain chocolate
1 tablespoon coffee essence
1 teaspoon vanilla essence
200 g/7 oz butter
275/10 oz icing sugar, sifted
6 eggs, separated
4 tablespoons ground almonds
65 g/2½ oz plain flour, sifted 3 times
apricot jam
3 tablespoons warm black coffee

American
10 squares (10 oz) semi-sweet
   chocolate
1 tablespoon coffee flavoring
1 teaspoon vanilla extract
14 tablespoons butter
2½ cups confectioners' sugar, sifted
6 eggs, separated
¼ cup ground almonds
½ cup plus 2 tablespoons all-purpose
   flour, sifted 3 times
apricot jam
3 tablespoons warm black coffee

Put 175 g/6 oz (6 squares) of the chocolate, the coffee essence (flavoring) and vanilla in a saucepan and melt gently. Cool.

Cream the butter with 90 g/3½ oz (1 cup less 2 tablespoons) of the sugar until light and fluffy. Beat in the egg yolks, almonds and melted chocolate mixture.

Beat the egg whites until stiff, then gradually beat in 75 g/3 oz (¾ cup) of the remaining sugar. Fold the egg whites into the chocolate mixture alternately with the flour.

Spoon into a greased and floured 20 cm/8 inch round deep cake pan. Bake in a preheated moderate oven (180°C/350°F, Gas Mark 4) for 1 hour or until a skewer inserted into the centre of the cake comes out clean.

Cool in the pan for 15 minutes, then turn out onto a wire rack to cool completely.

Cut the cake into two layers and sandwich them back together again with apricot jam. Melt a little more jam and brush this all over the top and sides of the cake.

Melt the remaining chocolate gently with the coffee. Remove from the heat. Gradually stir in the remaining sugar to make a thickish icing. Spread the icing over the top and sides of the cake and leave until set before cutting.

Kugelhopf

Metric/Imperial
75 g/3 oz raisins
3 tablespoons kirsch
25 g/1 oz fresh yeast
250 ml/8 fl oz lukewarm milk
75 g/3 oz sugar
500 g/1 lb 2 oz plain flour
½ teaspoon salt
2 eggs, beaten
200 g/7 oz butter, softened
50 g/2 oz blanched almonds,
    chopped
sifted icing sugar

American
½ cup raisins
3 tablespoons kirsch
1 cake compressed yeast
1 cup lukewarm milk
6 tablespoons sugar
4½ cups all-purpose flour
½ teaspoon salt
2 eggs, beaten
14 tablespoons butter, softened
½ cup chopped blanched almonds
sifted confectioners' sugar

Soak the raisins in the kirsch for 20 minutes. Mix the yeast with 120 ml/4 fl oz (½ cup) of the milk, 1 teaspoon of the sugar and just enough of the flour to make a thin cream. Leave in a warm place for 20 minutes or until frothy.

Sift the remaining flour and the salt into a bowl. Stir in the remaining sugar, then beat in the eggs and the rest of the milk. Work in the butter and knead the dough until it comes cleanly away from the sides of the bowl. Beat in the yeast mixture. Cover and leave to rise in a warm place for 1 hour.

Knead the dough lightly, then knead in the raisins. Scatter the almonds over the bottom and sides of a greased kugelhopf mould or a 30 cm/12 inch ring mould. Press in the dough; it should only half fill the mould. Cover and leave in a warm place until risen to the top of the mould.

Bake in a preheated moderate oven (160°C/325°F, Gas Mark 3) for 45 minutes. Cool in the mould for 30 minutes before turning out. When cool, dust with icing (confectioners') sugar.
Serves 10
Note: dried yeast may be substituted for fresh – use 4 teaspoons dried yeast (2 packages active dry yeast) and follow the package instructions for dissolving it.

Fluden

Metric/Imperial	American
1 quantity rich sweet shortcrust pastry (see page 104), made with 225 g/8 oz sugar	1 quantity rich sweet pie pastry (see page 104), made with 1 cup sugar
100 g/4 oz apricot jam	⅓ cup apricot jam
100 g/4 oz stoned dates, chopped	⅔ cup chopped pitted dates
100 g/4 oz nuts, chopped	1 cup chopped nuts
1 teaspoon ground cinnamon	1 teaspoon ground cinnamon
1 tablespoon orange juice	1 tablespoon orange juice
500 g/1 lb cooking apples, peeled, cored and chopped	1 lb tart apples, peeled, cored and chopped
50 g/2 oz brown sugar	⅓ cup brown sugar
grated rind of ¼ lemon	grated rind of ¼ lemon
juice of 1 lemon	juice of 1 lemon
1 egg white, lightly beaten	1 egg white, lightly beaten
sugar to dredge	sugar to dredge

Divide the dough into three portions, one portion larger than the other two. Roll out the larger portion and use to line a greased 28 × 18 cm/11 × 7 inch cake pan.

Spread half the jam over the bottom of the pastry case. Mix together the dates, nuts, cinnamon and orange juice and sprinkle over the jam.

Roll out another portion of dough and lay over the date mixture. Spread with the rest of the jam. Mix together the apples, brown sugar and lemon rind and juice and sprinkle over the jam. Roll out the remaining portion of dough and lay over the apple mixture.

Brush the egg white over the dough and sprinkle with sugar. Bake in a preheated moderate oven (180°C/350°F, Gas Mark 4) for 30 minutes, then reduce the temperature to 160°C/325°F, Gas Mark 3 and continue baking for 1½ hours.

Fleurons

Metric/Imperial	American
1 quantity flaky pastry (see page 105)	1 quantity flaky pastry (see page 105)

Roll out the dough thinly and cut into crescents or other decorative shapes with pastry (cookie) cutters. Place on a baking sheet.

Bake in a preheated very hot oven (230°C/450°F, Gas Mark 8) for 15 to 20 minutes or until well risen and golden brown.
Makes 8–12

Kiddush Sultana (Raisin) Cake

Metric/Imperial
150 g/5 oz margarine
150 g/5 oz caster sugar
2 drops of vanilla essence
¼ teaspoon grated lemon rind
2 eggs, beaten
225 g/8 oz self-raising flour, sifted
4 tablespoons warm water
100 g/4 oz sultanas
1 tablespoon flaked almonds

American
10 tablespoons margarine
⅔ cup sugar
2 drops of vanilla extract
¼ teaspoon grated lemon rind
2 eggs, beaten
2 cups self-rising flour, sifted
¼ cup warm water
⅔ cup seedless white raisins
1 tablespoon slivered almonds

Cream together the margarine, sugar, vanilla and lemon rind until light and fluffy. Beat in the eggs, then fold in the flour alternately with the water. Fold in the sultanas (raisins). Pour into a greased 28 × 18 cm/11 × 7 inch cake pan. Sprinkle with the almonds.

Bake in a preheated moderate oven (180°C/350°F, Gas Mark 4) for 45 minutes.

Variations:
Instead of the sultanas (raisins), use a mixture of currants, raisins, chopped mixed candied peel, chopped glacé (candied) cherries and sultanas (seedless white raisins).

Tortillas de Maiz

Metric/Imperial
275 g/10 oz cornmeal flour (masa harina)
pinch of salt
about 350 ml/12 fl oz warm water

American
2 cups cornmeal (masa harina)
pinch of salt
about 1½ cups warm water

Put the cornmeal flour and salt in a bowl and gradually knead in the water to form a smooth soft dough. Divide into 14 to 16 portions and leave for 1 hour.

Place each portion of dough between sheets of cling film (plastic wrap) and flatten with a rolling pin into a thin cake about 13 cm/5 inches in diameter.

Heat an ungreased frying pan. Put a tortilla in the pan and cook for about 1 minute or until golden speckles appear on the surface. Turn over and cook the other side for 1 to 1½ minutes. Serve hot.

Makes 14–16
Note: If the tortillas become cool and dry, moisten them with a little water and reheat in the frying pan.

Schnecken

Metric/Imperial
25 g/1 oz plus 1 teaspoon sugar
3–4 tablespoons lukewarm water
2 teaspoons dried yeast
225 g/8 oz plain flour
½ teaspoon salt
25 g/1 oz butter
1 egg, beaten
Filling:
50 g/2 oz butter, melted
50 g/2 oz sultanas
25 g/1 oz nuts, chopped
1 teaspoon ground cinnamon
4 tablespoons brown sugar
2 tablespoons water
Glaze:
2 tablespoons sugar
boiling water

American
2 tablespoons plus 1 teaspoon sugar
3–4 tablespoons lukewarm water
1 package active dry yeast
2 cups all-purpose flour
½ teaspoon salt
2 tablespoons butter
1 egg, beaten
Filling:
4 tablespoons butter, melted
⅓ cup seedless white raisins
¼ cup chopped nuts
1 teaspoon ground cinnamon
¼ cup brown sugar
2 tablespoons water
Glaze:
2 tablespoons sugar
boiling water

Dissolve the 1 teaspoon sugar in 1 tablespoon of the water. Sprinkle the yeast on top and leave in a warm place for about 20 minutes or until frothy.

Sift the flour and salt into a bowl and rub in the butter. Stir in the remaining sugar. Make a well in the centre and put in the yeast liquid, egg and remaining water. Gradually draw the flour into the liquids and mix to a stiff dough. Knead until the dough is smooth and elastic, then roll it out to a square.

Brush the dough with about 1 tablespoon of the melted butter. Sprinkle over the sultanas (raisins), nuts, cinnamon and 2½ tablespoons of the brown sugar. Dampen the edges and roll up tightly like a Swiss (jelly) roll. Brush with another tablespoon of the melted butter, then cut into 2.5 cm/1 inch thick slices.

Use the remaining butter to grease a deep cake pan. Sprinkle over the remaining brown sugar followed by the water. Place the slices in the pan, cut sides down. Leave to rise in a warm place until doubled in size.

Bake in a preheated hot oven (220°C/425°F, Gas Mark 7) for 20 to 30 minutes. Cool.

Dissolve 1 tablespoon of the sugar for the glaze in a little boiling water and brush over the slices while warm. Sprinkle with the remaining sugar.
Makes 12

Variations:

Chocolate Roll: Make up half the quantity of dough as above and roll it out into an oblong. Melt 50 g/2 oz (4 tablespoons) butter in a saucepan and stir in 2 tablespoons (unsweetened) cocoa powder and 50 g/2 oz (⅓ cup) brown sugar. Bring to the boil, stirring to dissolve the sugar. Stir in a few drops of vanilla essence (extract) and cool. Spread this filling over the dough oblong. Dampen the edges and roll up tightly like a Swiss (jelly) roll. Rise as above, then bake in a preheated moderately hot oven (200°C/400°F, Gas Mark 6) for 30 minutes. Glaze as above.

Purim Kalisch: Make up double the quantity of dough as above and divide into four portions. Roll into long sausages and plait (braid) together. Rise as above, then bake in a preheated moderately hot oven (200°C/400°F, Gas Mark 6) for 30 to 40 minutes. Brush with about 4 tablespoons of thin glacé icing (see page 42) and sprinkle over coloured hundreds-and-thousands.

Challah

Metric/Imperial	American
1 teaspoon sugar	1 teaspoon sugar
2 tablespoons lukewarm water	2 tablespoons lukewarm water
2 teaspoons dried yeast	1 package active dry yeast
500 g/1 lb strong plain flour	4 cups all-purpose flour
1 teaspoon salt	1 teaspoon salt
1 egg, beaten	1 egg, beaten
2 tablespoons oil	2 tablespoons oil
beaten egg to glaze	beaten egg to glaze
poppy seeds	poppy seeds

Dissolve the sugar in the water. Sprinkle the yeast on top and leave in a warm place for about 20 minutes or until frothy.

Sift the flour and salt into a bowl. Make a well in the centre and put in the yeast liquid, egg and oil. Gradually draw the flour into the liquid and mix to a stiff dough, adding more water if necessary. Knead until the dough is smooth and elastic, then divide it into eight portions. Roll each into a long sausage. Make into two loaves by plaiting (braiding). Brush with water, then leave to rise in a warm place until doubled in size.

Brush with beaten egg and sprinkle with poppy seeds. Bake in a preheated moderately hot oven (200°C/400°F, Gas Mark 6) for 10 minutes, then reduce the temperature to moderate (180°C/350°F, Gas Mark 4) and continue baking for 45 minutes.

Makes 2

Variation:

For a richer challah, replace the water with 175 g/6 fl oz (¾ cup) lukewarm milk and increase the eggs to 4. Omit the oil. Make into one large plaited (braided) loaf. Bake in a preheated hot oven (220°C/425°F, Gas Mark 7) for 15 minutes, then reduce the temperature to moderately hot (190°C/375°F, Gas Mark 5) and continue baking for 20 to 30 minutes.

Hamantaschen

Metric/Imperial
150 g/5 oz margarine
150 g/5 oz caster sugar
1 egg yolk
100 g/4 oz self-raising flour, sifted
melted honey to glaze
Filling:
100 g/4 oz poppy seeds, ground
grated rind of 1 lemon
150 ml/¼ pint water
50 g/2 oz sugar
25 g/1 oz margarine
25 g/1 oz sultanas
2 teaspoons wine

American
10 tablespoons margarine
½ cup plus 2 tablespoons sugar
1 egg yolk
1 cup self-rising flour, sifted
melted honey to glaze
Filling:
⅓ cup ground poppy seeds
grated rind of 1 lemon
⅔ cup water
¼ cup sugar
2 tablespoons margarine
2½ tablespoons seedless white
   raisins
2 teaspoons wine

Cream the margarine with the sugar until light and fluffy. Beat in the egg yolk, then fold in the flour to make a very stiff dough. Roll out the dough thinly and cut into 7.5 cm/3 inch rounds.

For the filling, put all the ingredients in a saucepan and bring to the boil, stirring. Simmer until thickened, then cool.

Put a spoonful of the filling in the centre of each dough round. Dampen the edges and bring them into the centre to form triangles. Place on a greased baking sheet.

Bake in a preheated hot oven (220°C/425°F, Gas Mark 7) for 20 minutes. Brush with the honey and cool.
Makes about 24
Variations:
Glaze the baked pastries with glacé icing (see page 42) instead of the honey. Instead of the poppy seed filling given above, use 100 g/4 oz sultanas (⅔ cup seedless white raisins), 100 g/4 oz (⅔ cup) raisins, 50 g/2 oz (⅓ cup) currants, 50 g/2 oz (¼ cup) sugar, 1 teaspoon ground cinnamon, 1 peeled and cored cooking (tart) apple and the grated rind and juice of 1 lemon, all minced (ground) together.

Instead of the poppy seed filling given above, use a prune filling made as follows: Soak 225 g/8 oz prunes overnight with the pared rinds of 1 lemon and 1 orange, 50 g/2 oz (⅓ cup) brown sugar and water to cover. The next day, cook the mixture until any liquid has evaporated. Discard the lemon and orange rinds and the prune stones (pits) and finely chop or mince (grind) the prunes. Alternatively, use drained, canned prunes mixed with finely grated lemon and orange rinds.

Matzo Puffs

Metric/Imperial
150 ml/¼ pint water
40 g/1½ oz margarine
¼ teaspoon salt
100 g/4 oz fine matzo meal
3 eggs
Filling:
50 g/2 oz margarine
100 g/4 oz icing sugar, sifted
few drops of vanilla essence
1 tablespoon wine
Icing:
50 g/2 oz plain chocolate
25 g/1 oz margarine
1 tablespoon brandy or wine
50 g/2 oz icing sugar, sifted
1 tablespoon cocoa powder

American
⅔ cup water
3 tablespoons margarine
¼ teaspoon salt
1 cup fine matzo meal
3 eggs
Filling:
4 tablespoons margarine
1 cup confectioners' sugar, sifted
few drops of vanilla extract
1 tablespoon wine
Frosting:
2 oz dark sweet chocolate
2 tablespoons margarine
1 tablespoon brandy or wine
½ cup confectioners' sugar, sifted
1 tablespoon unsweetened cocoa

Put the water, margarine and salt in a saucepan and bring to the boil. Remove from the heat and stir in the matzo meal. Cool slightly, then beat in the eggs one at a time.

Drop tablespoons of the mixture onto a greased baking sheet. Bake in a preheated moderately hot oven (190°C/375°F, Gas Mark 5) for 40 minutes. Slit each puff to allow the steam to escape, then leave to cool in the turned-off oven.

For the filling, cream the margarine with the sugar and vanilla until light and fluffy. Beat in the wine. Use to fill the puffs.

For the icing, melt the chocolate gently with the margarine. Remove from the heat and beat in the remaining ingredients. Spread the icing over the puffs.

Kipfel

Metric/Imperial
225 g/8 oz butter
75 g/3 oz sugar
2 teaspoons hot water
2–3 drops of vanilla essence
350 g/12 oz plain flour, sifted
50 g/2 oz nuts, chopped
sifted icing sugar

American
½ lb (2 sticks) butter
6 tablespoons sugar
2 teaspoons hot water
2–3 drops of vanilla extract
3 cups all-purpose flour, sifted
½ cup chopped nuts
sifted confectioners' sugar

Cream the butter with the sugar until light and fluffy. Beat in the water and vanilla, then mix in the flour and nuts. Chill well, overnight if possible.

Form the mixture into small rolls about 7.5 cm/3 inches long and pencil thin. Shape into crescents and place on greased baking sheets.

Bake in a preheated moderately hot oven (200°C/400°F, Gas Mark 6) for 15 minutes. Coat with icing (confectioners') sugar.
Makes about 60

Tarte Normande

Metric/Imperial
100 g/4 oz sugar
4 tablespoons water
6 apples, peeled and cored
1 quantity pâte sucrée (see page 107)
½ quantity crème pâtissière (see page 42)
6 small pancakes (see page 105)
6 tablespoons Calvados, warmed
cream to serve

American
½ cup sugar
¼ cup water
6 apples, peeled and cored
1 quantity pâte sucrée (see page 107)
½ quantity crème pâtissière (see page 42)
6 small crêpes (see page 105)
6 tablespoons applejack, warmed
cream to serve

Dissolve the sugar in the water in a saucepan. Add the apples, cover the pan and cook gently until the apples are tender, turning them from time to time and basting with the syrup.

Meanwhile, roll out the pastry dough thinly and use to line six 10 cm/4 inch fluted tins. Bake blind (unfilled) in a preheated moderately hot oven (190°C/375°F, Gas Mark 5) for 10 minutes. Remove the beans and foil lining and bake for a further 5 minutes or until lightly browned. Cool.

Put 1 to 2 tablespoons crème pâtissière in each pastry case and place an apple on top. Coat with a little of the apple syrup, then cover with a pancake (crêpe). Pour over the Calvados (applejack) and set alight. Serve flaming, with cream.
Serves 6

Bulgarian Orange Yogurt Cake

Metric/Imperial
175 g/6 oz self-raising flour
pinch of salt
100 g/4 oz butter
175 g/6 oz caster sugar
2 eggs
½ × 175 g/6 oz carton frozen
  concentrated orange juice, thawed
150 ml/¼ pint natural yogurt
Filling:
50 g/2 oz butter
175 g/6 oz icing sugar, sifted
about 2 tablespoons thawed frozen
  concentrated orange juice

American
1½ cups self-rising flour
pinch of salt
8 tablespoons (1 stick) butter
¾ cup sugar
2 eggs
½ × 6 oz carton frozen concentrated
  orange juice, thawed
⅔ cup unflavored yogurt
Filling:
4 tablespoons butter
1½ cups confectioners' sugar, sifted
about 2 tablespoons thawed frozen
  concentrated orange juice

Sift the flour with the salt. Cream the butter with the sugar until light and fluffy.
Beat in the eggs one at a time, adding a tablespoon of flour with each egg.
Fold in the remaining flour alternately with the orange juice concentrate and
yogurt.

Divide between two greased and floured 20 cm/8 inch sandwich tins (layer
cake pans). Bake in a preheated moderately hot oven (190°C/375°F, Gas
Mark 5) for 30 to 35 minutes or until well risen and golden. Cool on a wire
rack.

For the filling, beat the butter until soft, then gradually beat in the sugar with
the orange juice concentrate.

Sandwich together the cake layers with some of the filling and use the rest
to cover the top of the cake.

Australian Apple Charlotte

Metric/Imperial
100 g/4 oz plain flour
50 g/2 oz self-raising flour
25 g/1 oz custard powder
25 g/1 oz cornflour
2 tablespoons icing sugar
100 g/4 oz butter
3–4 tablespoons water
Filling:
900 ml/1 ½ pints sweetened apple
  purée
1 tablespoon lemon juice
½ teaspoon grated nutmeg
Icing:
175 g/6 oz icing sugar
milk
green food colouring
25 g/1 oz candied angelica, chopped

American
1 cup all-purpose flour
½ cup self-rising flour
¼ cup custard powder
¼ cup cornstarch
2 tablespoons confectioners' sugar
8 tablespoons (1 stick) butter
3–4 tablespoons water
Filling:
4 cups sweetened apple sauce
1 tablespoon lemon juice
½ teaspoon grated nutmeg
Frosting:
1 ½ cups confectioners' sugar
milk
green food coloring
2 ½ tablespoons chopped candied
  angelica

Sift the flours, custard powder, cornflour (cornstarch) and sugar into a bowl.
Rub in the butter then bind to a firm but pliable dough with the water. Roll out
two-thirds of the dough and use to line an 18 cm/7 inch springform pan.

Mix together the filling ingredients and pour into the pastry case. Roll out
the rest of the dough and lay over the filling. Pinch the edges together to seal
and make two slits in the centre of the lid.

Bake in a preheated hot oven (220°C/425°F, Gas Mark 7) for 10 minutes,
then reduce the heat to moderate (180°C/350°F, Gas Mark 4) and bake for a
further 20 minutes or until the pastry is golden brown. Cool.

Mix the icing (confectioners') sugar with enough milk to give a thick
coating consistency. Tint it pale green with a few drops of food colouring,
then fold in the angelica. Spread over the pastry lid and leave until set.
Serves 6

Baklava

Metric/Imperial
225 g/8 oz plain flour
pinch of salt
175 g/6 oz butter
about 250 ml/8 fl oz water
1½ teaspoons vinegar
Filling:
melted butter
225 g/8 oz almonds, walnuts or
   pecans, finely chopped
50 g/2 oz brown sugar
Syrup:
5 tablespoons water
225 g/8 oz sugar
juice of 1 lemon

American
2 cups all-purpose flour
pinch of salt
12 tablespoons (1½ sticks) butter
about 1 cup water
1½ teaspoons vinegar
Filling:
melted butter
2 cups finely chopped almonds,
   walnuts or pecans
⅓ cup brown sugar
Syrup:
5 tablespoons water
1 cup sugar
juice of 1 lemon

Sift the flour and salt into a bowl. Cut the butter into small nut-sized pieces and add to the flour. Mix the water with the vinegar and add to the bowl. Mix to a stiff, lumpy dough.

Roll out the dough to an oblong. Fold it in three and press the edges together to seal. Turn so the raw edges are to the sides. Roll out again into an oblong. Repeat the folding, rolling out and turning twice, then chill for 30 minutes.

Divide the dough into four portions and roll out each to an 18 cm/7 inch square. Place one dough square in the bottom of a greased 18 cm/7 inch square cake pan. Brush with melted butter and sprinkle with about one-third of the nuts and brown sugar. Continue making layers in this way, ending with the last dough square. Brush with more melted butter and cut into squares or diamonds.

Bake in a preheated moderately hot oven (190°C/375°F, Gas Mark 5) for 30 minutes or until the pastry is crisp.

Meanwhile, put the ingredients for the syrup in a saucepan and bring to the boil, stirring to dissolve the sugar. Boil until syrupy. Spoon the hot syrup over the baklava and cool.

Index

227

Notes

Notes

Notes

Notes